40.00

VOTING
IN AMERICA

A Reference Handbook

Other Titles in ABC-CLIO's
**Contemporary
World Issues**
Series

Books in the Contemporary World Issues series address vital issues in today's society such as genetic engineering, pollution, and biodiversity. Written by professional writers, scholars, and nonacademic experts, these books are authoritative, clearly written, up-to-date, and objective. They provide a good starting point for research by high school and college students, scholars, and general readers as well as by legislators, businesspeople, activists, and others.

Each book, carefully organized and easy to use, contains an overview of the subject, a detailed chronology, biographical sketches, facts and data and/or documents and other primary-source material, a directory of organizations and agencies, annotated lists of print and nonprint resources, and an index.

Readers of books in the Contemporary World Issues series will find the information they need in order to have a better understanding of the social, political, environmental, and economic issues facing the world today.

VOTING
IN AMERICA

A Reference Handbook

Robert E. DiClerico

**CONTEMPORARY
WORLD ISSUES**

ABC-CLIO

Santa Barbara, California   Denver, Colorado   Oxford, England

Library of Congress Cataloging-in-Publication Data
DiClerico, Robert E.
   Voting in America : a reference handbook / Robert E. DiClerico
      p.   cm. — (ABC-CLIO's contemporary world issues series)
   Includes bibliographical references and index.
   ISBN 1-57607-931-7 (hardcover : alk. paper); 1-57607-932-5 (eBook)
   1. Voting—United States.   2. Elections—United States.   I. Title.
II. Series: Contemporary world issues.

JK1976.D53   2004
324.6'0973—dc22

                                                       2004005416

08   07   06   05   10   9   8   7   6   5   4   3   2

This book is also available on the World Wide Web as an eBook. Visit abc-clio.com for details.

ABC-CLIO, Inc.
130 Cremona Drive, P.O. Box 1911
Santa Barbara, California 93116-1911

This book is printed on acid-free paper ∞.
Manufactured in the United States of America.

Contents

Preface

The presidential election of 1800 was a momentous event in American history, for it marked the first time under our new constitutional structure that the party in power up to that point (Federalists) had to relinquish it to the opposition (Republicans) led by Thomas Jefferson. Despite the fact that Jefferson and his supporters were regarded by Federalists as dangerous radicals, the transfer of power occurred without riots in the streets or the firing of a single shot. The presidential election of 2000, coming two hundred years later, marked the fiftieth occasion on which the party controlling the White House was either replaced or reconfirmed, and the 2002 midterm election, the fiftieth time that the parties controlling the Houses of Congress were continued or changed. Although some of these elections were not without controversy, including the elections of 1800 and 2000, all were characterized by a peaceful transfer of power.

The mechanism that achieved these transfers was, of course, the electoral process—a process that, through the casting of votes, periodically allows the citizenry to change or reconfirm those by whom they wish to be governed (recognizing, of course, that for parts of our history presidential electors and U.S. senators were picked by the elected representatives of the people, namely, state legislatures). The fact that our transfers of power took place without violent disruption was crucially linked to the widespread perception that the electoral process used to accomplish this task was seen to be fair—at least at the times those elections occurred. There were, needless to say, those who did not share that view, often because they were excluded from the franchise altogether, or else frustrated in their attempts to exercise it. But they accepted, or at least tolerated, decisions made at the polls because the political process, for all of its failings, accorded them and their champions the freedom to organize and convince others of the inequities present in the election process, and to demand that they be eliminated.

This book is fundamentally about that lengthy and often circuitous journey toward a more democratic electoral process—a journey that has seen not only profound changes in *who* can vote, but also in *whom* and *what* we can vote for, as well as *how, when,* and *where* we can vote. Many insist that the journey is far from over, however, warning that our electoral process continues to be compromised by a number of festering problems, including the two-party monopoly, a chaotic primary process, low voter turnout, the distortive effects of money, a dysfunctional electoral college, outmoded voting machinery, arbitrary redistricting, and an epidemic of direct legislation. This book is also about these issues, and the divergence of opinion over how much they impede the electoral process and how amenable they are to correction.

Acknowledgments

In the course of completing this three-year project, I have received invaluable assistance from the editorial staff at ABC-CLIO, none greater than that provided by senior editor Alicia Merritt. Not only did she spark my interest in contributing to ABC-CLIO's Contemporary World Issues Series, but offered as well timely and wise advice on a host of issues ranging from the book's subject matter to questions of scheduling. Sincere thanks are also due copyeditor Michelle Asakawa. She was unfailingly thorough in her review of the manuscript, and on more than a few occasions rescued my less felicitous phrasing. Hearty thanks are also due the production editor, Carla Roberts, whose skillful oversight of the project is evidenced by the fact it was brought to completion ahead of schedule. Last, but by no means least, I am deeply indebted to my graduate assistant, Gayle Funt, who was relentless in tracking down elusive facts and getting them to me in a timely fashion.

Robert E. DiClerico
Morgantown, WV
January 2004

1

A History of Voting Rights in America

Although periodic elections do not by themselves guarantee that a nation's political system will be democratic, it is impossible to imagine any government being so characterized in the absence of elections. Indeed, the collective act of voting is the crucial mechanism we use for both determining who is going to do the deciding for us and, just as important, holding those deciders accountable.

H. G. Wells aptly noted that "election is democracy's ceremonial, its feast, its great function." As we shall see in this chapter, the number of people invited to that feast in the United States has varied considerably over time. Some have had a seat at the table from the very beginning, while others had to struggle to win it; and still others were invited, only to be disinvited at subsequent feasts, forcing them also to fight for a permanent seat at the table.

Beyond examining who has had a right to attend the feast, this chapter will also consider the expansion over time in the number of feasts held, as well as the number of courses available to choose from, and even voters' ability to determine what those courses will be.

The Quest for the Right to Vote

The Colonial Period

As with so many features of our political system, the development of suffrage in Colonial America was heavily influenced by the British experience. Under a law instituted in 1430, the franchise in England was conditioned upon the ownership of land (i.e., freehold) worth at least "40 shillings a year in rental value or in income, or the lawful or customary equivalents" (Williamson 1960, 5). Seven of the American colonies (Georgia, New Hampshire, New Jersey, New York, North Carolina, Rhode Island, and Virginia) likewise instituted a freehold requirement for colony elections, although the amount and value of the land varied by colony. In other colonies personal property of a stated value or the payment of taxes was deemed a valid substitute for owning land. In Connecticut, Massachusetts, and Maryland, for example, personal worth of 40 pounds was required, while in South Carolina the payment of 20 shillings in taxes in an election year was sufficient (Williamson 1960, 5). For local and county elections, as opposed to colony elections, property requirements were generally less burdensome.

The reasons for insisting that the franchise be tied to property ownership of some kind were several. For one thing, it insured that the voting population would have a permanent stake in the community and would thereby be affected by who or what was being voted on, which would in turn foster a concern for the community. Landownership, moreover, was viewed in an especially favorable light because farming was judged to be an enobling undertaking that fostered character, independence, stability, and a concern for the property rights of others—all qualities to be valued when applied to the political sphere (Williamson 1960, 5).

In the words of a Virginia banker responding to a colleague who spoke against the freehold requirement:

> I do not pretend that great virtues may not be found in all professions and walks of life. But I do believe, if there are any chosen people of God, they are the cultivators of the soil. If there be virtue to be found any where, it would be amongst the middling farmers, who constitute the yeomanry, the bone and sinew of our country. Sir, they are men of moderate desires, they have to labor for their subsistence, and the support of their families; their wishes are bounded by the limits of their small possessions; they are not harassed by envy, by the love and show of splendor, nor agitated by the restless and insatiable passion of ambition. (Peterson 1966, 393)

Property was valued as well because it helped to inoculate citizens against the possibility that their voting decision might be influenced by others. In the words of acclaimed British legal scholar Sir William Blackstone, the "true reason of requiring any qualification with regard to property in voters is to exclude such persons as are in so mean a situation as to be esteemed to have no will of their own" (Peterson 1966, 11). Those living on the estate of another, for example, dependent upon him for their domicile and livelihood, might feel very considerable pressure to make his views and voting preferences their own. Property restrictions on the right to vote were also justified on grounds of "virtual representation," the notion that those who were barred from the franchise would nevertheless have their interests represented by those who were eligible to vote. A final rationale behind the property requirement was rooted in the issue of competence. In a land where opportunity presented itself at every turn, if you were not competent enough to acquire property of some kind, then you probably were not competent enough to vote, either (Keyssar 2000, 5, 9).

There were other restrictions on the franchise as well. Just six of the colonies made voting conditional on attaining twenty-one years of age. With respect to residency, Pennsylvania was the toughest, requiring two years, while four states imposed no residency at all. Other restrictions on the franchise were self-evidently invidious in nature. Freed Negroes were prohibited from voting in four southern colonies (Georgia, North Carolina, South Carolina, and Virginia); women in three (Delaware, Pennsylvania, and South Carolina); Catholics in five, including Maryland, New York, and New Jersey; and Jews in four (Maryland, New York, South Carolina, and Rhode Island) (Williamson 1960, 6).

The colonies' rapidly deteriorating relations with England would ultimately have an impact upon attitudes toward the right to vote. The forces giving rise to this reality were both philosophical and practical in nature. The principle of natural rights, which grew in its appeal in the eighteenth century and asserted that certain rights attach to all individuals as human beings, was now seized upon as a rationale for arguing that voting was one of these rights—"a right that inhered in individuals rather than property" (Keyssar 2000, 12). The folly of believing otherwise was brought home with stunning clarity by Benjamin Franklin:

> Today a man owns a jackass worth fifty dollars and he
> is entitled to vote; but before the next election the

jackass dies. The man in the meantime has become more experienced, his knowledge of the principles of government, and his acquaintance with mankind, are more extensive, and he is therefore better qualified to make a proper selection of rulers—but the jackass is dead and the man cannot vote. Now gentlemen, pray inform me, in whom is the right of suffrage? In the man or in the jackass? (Keyssar 2000, 3)

Then, too, the colonists' demand of "no taxation without representation," around which much of their anger against the mother country coalesced, had a diminished claim to validity if *taxpaying* Americans themselves had no say in choosing their representatives only because they happened not to own land. Likewise, if the colonists rejected, as they did, claims by the British parliament that their interests enjoyed "virtual," if not actual, representation within that body, then it would become difficult to defend the property qualification partly on the ground that those Americans without it nevertheless had their interests represented by those voters who did own property (Wood 1969, 79). To these points of principle must also be added a more practical concern that forced a rethinking of restrictions upon the franchise, namely, the importance of attracting as much popular support as possible in facing off against the British. And nowhere was that support more critical than among the ranks of those militias and armies who would be doing the fighting—a disproportionate number of whom were young in years and decidedly less likely to meet the property qualification for voting. Likewise, no group within the population could make a greater claim to the right to vote because they were, after all, defending the liberties and freedoms of the colonies. And claim it they would, starting with the right to elect their own officers (Williamson 1960, 80–82).

The British were especially angered by the Boston Tea Party (1773), prompting them to respond with five separate acts designed to punish the colonists in one way or another. Referred to by the colonists as the Intolerable Acts (1774), this appellation suggested the extent to which the colonists were likewise outraged by the British response. Indeed, these actions precipitated calls within America for the creation of alternative legislative bodies. One was the Continental Congress, convening in Philadelphia, and to which the colonies sent representatives. The others were provincial congresses established within each colony.

With respect to the provincial congresses especially, there grew demands to have their members chosen by the people—more specifically by people who paid taxes, even though they did not own land. New York City, and the colonies of Georgia, New Hampshire, and New Jersey responded favorably to those calls.

Following the decision by the colonies to declare their independence from England on July 4, 1776, they were faced with having to create new governments for themselves—an exercise that inevitably led their constitutional conventions to wrestle with the question of who was qualified to decide who the members of these new governments ought to be. Five states (Connecticut, Delaware, Massachusetts, Rhode Island, and Virginia) were content to maintain the previous property restrictions, with Massachusetts even raising them while also doing away with its prohibition against blacks. South Carolina, meanwhile, made only a slight reduction in the property qualification. In contrast, Maryland now decided to allow taxpaying or landownership as a qualification, while New Hampshire, Georgia, New Jersey, and Pennsylvania abandoned the freehold qualification entirely and replaced it with a taxpaying requirement for males and females. In an effort to reach a compromise among conflicting views on the importance of the freehold restriction, New York and North Carolina came up with a mixed arrangement, with the former maintaining the freehold requirement but reducing it by half for election of members to its assembly, as opposed to the senate and governorship. North Carolina accepted a taxpaying requirement for the lower house but maintained the freehold restriction for the senate and governorship. Only the state of Vermont allowed all free white males to vote without regard to their ability to pay taxes or own property. By the 1780s, denial of the franchise to Jews had been repealed, and free blacks were permitted to vote in six states (North Carolina, Massachusetts, New York, Pennsylvania, Maryland, and Vermont) (Keyssar 2000, 92–113).

The 1787 Constitutional Convention

With views in the country still divided on the desirability of a property requirement for voting, it is not surprising that such divisions were in evidence as the Founding Fathers debated the form and structure of our new government. Some, looking ahead to the day when the country would be more and more populated by laborers without property, saw a property requirement as a protection against, in the words of John Dickinson, "the dangerous influence of those multitudes without property and without principle" (Padover 1962, 239). Although James Madison stated that his position on the freehold would be guided by how such a constitutional provision would be received in the states, on the merits of the matter alone he shared Dickinson's views, warning that the time would come when most citizens would lack property of any kind, and thus "the rights of liberty and property will not be secure in their hands" and they "will become the tools of opulence and ambition" (Padover 1962, 239). Gouverneur Morris weighed in with the prediction that allowing those without property to elect members of the House of Representatives would convert that body into an aristocracy: "Give the votes to people who have no property and they will sell them to the rich who will be able to buy them. We should not confine our attention to the present moment. The time is not distant when this country will abound with mechanics and manufacturers who will receive their bread from their employers. Will such men be the secure guardians of liberty?" (Padover 1962, 240). He thought not. Other delegates such as Nathaniel Goreham, Oliver Ellsworth, and George Mason believed otherwise, reasoning that it would be highly unwise for the new constitution to deny to citizens through a freehold requirement a right that had already been extended to citizens in many states. Benjamin Franklin also argued against any such restriction, noting that during the war the common people had admirably demonstrated their virtue and public spirit, without which it would not have been won. In the final analysis, the Founding Fathers appeared to accept the assessment of Oliver Ellsworth on this divisive issue: "The states are the best judges of the circumstances and tempers of their own people" (Padover 1962, 240). Accordingly, they adopted the proposal that the electors for the House of Representatives shall have the same qualifications as those who elect the most numerous branch of the state legislatures (Article I, Sec. 2), which is to say that qualifications for voting would be left in the hands of the states.

Bear in mind, however, that the House was the only branch that would be elected by the people. Members of the Senate, an institution viewed by the Founding Fathers as a break upon the potentially factional passions of the House, were to be appointed by each state's legislature. The president, meanwhile, was to be chosen by a group of presidential electors, with each state legislature determining how its presidential electors would be chosen.

That the people were not permitted to elect the president did indeed reflect an inclination by some delegates to limit their role as much as possible, but the matter was considerably more complicated than this simple explanation. Madison, for example, the preeminent figure at the convention, supported popular election in theory but thought it impractical in current circumstances, where transportation and communication were so poor as to prevent most citizens from having an acquaintance with the candidates for president. For others the reluctance to support direct election had more to do with self-interest than an inherent disdain for the populace. More precisely, delegates from the small states, obsessed with the fear that the large states would control the new government, fiercely opposed popular election, believing that such an arrangement would invariably produce presidents from large states. They were joined by southern delegates who were convinced that with more voters eligible to vote in the North than the South, a popular vote would routinely yield presidents from northern states (Diamond 1977, 1–5). (Such fears, as history would ultimately demonstrate, proved misplaced.). The manner of electing the president proved to be the most difficult issue for the delegates to resolve, yielding to solution only after the proposal for an electoral college—a peculiar arrangement, carefully crafted so as to gain the support of all the competing factions that developed around this issue.

During the Constitutional Convention's deliberations on suffrage, Madison rightly observed at one point that "the right of suffrage is certainly one of the fundamental articles of republican government" (Padover 1962, 241). In leaving the matter of suffrage to the states, all but one of which (Vermont) retained a property/taxpaying requirement of some sort, were not the Founding Fathers seriously circumscribing the number of free white males who would be able to participate in the new government they had fashioned? The answer to this question has generated considerable debate among scholars. Eminent historian Charles Beard concluded that the property requirements, be they land or personal, were sufficiently onerous as to prevent most white males from qualifying to vote (Beard 1913). In a thoroughgoing challenge to both Beard's methodology and findings, Charles Brown finds that ownership of land was extensive, thereby excluding never more than 25 percent, and typically no more than 5 to 10 percent. In his study of property requirements in three states (Massachusetts, New Jersey, and Virginia), Chilton

Williamson reaches a similar conclusion, noting that "the diffusion of real and personal property was so great as to render the property tests for voting much less restrictive than they appear to be" (Brown 1956, 194–200; Diamond 1966, 15; Williamson 1960, 5).

Forces for Expansion

Between 1790 and 1850, five states eliminated the property requirement for voting, and as the 1850s came to a close the only vestiges of that restriction were in Rhode Island, where foreigners born in the United States were required to own property; and in New York, which required that African Americans meet a property test to vote. No new state admitted to the Union after 1790, however, included in its original constitution any kind of property test for voting (Crotty 1977, 29).

A number of factors conspired to bring about these changes, not the least of which was the population growth occurring in the cities—up from four to twenty million in the first fifty years of the nineteenth century. Accordingly, the mechanics, laborers, and artisans, about whom some of the Founding Fathers had expressed fears at the Constitutional Convention and who now populated our cities, found it impossible to meet a freehold requirement of several acres and therefore voiced their strong objections to it. To their voices were added those who were farming the land; some, tenant farmers in the north leasing land; others, purchasing land with a mortgage and not entitled to vote until it was paid off; still others, farmers in the west frustrated by the inordinate length of time required to take title to property.

The War of 1812 drove home with renewed force an argument that had already been made for some time against the property requirement, namely, that those being asked to defend the freedoms of others, including the right to vote, should not themselves be denied those very freedoms. Thus, as men signed up to fight the British, they could also be found in some states signing petitions objecting to the freehold requirement. When states such as Connecticut, New York, and Mississippi decided to waive property and taxpaying requirements for army and militia members, the matter of self-interest weighed as heavily as elemental fairness in the decision to do so. The government had experienced no easy time getting men to enlist in the fight against the British, and it was not altogether satisfied with how they performed once in the ranks. Thus, extending the franchise to the unpropertied was seen as a means of instilling greater commitment by them to the defense of the nation. For southern states, moreover, there was an additional incentive—by inviting poor whites into the franchise, there was a greater likelihood that they would join the militias that might be summoned to put down any uprising by the slave population (Keyssar 2000, 35–37).

The expansion of the nation westward also contributed to the broadening of the franchise. Inequalities in status and wealth were decidedly less pronounced in the territories than in the older states of the East. Upon entry into the Union, "These newer states took the democratic rhetoric seriously and incorporated provisions protecting individual rights (including voting) into their state constitutions" (Crotty 1977, 11). On more practical grounds, the new states also saw an inclusive suffrage as an added inducement to draw people into their states, thereby driving up land values and spurring on economic development. Indeed, some states even went so far as to extend the voting privilege to legal aliens. In 1848, Wisconsin enfranchised aliens provided they had resided there for two years and announced their intention to become U.S. citizens. Michigan and Indiana took similar steps, as did the congress for the Minnesota and Oregon territories (Keyssar 2000, 33).

By the 1830s the country had two competitive political parties, the Democrats and the National Republicans. Because the primary goal of a political party is to win, it should occasion no surprise that in a competitive party environment, one or the other would have a strong incentive to expand the potential universe of voters if it stood to gain at the polls by doing so. The Democrats took the lead in calling for an abolition of the property requirement, but the National Republicans, not wanting to antagonize a potential new bloc of voters, ultimately felt compelled to go along as well. If a state party, moreover, was not out front on abolishing the property requirement, it could well be punished by citizens voting in local elections, where voting requirements were typically much less stringent than at the state level (Keyssar 2000, 39–41).

A final consideration that weighed in the movement to abolish the property requirement was the fact that states that had already done so seemed not to have suffered any untoward consequences.

In politics as in physics, for every action there is a reaction, and the abolition of the property requirement was no exception.

Residency requirements were increased by many governments at the state (one year) and local (three months) levels on the grounds that length of residence indicated some degree of permanence in and knowledge of the community—benefits previously said to flow from the property requirement. Some twelve states, while willing to dispense with any property qualification for voting, nevertheless passed laws denying the vote to paupers (i.e., those supported at the public's expense) on the grounds that they should not be able to choose the government if they were not contributing to its maintenance. Most disturbing, however, was the impact of the property qualification on blacks. The decision by more and more states during the first half of the nineteenth century to prevent blacks from voting was rooted in the belief that they were fundamentally inferior to whites, but also in the fear that abolition of the property requirement would encourage more blacks to move north. Every state brought into the Union after 1819 denied the franchise to blacks, and by 1855 there were only five states left (Maine, Massachusetts, New Hampshire, Vermont, and Rhode Island) that extended them that right (Keyssar 2000, 55, 57, 61, 65). Nor, need it be said, was the cause of blacks helped by an egregious Supreme Court decision in 1857 (*Dred Scott v. Sandford*) ruling that blacks, whether slave or free, were not citizens of the United States (Kelly and Harbison 1963, 384–391).

The welcoming of foreigners, even to the point where six states and the Washington territory were willing to grant voting privileges to those intending to become U.S. citizens, also was destined to produce a counterreaction that began in the 1850s and, as we shall see later, became more acute in the early part of the twentieth century. The influx of foreigners, which began in the 1820s, had reached close to three million by 1854—15 percent of the entire U.S. population. Although there were fault lines of antagonism among them, with German Catholics disdainful of their Irish counterparts, and those from the British Isles suspicious of those from continental Europe, the most prominent faultline was between native Americans and foreigners. Offended by their customs, religion, speech, and drinking, this nativist sentiment was most apparent in the cities of the Northeast in which many newly arrived immigrants located (Crotty 1977, 14–16; Keyssar 2000, 82, 83; Burns 1982, 547). This bigotry found a home in a secret society known as the "Know Nothings," which ultimately went public as the American Party, showing particular strength in the North. Though hostile to foreigners generally, it had a special antipathy toward Roman Catholics, as evidenced by its program of "Anti-Romanism, Anti-Bedinism, Anti-Pope's Toeism, Anti-Nunneryism, Anti-Winking Virginism, Anti-Jesuitism, and Anti-the-Whole-Sacerdotal-Hierarchism with all its humbugging mummeries" (Burns 1982, 547). Fortunately, the American Party fell as quickly as it rose, but not before securing nine governorships, winning control of legislatures in six states, and helping to elect a nativist speaker of the U.S. House.

The antipathy to foreigners, which started to rear its head in the 1850s, affected the laws in some states. Oregon, whose immigrant population was primarily Chinese, decided to limit the franchise to whites only. Massachusetts, meanwhile, mandated that any voter be able to write his name and read from the Constitution. Connecticut did much the same and also insisted that immigrants seeking to be naturalized wait two years. Illinois, whose biggest city (Chicago) had a significant immigrant population, repealed its law allowing the vote to immigrants intending to become U.S. citizens.

Suffrage for African Americans: Granted and Taken Away

With the termination of the Civil War came renewed hope among blacks that they would now be accorded full citizenship in American society, including one of the most basic rights that attaches to that privilege—the right to vote. Slaves, of course, had never had the right to vote, but free blacks had been able to vote in several northern states and Tennessee; that started to change, however, during the early part of the nineteenth century, and by the time of the Civil War only five states accorded free blacks the franchise (Maine, Massachusetts, New Hampshire, Vermont, and Rhode Island). New York did as well but only if a black met a property qualification of $250 and a three-year residency requirement.

The push for suffrage came not only from freed slaves but also from the 180,000 blacks who had fought in the Civil War. The Republican Party, meanwhile, though not unmoved by concerns for fundamental fairness—"The first great and sufficient reason why the negro should be admitted to the right of suffrage is that it is right" (Senator Edmund Ross of Kansas, cited in Maltz 1990, 143)—also saw the opportunity to champion the cause of black suffrage as a vehicle for strengthening the party in both northern and southern states (Franklin 1967, 325). Accordingly, the Republican-controlled Congress moved on several fronts. It proposed in 1866 the Fourteenth Amendment (1868), which set forth a definition of U.S. citizenship that included blacks and stated that citizens may not be denied privileges and immunities or equal protection of the laws. Furthermore, any state denying the right to vote in federal elections to any of its citizens would have its representation in Congress reduced by the percentage of those being so denied. This was followed by the Reconstruction Act (1867), which made readmission to the Union contingent upon ratifying the Fourteenth Amendment and ratifying state constitutions that accorded blacks the same voting privileges as whites. But Republicans were wary that even these steps would be sufficient to protect the franchise for blacks. The Democratic Party was starting to show some strength in state legislatures (e.g., Ohio, New Jersey, Minnesota), the election of 1868 returned the Republicans to power in Congress but with fewer seats, and there were disturbing new signs of southern resistance, including the rise of the Ku Klux Klan, attempts to unseat black legislators in Georgia, and harassment of blacks in Louisiana. Thus, a number of congressional Republicans thought it essential to move quickly toward passage of a constitutional amendment that would *specifically* prohibit the denial of the vote on the basis of race. In 1869, Congress did precisely that in the form of the Fifteenth Amendment (1870), which prohibited the federal and state governments from denying or abridging the right to vote for reasons of "race, color, or previous condition of servitude," and gave to Congress the power to enforce this provision.

Reconstruction in the South brought with it a flowering of secret societies, including the notorious Ku Klux Klan and Knights of the White Camellia, all designed to thwart the incorporation of blacks into the political process. When blacks turned out to vote, they were sometimes beaten, driven from their communities, and even hanged. Congress responded with the Enforcement Acts of 1870 and 1871, the first of which made interfering with the right to vote a federal crime punishable in a federal court, and the second, authorizing the president to send troops in order to protect the electoral process. In South Carolina alone, hundreds were arrested and no fewer than one hundred individuals fined and sentenced.

Southern Democrats, however, soon found conditions more conducive to their resurgence. In 1871 and 1872 Congress made it possible for most Confederates to regain their suffrage, which had been all but removed from them at the start of Reconstruction. The effect of this restoration was to greatly increase the ranks of the Democratic Party, which by 1876 became dominant again except in the states of Florida, South Carolina, and Louisiana (Franklin 1967, 327–329). Nor did the Republicans in the South help their cause any by being associated with governments that had become notoriously corrupt, and thus plump and ready targets of attack by the Democratic Party. The Supreme Court, as it frequently did during this period, made matters even worse by bringing down the curtain on the Enforcement Acts, ruling in 1876 that they were not enforceable under the Fourteenth (*United States v. Cruikshank*) or Fifteenth (*United States v. Reese*) Amendment, thereby declaring unconstitutional two statutes that had proved very useful in addressing white intimidation of blacks. Bear in mind also that as part of the deal worked out in the highly disputed election of 1876, southern Democrats in the House agreed to allow the electoral vote count to go forward unobstructed, provided that President Rutherford Hayes agreed to withdraw federal troops from the South, thereby ending Reconstruction. The Democrats, in return, would agree to protect the rights of blacks. Hayes kept his word. The Democrats, however, proved unable to make good on their pledge.

The fact that the Democrats were once again on the ascendancy in the South did not end the physical violence entirely, but other more subtle methods of discouraging blacks from voting were becoming more common: placing polling places away from black communities; changing polling locations at the last minute; stuffing ballot boxes; or, as one Democrat bragged, altering the count: "the white and black Republicans may outvote us, but we can outcount them" (cited in Franklin 1967, 333). Where possible, state legislatures were also complicit in a variety of ways, including gerrymandering voting districts in order to dilute black voting power—Virginia, for example, redefined its voting districts five times in a seventeen-year period. Petty larceny became grounds for being denied the vote, poll taxes were instituted in some places, and ballots were made deliberately confusing.

The assault on black suffrage ultimately went beyond tactics of intimidation and the passage of laws designed to obstruct, and moved into the constitutional arena. A number of attempts were made to seed state constitutions with provisions having as their sole purpose the goal of disenfranchising blacks, but in order not to run afoul of the Fifteenth Amendment, these restrictions were not specifically targeted at blacks, even though they were fashioned in such a way as to make blacks unable to comply. The most onerous restrictions were in those states where black populations were largest. In 1890, Mississippi, a majority of whose population was black, took the first steps by mandating a poll tax and literacy test. Five years later South Carolina followed suit, while allowing an exception to those who owned or paid taxes on property the previous year valued at $300 or more. In 1898, Louisiana not only imposed a literacy and poll tax but introduced a new constitutional wrinkle known as the "grandfather clause," which exempted from these requirements any males whose fathers and grandfathers were qualified to vote as of January 1, 1867. Needless to say, no blacks in the state had been qualified to vote on that date (Key 1949, 339–341).

These constitutional impediments had their intended effects. In the state of Mississippi, for example, only 9,000 of 147,000 voting-age blacks were registered to vote after 1890. In Louisiana, where there were 130,344 blacks registered in 1896, that number dropped to 5,320 in 1900, and down to 1,342 by 1904. Alabama, too, achieved its purpose, with only 3,000 blacks making the registration rolls a year after its new constitution went into effect in 1901, out of some 181,471 eligible to vote (Keyssar 2000, 341). Although the U.S. Supreme Court would ultimately rule the "grandfather clause" unconstitutional in 1915, in an 1898 decision (*Williams v. Mississippi*) it found no Fifteenth Amendment violation in either the literacy test or the poll tax. The Republican Party, meanwhile, having won a resounding victory in the election of 1896 in which it demonstrated unexpected strength in the northern states, now seemed much less concerned about preserving its black constituency in the South.

Tightening Voting Procedures in the North

As the southern states were making a concerted effort to contract the universe of voters to include whites only, northern states were embarking upon a series of their own reforms, which would also have the effect of reshaping its electorate. The motive behind these changes was not race, however. Rather, it was fueled in part by a desire to clean up government at the state and local levels, as well as make it more efficient. Members in both the Republican and Democratic parties who took up the cause at around the turn of the century became known as the "Progressives" and included business professionals, ministers, intellectuals, and journalists (Converse 1972, 297). The nearly fifteen-year period during which they exerted influence was called the Progressive Era.

The major target of the reformers was the Democratic Party political machines, which, with the loyal support of immigrant working-class voters, managed to gain control of municipal governments and even some state offices. Many of these municipal governments were rampant with graft and corruption and evinced little concern for conducting their affairs according to sound management principles. Nor were the parties, which printed and monitored the public casting of ballots in elections, averse to manipulating the process in order to insure that they remained in power. These activities included encouraging loyal supporters to vote more than once, giving individuals ballots to cast that had already been marked, defacing ballots cast for opponents, correcting spoiled ballots, stuffing ballot boxes, and, if all else failed, misreporting the official tally of votes (Benson 1978, 173).

One of the major reforms targeted at the political machines was the introduction of the Australian ballot. First used in Louisville, Kentucky, in 1888, this ballot is cast in secret and prepared, distributed, and tabulated by public officials at public expense. Both the Progressives and Populists lined up strongly behind this reform, which by 1910 had been adopted by every state in the Union (Mowry 1958, 80). Other changes struck serious blows against the political machines as well, including the change to nonpartisan elections at the local level, the replacement of patronage politics with a civil service system, and relocating some key government functions in independent agencies, thereby removing them from the rough and tumble of politics. Also, as a means of curbing party control over the nomination of candidates, the direct primary was introduced, which will be detailed later in this chapter.

To suggest that the Progressives were motivated solely by the high-minded principle of "clean government" would be to misstate reality, however, for lurking beneath the surface were also concerns that working-class laborers in the cities and farmers in the rural areas were espousing views that potentially threatened the economic interests of established elites. Farmers, increasingly irate over what railroad companies were charging them to take goods to market, initially organized into Granges, later to be replaced in the late 1870s by the Farmers' Alliance, which was the genesis of the Populist movement. Even in the South, white dirt farmers could be found joining for a time with their black counterparts to protest high interest rates and the railroad companies. With industrial competition growing by leaps and bounds, manufacturers sought to keep down costs by lowering wages, and this step in turn precipitated worker strikes in the 1880s and efforts by companies to halt union activity. In some instances, federal troops were even called in to disperse striking workers, and considerable loss of life ensued; by 1894 labor action of this kind had reached epidemic proportions (Piven and Cloward 2000, 56–60).

As one might expect, these farmer and worker concerns found expression in the political process and took the form of various third-party movements, including the Labor Reform Party (1872), the Greenback-Labor Party (1876), the Anti-Monopoly Party (1884), and the People's Party (1892), which was farmer-based and called for, among other things, the elimination of national banks, government ownership of transportation, and a fair system of taxation—a platform that proved attractive enough to garner the party twenty-two electoral votes for its nominee, James Weaver. In the campaign of 1896, the Populist movement reached its peak when the People's Party joined the Democrats in nominating William Jennings Bryan to run against Republican William McKinley, who saw considerable danger in the Populist rhetoric of the time and whose candidacy was strongly backed by corporate and financial interests in the country (Piven and Cloward 2000, 57, 58).

For the Progressives, their concerns over "untutored" voters were particularly palpable in connection with the working-class voters of the cities. In the words of eminent historian Francis Parkman, a leading Progressive intellectual of the period, "It is in the cities that the diseases of the body politic are gathered to a head, and it is here that the need of attacking them is most urgent. Here the dangerous classes are most numerous and strong, and the effects of flinging the suffrage to the mob are most disastrous" (cited in Piven and Cloward 2000, 90, 91). Not surprisingly, eleven states repealed laws that had extended the vote to immigrants intending to become U.S. citizens. But what to do about those citizens who already had the vote? Quite obviously, it could not be taken away, so means were found to make its exercise more difficult. Seven states outside the South increased their residency requirements—a change that had some real merit as a means of trying to prevent parties from shipping voters into a district solely for the purpose of voting, and then shipping them out again. In addition, by 1920 nine nonsouthern states had adopted literacy tests, with New York following suit in 1922, and Oregon in 1926. Although Massachusetts (1801) and New Jersey (1866) had adopted voter registration before any other states, more and more states began doing so in the latter part of the nineteenth century. Moreover, the procedures to register became considerably more onerous. Thus, rather than the government taking the initiative for registering citizens, that responsibility now fell to citizens themselves. Moreover, instead of registration being permanent, individuals now had to periodically re-register, and dates for cutting off the registration period were moved further back from election day. By 1929, all but three states had instituted voter registration procedures (Piven and Cloward 2000, 89–92; Kleppner 1982, 60; Keyssar 2000, 151).

Although some of the above changes certainly made sense, and indeed were motivated in part as a means of combating the voter fraud so apparent with the rise of political machines, it is equally clear that placing more hurdles between the voter and the ballot box contributed to the subsequent decline in voting turnout, particularly among those of lower socioeconomic status (Piven and Cloward 2000, 92, 93; Kleppner 1982, 60–64)—a result that was not unwelcome among some elements in the Progressive movement.

Women and Native Americans

Women. In 1878 a constitutional amendment was introduced in the U.S. Senate prohibiting the denial of the vote on the basis of sex. Although each house of Congress created a committee to study the matter, and both gave the amendment a favorable recommendation, it would be soundly trounced on the floor of the Senate. That an issue so central to women's rights had finally made it onto the agenda of the U.S. Congress at all was a function of events that preceded it.

Thirty years earlier in Seneca, New York, two women who had been active in the antislavery movement found themselves leading a conference on the rights of women. One was Lucretia Mott; the other, Elizabeth Cady Stanton. Their decision to do so had its origins in a meeting of the World's Anti-Slavery Convention held in London in 1840, which they both attended as delegates, although they were prohibited from being seated with the male delegates. This indignity persuaded them to commit to organizing a convention of women's rights upon their return to the states. In actual fact, the conference did not take place until some eight years later, but its "Declaration of Sentiments" marked the beginning of women's struggle for the right to vote:

> When, in the course of human events, it becomes necessary for one portion of the family of man to assume among the people of the earth a position . . . to which the laws of nature and of nature's God entitle them. . . . We hold these truths to be self-evident: that all men and women are created equal. . . . The history of mankind is a history of repeated injuries and usurpations on the part of man toward woman, having in direct object the establishment of an absolute tyranny over her. To prove this let facts be submitted to a candid world. (cited in Burns 1982, 401)

The bill of particulars that followed began with the denial of the right to vote. In a sign of how much work remained to be done, however, the right-to-vote grievance passed with only a narrow majority, and without the support of Lucretia Mott. Of the women in attendance that weekend in 1848, only one would ultimately live long enough to be able to vote for a president.

This meeting would be followed by others in Syracuse and Rochester, New York; in Akron, Ohio; and in Salem and Worcester, Massachusetts, where the first National Women's Rights meeting convened in 1850. Prior to the Civil War, prominent abolitionists such as Frederick Douglass, Horace Greeley, and Wendell Phillips had committed to pushing women's suffrage, but they later declined to do so, believing that it would detract from the effort needed to advance the cause of blacks (Smith 1997, 311–312). Over the next twenty years women, invoking the principle of "no taxation without representation," would decline to pay taxes in some states, and two new organizations emerged in 1869, reflecting a more systematic approach to their campaign. The National Woman Suffrage Association, under the leadership of Susan B. Anthony and Elizabeth Cady Stanton, focused all of its attention at the national level; the American Woman Suffrage Association, led by Lucy Stone and Henry Blackwell, worked in both the state legislatures and state constitutional conventions. Their cause received another boost when the territories of Wyoming and Utah decided to enfranchise women in 1869 and 1870, respectively, followed in 1883 by the state of Washington. Upon achieving statehood in 1890, Wyoming became the first state in the Union to grant the full franchise to women, with Utah, Colorado, and Idaho doing likewise over the subsequent five years. That western states took the lead in enfranchising women is understandable given the greater sense of egalitarianism that infused frontier communities and the desire to attract more settlers to them. There were also a great many states, counties, or municipalities that extended a limited vote to women on school boards, liquor licensing, and even municipal elections (Keyssar 2000, 184–186). (As far back as 1838, Kentucky decided to allow widowed property owners and unmarried women the right to vote in school board elections.)

If the push for women's suffrage was fought on grounds of simple fairness, it must also be said that in some elements of the movement this argument was joined by other decidedly less noble ones; namely, that the more virtuous nature of the female sex would serve at the ballot box as a protection against the undesirable attitudes found in members of the working class and foreigners; that one could hardly justify allowing "ignorant" blacks and foreigners to vote and not accord the same right to women; and that by extending the suffrage to women, according to the National American Woman Suffrage Association (NAWSA, created in 1890 from a merger of both earlier women's suffrage groups), Americans would insure that the white race would continue to rule. Fortunately, at the 1906 convention of the NAWSA, child labor reformer Florence Kelley repudiated and condemned such attitudes and succeeded in redirecting the organization in a more positive direction (Keyssar 2000, 188, 189, 198, 199).

Over the next several years women's rights groups became much more skilled in organizing at the grassroots level. Add to this the fact that women now made up one-fifth of the work force—a development that had two salutary effects. First, more women now became active in the movement, believing that the vote could provide them with political leverage that would make state governments more attentive to their working conditions specifically, and economic interests generally. Second, as women joined unions, their cause was taken up by organized labor, and thus what had been a tepid endorsement of the

American Federation of Labor given back in 1892 was now trumpeted by Samuel Gompers in 1915 and, incidentally, by socialist organizer Eugene Debs. Between 1910 and 1914 eight states voted to grant women the right to vote, the Progressive Party endorsed it, a right to vote amendment actually made it onto the floors of Congress, and President William Taft even agreed to speak before the NAWSA. Not even these developments, however, were enough to create an unstoppable momentum, and the East proved a particularly hard nut to crack, with Massachusetts, New York, New Jersey, and Pennsylvania all voting down the female franchise (Keyssar 2000, 204–207).

In 1916, both the Democratic and Republican parties endorsed the franchise for women but stated that it was a decision that should be left to the states. Although this view was also held by President Woodrow Wilson initially, he ultimately felt compelled to call upon the House of Representatives in 1917 to create a committee on women's suffrage. That he did so was no doubt a function of the fact that women's groups were protesting outside the White House; in the twelve states where women could vote in the presidential election of 1916, his narrow election victory resulted from narrowly carrying ten of them. But perhaps most crucially, with the onslaught of World War I in 1918, women were showing their patriotism by contributing to the war effort through such activities as knitting clothes and selling war bonds and thrift stamps; and in so doing, they neutralized the all-too-familiar claim that if you don't fight, you shouldn't vote (Kyvig 1996, 216).

As the House of Representatives debated a constitutional amendment in 1918, President Wilson, going against the platform of his party, advised the House that a federal solution was required to address women's suffrage, and he urged the membership to endorse it as "an act of right and justice." In the Senate, which proved more resistant, Wilson took the unprecedented step of appearing before that body and asking them to follow the House and approve the amendment as "necessary to the successful prosecution of the war" and "vital to the right solution of the great problems which we must settle, and settle immediately, when the war is over" (cited in Kyvig 1996, 233, 234). The Senate remained unpersuaded, however, but not for long. There were simply too many forces now arrayed in favor of women's suffrage: the increasingly sophisticated and aggressive organizational abilities of the movement, the fact that the many states that now allowed women to vote had not suffered any untoward consequences, the growing involvement of women in the war effort, and, perhaps most important, the growing sense among politicians at all levels that women's suffrage was inevitable and that in the interest of avoiding the electoral wrath of a new group of voters, it was best to get on the train before it left the station. The following year both houses of Congress passed the Nineteenth Amendment, and with the ratification by Tennessee on August 18, 1920, roughly one-half of our nation's population had now gained a federally protected right to vote. By one suffragette's calculation this achievement was possible only after "fifty-six state referendum campaigns and 480 drives to get state legislatures to hold those referendums, 47 campaigns to get state constitutional conventions to write women's suffrage into state constitutions, 277 campaigns to get state party conventions to include women's suffrage planks, 30 campaigns to get presidential party campaigns to include women's suffrage planks in their platforms and 19 campaigns with 19 successive Congresses" (Collins 2002).

Native Americans. The ability of Native Americans to vote had been hamstrung by the difficulties they experienced in securing citizenship. As far back as the 1830s, the U.S. Supreme Court had ruled that Native Americans were not American citizens because they were a dependent nation within the United States. Their root citizenship seemed to lie in treaty agreements with the United States. Nor did the Fourteenth Amendment facilitate the acquisition of citizenship for Indians, for the Supreme Court concluded in 1884 that the amendment was not applicable to the Native American population. The government, however, decided that it was desirable to extend citizenship to Indians provided certain conditions were met. Thus, in 1887 Congress passed the General Allotment Act, which allowed the establishment of Indian citizenship provided they had adopted a "civilized way of life" and had agreed to private allotments of their tribal lands. By 1905, the number of Native Americans achieving citizenship exceeded half the number eligible. Moreover, just as war had provided a boost to other groups seeking the right to vote, so it did with Native Americans, for Congress moved to extend citizenship to all American Indians who had served in the First World War and were honorably discharged. In 1924, Congress took more sweeping action by passing the Citizenship Act, which awarded citizenship automatically to any Native American born in the United States. Although this law should have settled the matter, ways were found to frustrate the franchise for this group of Americans. Some states (e.g., New Mexico) declined to let them vote because they did not pay taxes. Others concluded that because Indians were living on reservations, they failed to meet residency requirements; or, as in the case of Arizona, their reservation status put them under guardianship, which disqualified them from voting under the state's constitution. Both Arizona and Mexico halted their discriminatory practices shortly after they were singled out for rebuke by the Committee on Civil Rights, established by President Harry Truman in 1946. The courts also stepped in, declaring in 1948 that the denial of the vote on grounds of not paying taxes was a contravention of both the Fourteenth and Fifteenth Amendments; the denial of residency to American Indians living on reservations was also challenged in the courts and subsequently repealed (Keyssar 2000, 60, 164–164, 253–255).

Unfinished Business: Blacks, the Young, and the Mobile

Blacks. The efforts of southern states to exclude blacks by legal and extralegal means, begun after the Civil War, persisted well into the twentieth century. Although all northern states had abandoned the poll tax by 1940, it persisted in the South except for the states of North Carolina, Georgia, and Florida. Efforts by Congress to legislate against the poll tax in 1942 and 1944 fell victim to southern filibusters. The best it could do was to include an exemption from paying the poll tax in the Soldiering Act, passed in 1942 to allow members of the armed forces to vote absentee.

Literacy tests were still on the books in the 1940s in no fewer than eighteen states, but their application was most arbitrary and capricious in the South (Key 1949). But when Alabama went so far as to expand its literacy test beyond reading to include an "understanding and explaining" of what was read, the U.S. Supreme Court in 1949 let stand a lower court decision (*Schnell v. Davis*) ruling the requirement unconstitutional.

With the advent of the direct primary, an offspring of the Progressive movement, southern states saw yet another opportunity to frustrate black suffrage by declaring the primaries open to whites only—the rationale being that political parties were private associations and thus free to decide whom they wanted to include in their party activities. The Supreme Court, overturning an earlier 1935 decision (*Grovey v. Townsend*) in which it concurred in the view that political parties were private organizations, declared in 1944 (*Smith v. Allrwight)* that parties conducting primaries were engaging in a state function and thus could not ban blacks from participating. Although this ruling ended the "white primary" in a number of states, those in the deep South still found ways around the ruling (Key 1949, 625–632). Finally, to all these impediments must be added continued efforts by whites to discourage black voter participation in far less subtle ways through economic and physical intimidation.

Changing circumstances, however, were to force the plight of blacks back onto the national agenda. As it had at previous times in our history, war once again served to concentrate the mind. Not only was there the obvious outrage of denying civil rights to blacks who had fought in World War II—and the Korean War—but the war itself was fought to rid the world of a Nazi regime that had practiced the most appalling acts of discrimination in human history. How, then, could the United States tolerate acts of racism within its own boundaries? With blacks becoming a more prominent voting force in the North, it also behooved the parties to take a more vigorous stand for civil rights in their platforms. This they did, particularly the Republicans (Keyssar 2000, 244–251).

Harry Truman, the first president of the twentieth century to address the issue of discrimination straight on, appointed a Committee on Civil Rights in 1946, which in its report titled *To Secure These Rights* drew attention to the failure of our political process to guarantee the franchise to all citizens. It was, moreover, at pains to point out that as the United States now confronted a new international adversary in the form of communism, its moral posture would be seriously compromised if basic civil rights were being denied to its own citizens. The committee called for, among other things, the elimination of the poll tax and all forms of discrimination in state and federal elections. Although Truman by executive order was able to end segregation in the armed forces and mandate fair employment practices in the federal government, there was no significant action taken in connection with voting rights.

Following Truman's actions, however, Congress did begin to address civil rights, with the House of Representatives enacting civil rights legislation on several occasions between 1953 and 1957, only to have it die in the Senate. Meanwhile, the abuses continued, including purging black voters from registration rolls, denying registration to people of "bad character," requiring that blacks be accompanied by somebody white who could testify to their good character, and, of course, the outright refusal to register blacks.

At the initiative of the Eisenhower administration, Congress passed the Civil Rights Act of 1957, the first such legislation since 1875. Its provisions included the creation of a temporary Commission on Civil Rights charged with investigating instances of voting irregularities based upon race, and reporting back to Congress within two years; granting to the federal government the authority to bring civil suits and obtain injunctions in federal court where the right to vote was either threatened or denied; and elevating the Civil Rights section of the Department of Justice to a division, to be supervised by a newly appointed assistant attorney general. This legislation, while it represented some progress, allowed only for civil and not criminal action against violators, and, as the Justice Department discovered, federal judges were not always cooperative on matters of enforcement (Brauer 1977, 159, 160).

In the first half of the 1960s, progress on black voting rights accelerated rapidly. The Civil Rights Act of 1960 extended the life of the Civil Rights Commission, which continued its role of drawing national attention to voting rights abuses in southern states. In addition, federal courts were authorized to appoint voter referees, and the voting records of a primary, special, or general election were required to be preserved for twenty-two months. The Kennedy administration also undertook a Voter Education Project in 1962, which managed to register 287,000 blacks in twenty-one months. In many counties within the South's Black Belt, bitter opposition to black registration still persisted, but registration drives nevertheless had the salutary effect of heightening black activism in those areas (Brauer 1977, 115, 116). Less successful were the Kennedy administration's efforts in 1962 to have Congress pass legislation prohibiting the use of literacy tests in federal elections—a proposal that was opposed not only by many southern senators but by some liberal ones as well, and even some black leaders, who saw its restriction to federal elections alone as too tepid. Two years later, however, there was another victory—this time the ratification of the Twenty-fourth Amendment outlawing the poll tax in all federal elections. The crown jewel of voting rights legislation, however, came one year later. With a voter registration drive in Selma, Alabama, having led to the arrest of Martin Luther King and the slaying of two civil rights workers, President Lyndon Johnson went before a joint session of Congress and, in the most stirring speech of his presidency, implored the members to enact voting rights legislation that would assure blacks the unimpeded right to vote. Before the year was out Congress had complied, passing the most comprehensive and effective voting rights legislation in U.S. history.

The Voting Rights Act of 1965 provided for the immediate suspension of literacy tests and other devices in those states where fewer than 50 percent of the voters had voted in 1964; the attorney general was authorized to dispatch federal examiners to southern states for the purpose of enrolling blacks and observing registration practices; governments in the jurisdictions under scrutiny were prohibited from changing their election procedures unless given permission by the Justice Department; and finally, the Justice Department was instructed to challenge the constitutionality of the poll tax in court, which it did, convincing the Supreme Court in 1966 (*Harper et al. v. Virginia Board of Elections*) that the use of a poll tax in any election violated the Equal Protection Clause of the Fourteenth Amendment. (This ruling, incidentally, caused three of the eleven states that still retained laws against paupers voting to repeal them.)

In two of the states where violations of black voting rights had been most egregious, the impact of the Voting Rights Act became readily apparent. Prior to its implementation, black voter registration in Mississippi was under 10 percent in 1964 but had grown to 60 percent by 1968; in Alabama during the same period, it went from 24 to 57 percent (Keyssar 2000, 264).

Congress renewed the Voting Rights Act in 1970, 1975, and 1982, on this latter occasion extending it for an additional twenty-five years. These extensions added new provisions, including widening the ban on literacy tests to all states—a provision challenged but upheld in a 1970 ruling by the Supreme Court (*Oregon v. Mitchell*); lowering the voting age to eighteen, which the Supreme Court ruled Congress could mandate for federal elections only (*Oregon v. Mitchell*); mandating a residency requirement of no more than thirty days in presidential elections; creating uniform standards for registration and absentee voting in federal elections; extending provisions of the act to include "language minorities" (i.e., Hispanics, American Indians, Alaska Natives, and Asians); and mandating bilingual registration materials and ballots.

Although the legislation and Twenty-fourth Amendment passed in the 1960s would firmly secure for blacks and others the right to vote, as we shall see further on in this chapter, there were attempts by some southern states to dilute the impact of that vote.

The Young. If the 1960s saw extraordinary advances in voting rights for blacks and other minorities, it did for the young as well; and the Vietnam War provided the backdrop against which the push for lowering the voting age played out. War, of course, had always prompted the claim that "if you're old enough to fight, then you're old enough to vote." During World War II the issue gained enough visibility that resolutions were introduced in Congress. The House Judiciary Committee held hearings on an amendment authored by Senator Jennings Randolph (D-WV), Congressman Harley Kilgore (D-WV), and Senator Arthur Vandenburg (R-MI) calling for lowering the voting age to eighteen. The proposal went nowhere, however, and only the state of Georgia on its own initiative decided in 1943 to allow eighteen-year-olds to vote. Similar action would be taken in the next decade by Kentucky (eighteen), Alaska (nineteen), and Hawaii (twenty).

As the young were being sent off to Southeast Asia in the 1960s to fight the most controversial and divisive foreign war in our nation's history, the call for lowering the voting age assumed a special resonance—particularly on college campuses. Not surprisingly, the issue boiled over into the political process. A number of states decided to address the question in referenda, with decidedly mixed results. Between 1966 and 1969 some eighteen states rejected one or another proposal to lower the voting age by one, two, or three years. A few reacted more favorably. Maine and Nebraska decided to lower it to twenty; Massachusetts, Minnesota, and Montana to nineteen; and Alaska to eighteen (Kyvig 1996, 364, 365). The Senate Subcommittee on Constitutional Amendments convened in 1970 under the leadership of Birch Bayh (D-IN), long a supporter of the eighteen-year-old vote. By this time the nation had experienced massive and sometimes violent antiwar protests, to say nothing of urban riots within some of its inner cities. Bayh and others saw the ballot as a means of channeling the frustrations of the young from the streets into electoral politics.

Why the Senate leadership ultimately decided to legislate the eighteen-year-old vote by including it in the 1970 Civil Rights Act (see above) rather than by a constitutional amendment is not altogether clear, but it is fair to say that Emanuel Celler (D- NY), the chairman of the House Judiciary Committee, was an important factor. It was to his committee that the amendment would have been referred in the House, and his strong belief that states should decide the qualifications for voting insured that the amendment would face a very chilly reception indeed. Ironically, however, the decision to lower the voting age by legislation ultimately opened the way for accomplishing it through amendment. More specifically, when certain provisions of the 1970 Civil Rights Act were challenged in court, the Supreme Court ruled (in *Oregon v. Mitchell*) that while Congress was constitutionally permitted to regulate voting age requirements for *federal* elections, it could not do so for *state* elections.

In the aftermath of the Court's ruling, legislators were now presented with the frightening prospect that in the upcoming 1972 election, those under twenty-one would be able to vote for federal candidates but not (in most states) those running for state office. Aware of the confusion and expense that would attend an election under these conditions, Congress knew it had to act without delay. Because repealing the eighteen-year-old vote provision of the Civil Rights Act—thereby taking back a right it had already given to the young—was guaranteed to alienate them, the amendment route now struck many as the only viable option. With uncommon alacrity, Congress overwhelmingly approved the amendment in March 1971, and the thirty-eighth state ratified it just three months later (Kyvig 1996, 366, 367).

The Mobile. Residency requirements for voting had long been established in states as a means of preventing corruption and insuring that citizens resided in a jurisdiction long enough to be sufficiently familiar with local issues and candidates to cast an informed vote. In the second half of the twentieth century, however, the U.S. population had become far more mobile. Thus, residency requirements of up to a year, which was the case in twenty-one of the thirty-three states having some kind of residency qualification, served as a serious impediment to voting—in one study this restriction was said to have kept as many as fifteen million from the polls in the 1964 election (Crotty 1977, 39; Keyssar 2000, 275). The 1970 Civil Rights Act addressed this problem by mandating a residency qualification of no more than thirty days in federal elections, and those unable to meet even this cutoff were entitled to cast absentee ballots in the state where they had previously resided. Two years later the Supreme Court would rule (in *Dunn v. Blumstein*) as a violation of the Equal Protection Clause Tennessee's one-year residency requirement for state elections and ninety-day requirement for county elections. Although not mandating an alternative standard, the Court suggested that "30 days appears to be an ample period of time" for states to protect against election fraud.

The Weight of a Vote: Reapportionment and Redistricting

As the political process moved to secure the right to vote during the 1960s, it also sought to ensure that the votes of American citizens would be valued the same when choosing the membership of legislative bodies. The need to address this issue was acute.

The Constitution (Article I, Sec. 2) mandates that a census be conducted every ten years. On the basis of the results, the number of seats allocated to each state in the U.S. House of Representatives is adjusted accordingly, and the boundaries of congressional districts, and indeed state legislative districts, are redrawn to reflect the population shifts that have occurred during the previous decade. The responsibility for redefining a state's congressional districts lies with its state legislature.

For much of the nation's history the matter of reapportionment was not much of a problem because Congress would respond to population expansions and the addition of new states by increasing the number of seats in the U.S. House of Representatives. It also mandated in 1842 that districts contain "as nearly as possible an equal number of inhabitants," and in 1901 that districts be designed of "compact territory." By 1900 the House had increased in size from its original 106 members to 391. To prevent that body from becoming too unwieldy, Congress decided in 1910 to cap the number of seats at 435.

Most state legislatures were also obliged under their state constitutions to redraw state legislative districts and to do so with populations of equal size. Most did not comply, however, preferring instead to allow districts to become greatly malapportioned rather than run the risk of a redistricting process that could cost some of them their seats. In states such as Alabama, Tennessee, and Delaware, for example, there had been no redistricting of their state legislatures during the first sixty years of the twentieth century, leaving some legislative districts with one hundred times more people than others (Dudley and Gitelson 2002, 23). Although such glaring disparities would seem to accord votes in some legislative districts far more weight than those in others, the Supreme Court for many years declined to become involved, arguing that reapportionment was a "political question" and thus not appropriate for settlement by the Court (*Colgrove v. Green*, 1946). All that changed in 1962 when the Supreme Court was presented with a case *(Baker v. Carr)* in which residents of Tennessee's cities contended that the vast differences in the populations of the State Assembly districts violated both the state's constitution and the Equal Protection Clause of the Fourteenth Amendment.

The Supreme Court, reversing its previous position of non-involvement in redistricting questions, now took jurisdiction over the case and ruled in favor of the underrepresented city dwellers. Two years later *(Reynolds v. Sims*, 1964) the Court articulated a standard for reapportionment of state legislatures, requiring that it be done solely on the basis of population and noting that "the Equal Protection Clause requires that a State make an honest and good faith effort to construct districts, in both houses of its legislature, as nearly of equal population as is practicable."

In the same year the Supreme Court addressed redistricting of congressional districts and in doing so imposed a standard that was even stricter than the one it required of the states. In *Wesberry v. Sanders,* it required that "as nearly as practicable" one person's vote in a congressional election be worth as much as another's. The Court reemphasized this point in 1969 (*Kirkpatrick v. Preisler*), noting that "a state must make a good faith effort to achieve mathematical equality; they were also required to show why any deviation from perfect equality was unavoidable or was justified by sound reasons" (Cain and Butler 1997, 31).

Of course, the redrawing of district lines can produce districts of roughly equal population and yet still produce results that are unfair if the lines are drawn in such a way as to dilute the vote of one group and thereby strengthen the vote of another. A district can, for example, be redrawn to advantage one political party (political gerrymandering) or disadvantage a particular group (racial/ethnic gerrymandering). The Supreme Court stated in 1986 that it would entertain cases of political gerrymandering that raised Equal Protection Clause questions (*Davis v. Bandemer*), but its rulings in 1986 (*Davis v. Bandemer*) and 1989 (*Badham v. Eu*) suggested that it was not prepared to accept claims of partisan gerrymandering unless it produces discrimination against political groups "comparable to that experienced by racial minorities" (Cain and Butler 1997, 32).

In southern public officials' ongoing effort to squelch the influence of blacks at the ballot box, racial gerrymandering was yet another arrow in their quiver. A particularly egregious example of this occurred in 1957 when the Alabama state legislature redrew the borders of Tuskegee, transforming it from a four-sided city to a twenty-eight–sided one that now excluded almost every black voter, leaving it as virtually an all-white city. In *Gomillion v. Lightfoot* (1960), the Supreme Court ruled that the action was a clear intent to discriminate against black voters and a violation of the Fifteenth Amendment. Under the 1982 amendments to the Voting Rights Act (1965), however, the redrawing of district lines, even when having no intent to discriminate, could nevertheless be invalidated if they had the *effect* of diluting minority voting power. These 1982 amendments were construed by some states, and even to some degree by the Department of Justice, as mandating the drawing of majority-minority districts, which they in fact proceeded to do following the completion of the 1990 census (Dudley and Gitelson 2002, 25, 26). The state of North Carolina, which picked up a seat, intentionally created a majority black congressional district, which was cleared by the Justice Department—clearance it was required to seek under provisions of the 1965 Civil Rights Act identifying seventeen states and jurisdictions guilty of past discriminatory practices. The configuration of this newly designed district was, to say the least, odd: "165 miles long, winding snake-like through tobacco country, financial centers, and manufacturing areas. The district was so narrow that one candidate for the seat quipped, 'I can drive down Interstate 85 with both car doors open and hit every person in the district'"

(Dudley and Gitelson 2002, 26). The Supreme Court would ultimately declare the design of the district unconstitutional because it was drawn solely with racial considerations in mind and, therefore, in violation of the Fourteenth Amendment (*Shaw v. Hunt,* 1996). In both this case, however, and one decided three years later (*Hunt v. Cromartie,* 1999), the Court pointed out that it was not inappropriate to take race into consideration along with other factors in designing districts, but it was impermissible to allow it to be the dominant factor.

Making Voting Easier

It is ironic that the 1960s and 1970s, which saw extraordinary gains made in securing the right to vote and insuring that votes would count equally, also marked the start of a decline in the number of citizens availing themselves of the opportunity to exercise the franchise. Between the 1960 and 1988 presidential elections, voter turnout declined from 63 percent to 50.1 percent. Although the explanation for why this occurred is uncertain and much debated, considerable attention was focused on the procedural hurdles that were placed in the path of prospective voters—a matter that preoccupied voting reformers for the rest of the twentieth century.

The Commission on Registration and Voting Participation, appointed by President John Kennedy, had drawn attention to these problems back in 1963, some of which (literacy tests, poll taxes, residency requirements) were addressed in the Voting Rights Acts and the Twenty-fourth Amendment. There continued, however, to be wide state variation in other areas related to the mechanics of getting registered to vote: Were registration offices open at convenient times (evenings and on weekends) and in places of easy access (at the neighborhood level)? Was registration permitted up to a few days prior to the election? How often were registration lists purged? And how easy was it to apply for absentee voting? (Wolfinger and Rosenstone 1980, ch. 4).

In the late 1960s three states decided to allow mail-in registration, and by the early 1990s the number had grown to twenty-nine. But the impact upon registration in these states proved to be modest, largely because voters still had to pick up the registration form at a local office (Piven and Cloward 2000, 206). President Jimmy Carter also decided to address the issue. As part of his first legislative package in 1977, he submitted to Congress the National

Uniform Registration Act, calling for election-day registration—a practice already on the books in four states (Minnesota, Maine, Wisconsin, and Oregon, the latter which later repealed it), where it significantly increased the registration rolls. Many members of Congress, however, uncertain of how a potential influx of new voters might affect their own and their party's reelection prospects, evinced little support for the idea. Some nine years later, Congress would take a limited step, easing registration and voting for those living abroad. The Uniformed and Overseas Citizen Absentee Voting Act allowed Americans outside the country to both register and vote absentee.

Perhaps the most organized and persistent campaign to reform registration procedures had its genesis in 1982 when an organization known as Human Service Employees Registration and Voter Education (Human SERVE) was established to promote the registration of voters at various public agencies such as daycare centers and welfare offices, all with a view to increasing registration rates among those least represented in American elections, namely, the poor. Michigan had been the first state to experiment with registration at a state agency, passing legislation in 1975 allowing its citizens to do so when applying for or renewing their driver's license. Over a period of several years Human SERVE worked assiduously to persuade states and localities to allow registration at public agencies, believing that substantial use of the procedure at the state level would facilitate adoption of national legislation. The National Voter Registration Act (NVRA), more commonly known as "Motor Voter," won congressional approval in 1992 only to be vetoed by President George H. Bush. In 1993 it passed again and was signed into law by President Bill Clinton. That the legislation ultimately won approval was the result of the dogged determination exhibited by Human SERVE and other voting rights activists, the fact that Motor Voter programs had already been operating in some twenty-nine states, and the publication of a number of respected scholarly studies showing that an influx of new voters would not alter election results (Piven and Cloward 2000, 222, 223). Although the NVRA provided for registration when applying for or renewing a driver's license, as well as in state offices that provide welfare and disabled assistance, it also allowed registration by mail with use of a standardized form, and it prohibited the purging of voter rolls except for change of residence. As to the impact of this legislation, the evidence indicates that the number of registrants has increased anywhere from 3.7 to 11 percentage points, depending upon how one counts those on voting lists who fall into the "inactive" category (Piven and Cloward 2000, 261, 262). The increase in the number of registered voters, however, appears to have had no impact on the number of citizens who turn out to vote.

Election 2000: Making Votes Count

Despite the enormous progress made in achieving the right to vote, the first presidential election of the new century served to highlight that much remained to be done. The right to vote, after all, and the streamlining of registration procedures that qualify individuals to exercise that right are all for naught if their votes get counted for someone other than they intended, or don't get counted at all.

One study of the 2000 election found that four to six million votes from around the country were not counted due to faulty equipment, confusing ballots, and voter error (Seeyle 2001). The now notorious misfirings that occurred in Florida, though unfortunate, were scarcely unique to that state. With respect to voting equipment, for example, only four states in 2000 (New York, Oklahoma, Alaska, Hawaii) had the same voting equipment in all of their counties. Thirty-seven percent of all the counties in the nation used the punch-card machine, a voting method with an error rate five times higher than the paper ballot or optical scanner, and which in Florida produced dimpled, hanging, and punched chads, leading to a statewide undercount of 3 percent (Rapoport 2001a, 44; *Washington Post* 2001, A7). Moreover, when it came time to do the recount, Florida, like a number of other states, had established no uniform standards for determining how to count the ballots. Thus, vote counters were using different standards to determine voter intent from identical types of ballots or identical types of voting machines. There was also variation by county in how absentee overseas ballots were counted, even though state and federal statutes were quite clear on what constituted a valid ballot. Thus, in some Florida counties overseas ballots were counted despite lacking a postmark and witness signatures— both required by law. In other counties, they were not. Even though Florida law specifies that ballots must be dated and postmarked no later than election day, some counties accepted later postmarks while others did not (Keating and Lebling 2001; Berke 2001; *New York Times* 2001b, A18).

Voter confusion also led to ballots being disqualified, or votes being cast for candidates other than the voter had intended. Thousands of votes in Florida, for example, were disqualified because voters took literally the words "Write-in Candidate." Thus, after casting their vote for president they went on to write in his name (Sabato 2002, 10). Nor were polling places always staffed with enough people—a problem that, incidentally, plagued 57 percent of the voting jurisdictions throughout the country—to assist voters who were confused or unfamiliar with the mechanics of voting (Walsh 2001). In other instances, it was not voter ignorance but rather ballot design that was the source of confusion. The now infamous Palm Beach County "butterfly ballot" was constructed so ineptly that it led to different combinations of overvotes (i.e., voting for more than one candidate). Over 5,000 voters ended up voting for both Al Gore and Pat Buchanan, nearly 3,000 for Gore and the Socialist candidate, hundreds who punched holes for both Gore and vice presidential candidate Joe Lieberman, and over 1,600 who voted for both George W. Bush and Buchanan (Dershowitz 2001, 25).

There were also problems with the voter registration process. According to a study undertaken by the General Accounting Office, 43 percent of the voting jurisdictions in the country had problems with the Motor Voter Act, including forwarding to election officials voter registration forms that were illegible, incomplete, and/or late, thereby causing many voters to be turned away from the polls on election day (Walsh 2001; *New York Times* 2001a, A10). In addition, the computer system responsible for updating voter registration rolls in Florida instead purged a number of qualified voters as felons, who are prohibited from voting under Florida law.

It is also worth noting here that Florida is one of only fourteen states to impose a permanent voting ban on any individual convicted of a felony—a rather harsh penalty, it would seem, for those who have served their time in prison and returned to society. Only three states (Maine, New Hampshire, Vermont) allow someone to vote in prison; thirty-two bar it while on parole, and twenty-nine while on probation (Dudley and Gitelson 2002, 12). According to the Brennan Center for Justice, Florida's ban on voting for those convicted of a felony served to exclude some 500,000 voters from the polls in the 2000 election (Rapoport 2001b, 13).

The problems associated with the 2000 presidential election led to the creation of the National Commission on Election Reform, jointly chaired by former presidents Gerald R. Ford and Jimmy Carter. Following seven months of study, the group presented its report to President George W. Bush on July 31, 2001. Their recommendations called for every state to adopt a statewide system of voter registration, provisional voting for those who claim to be qualified to vote, restoration of voting rights to convicted felons who have served their sentences, and the creation of statewide standards for determining what constitutes a valid vote. The commission also called upon Congress to make election day a national holiday, ease requirements for overseas absentee voter registration, develop a comprehensive set of voter equipment standards, provide federal assistance to the states for election administration, and create an Election Administration Commission to assist in these matters (National Commission on Federal Election Reform 2001, 5–14). Although Congress did not follow all of these recommendations, in fall 2002 it passed the Help America Vote Act, which incorporated many of them: States were provided with federal money to assist them in replacing punch card and lever voting machines and were required to provide one voting machine per precinct for disabled voters, define what constitutes a legal vote for each type of voting machine, create a centralized and computerized state voter registration database, and provide for provisional voting. The act also created an Election Assistance Commission, appointed by the president, to assist states in complying with its provisions.

The Opportunities to Vote

Thus far, our attention has been focused on tracing expansions in the right to vote, assurances that the casting of the vote itself is not compromised, and the mechanics of qualifying to exercise that right. We now turn our focus to the purposes to which the vote is to be put, namely, making choices.

The Vote for President

For reasons addressed earlier in this chapter, the Founding Fathers did not contemplate direct election of the president. Rather, the chief executive was to be chosen by a group of presidential electors, and it would be left up to each state legislature to determine how its state's presidential electors would be chosen. Although state legislatures themselves initially made the selections, as the democratic spirit gained momentum throughout the country, legislatures faced growing pressure to allow the people within their states to do the choosing, and by 1832 every state except South Carolina (which held off until 1860) was now giving the choice of electors over to its citizens. In addition, as political parties grew in strength, they began to recruit presidential electors who were bound informally to their party's nominee. Hence, the presidential electors no longer exercised the independent judgment contemplated by the Founding Fathers. Although presidential electors today are legally bound by state law in twenty-six states—the constitutionality of which is highly questionable—only a minuscule number have proven to be "faithless," and in no instance have they determined the outcome of a presidential election. In short, popular election of pledged electors in essence created a system of popular election of the president. It is worth noting, however, that in contrast to popular election of members of the U.S. House, which is guaranteed in the original Constitution, and popular election of U.S. senators, guaranteed under the Seventeenth Amendment, there is no constitutional guarantee to the people to elect their president. Rather, that privilege is given to us by the state legislatures in our respective states, any one or all of which could theoretically reclaim that right at any time.

Direct Election of U.S. Senators

The Founding Fathers anticipated that the United States Senate would act as a brake upon the House of Representatives, whose members were to be directly elected by the people and for only two years, thereby rendering them much more sensitive to the public pulse. The Senate, in contrast, would be more insulated from temporary partisan storms, in part because its members would be serving six years and partly also because they would be chosen not directly by the people but by presumably more responsible members of state legislatures.

Congressman Henry Storrs of New York in 1826 became the first member of Congress to propose a constitutional amendment calling for direct election of U.S. senators. Andrew Johnson would do likewise as a congressman, senator, and president. As calls for expanding the role of the people in government began to grow in the 1890s, so too did the appeal of electing senators directly. Indeed, during the first session of the Fifty-second Congress (1892–1893) there were no fewer than twenty-five proposals calling for direct election (Kyvig 1996, 208–209). Nor did it hurt the cause that senators were increasingly seen as "fat cats" who owed their seats to their wealth and a willingness to sprinkle some of it among state legislators. Nor, further, did it hurt that several state legislatures were themselves derelict in carrying out their responsibility to choose their senators: "In no fewer than forty-five instances in twenty states between 1891 and 1905, legislatures, unable to reach agreement on candidates, delayed filling Senate seats. Fourteen seats remained empty for an entire legislative session or more. In the worst case, Delaware was represented by only one senator in three Congresses, and none at all from 1901 until 1908" (Kyvig 1996, 209).

Sensing the growing appeal of direct election, the People's Party and the Democratic Party took up the cause, and between 1893 and 1902 the House of Representatives expressed its support for direct election proposals on five different occasions; it was joined in 1897 by fifteen state legislatures. An amendment proposal must have two-thirds approval in both houses of Congress, however, and it should come as no surprise that the Senate, wary of the unpredictability that would attend a change in the way senators were selected, never permitted the matter to come to a vote. Direct election advocates now began to seek alternatives, one of which was a constitutional convention. Although attracting very considerable support, there was also some concern that a convention might open a Pandora's box for the introduction of all kinds of amendments. More effective was the tack taken by the state of Oregon, some variant of which would ultimately be adopted by more than half the states by 1909. Those filing petitions of candidacy for the state legislature were required to state whether they agreed to vote for the senatorial candidate who received the most votes in the primary election.

The cause received a further boost both from a bribery scandal that swirled around the legislative selection of an Illinois senator (William Lorimer) and from the addition of a new and relentless Kansas senator (Joseph L. Bristow), who unsuccessfully tried to attach a direct election amendment to a tax bill in 1909 but fared better the following year, when his proposal was referred to a more sympathetic Senate committee. After a year's consideration, the proposal was favorably reported out of committee and, for the first time, onto the floor of the Senate, where it came up for a vote in February 1911. Although the proposal failed to achieve the necessary two-thirds (54 to 33), the momentum behind the movement only grew, and the following year Congress approved the amendment. It became part of the Constitution following its ratification by the thirty-sixth state, Connecticut, on April 8, 1913.

Choosing Our Choices

In other democracies of the world, the nomination of government leaders is done by political party groups that range in inclusiveness from relatively small executive councils (e.g., Germany), to party members in the national legislature (e.g., Australia), to a national party convention that in some ways resembles our own (e.g., Canada). But even the most inclusive of processes to be found in other countries fall well short of the role accorded the American citizenry in determining who their choices will be on election day. The participatory character that now defines the presidential nominating process, however, did not exist at the time political parties were established in this country. The congressional caucus was the initial mode of nomination, with the members of each party in Congress meeting to decide who its standard-bearer would be in the general election. Employed from 1800 to 1824, the caucus method gradually fell into disrepute. It came under fire from such heavyweights as Andrew Jackson, Henry Clay, and John Quincy Adams, all of whom had been passed over as the Republican Party nominee in 1824. The nod was instead given to John Crawford, who went on to lose badly in the general election. An ever-growing number of state and local party officials also objected to the congressional caucus because it denied them any role whatsoever in selecting a nominee.

Following a brief transition period during which presidential candidates were nominated by state legislatures and local conventions, political parties instituted a new system known as national conventions. First employed in 1831, these conventions were made up of delegates chosen by each state's political party, with the process of delegate selection varying by state. In some states, the *appointment* method was used, with the governor or a party's state committee having the appointment power. The most common practice adopted, however, was the *caucus-convention*. Under this system, party members met in their precincts and selected delegates to a county-level caucus, which then picked delegates to attend a district caucus; the district caucus in turn chose delegates to the party's state convention, which then selected delegates to attend the party's national convention.

By the turn of the century, many voters had become disillusioned with this method of nomination as well. It was perceived as subject to near-total manipulation by the party bosses. Few regulations existed on convention procedures. Strong-arm tactics were used to prevent some delegates from entering the conventions and to intimidate others once they got there, and many of the delegates proved to be unsavory characters more than willing to sell their vote to the highest bidder. This state of affairs, along with other malfunctions in the political process, gave rise to a reform movement known as the Progressives (already discussed in this chapter) that, among other things, sought to involve voters more directly in the nominating process. As a means of achieving this goal, they called for the establishment of the primary to nominate presidential candidates and, incidentally, candidates for other public offices as well. Administered by the states rather than political parties, primaries enabled voters themselves to pick the individuals who would comprise their state's delegation to its party's national nominating convention. Four years later the state of Wisconsin, birthplace of the Progressive movement, went further, requiring that all its delegates to the Republican and Democratic national conventions be chosen by primary. Choosing delegates, however, did not enable voters to register their preferences for presidential candidates themselves. Accordingly, in 1910 the citizens of Oregon decided to establish the first presidential "preference" primary in which voters were given an opportunity to express their preference for a presidential candidate and then vote separately (on the same ballot) for individuals they wanted to serve as delegates. These delegates were legally bound to vote for the presidential candidate who won the preference vote.

The appeal of presidential primaries began to take hold, and by 1916 some twenty-five states had instituted primaries of one kind or another. The initial enthusiasm gradually waned, however, with only the state of Alabama adopting the primary method over the next thirty-two years, while eight others decided to abandon them. Several factors contributed to this change of heart: Party leaders showed little enthusiasm for them, the cost of running them was high, turnout was low, and many presidential candidates declined to enter or campaign in them. In subsequent years, some states returned to the primary and others repealed it, until by 1968 the number appeared to have stabilized at sixteen states plus the District of Columbia.

The 1968 Democratic national convention proved to be a defining event in the history of presidential nominating politics. President Lyndon Johnson took himself out of the race for the nomination after his challenger, anti–Vietnam War candidate Senator Eugene McCarthy (D-MN), appeared to be attracting a surprising level of support among Democrats—so much in fact that Senator Robert Kennedy (D-NY) decided to toss his hat into the ring as an antiwar candidate. With Lyndon Johnson's blessing, Vice President Hubert Humphrey decided to join the race, too—but entered no primaries—and was widely seen as the defender of the president's war policy. With the untimely assassination of Robert Kennedy on the evening of his big win in the California primary, the race was now between McCarthy and Humphrey. It was not much of a race, however, for by the time the first balloting of convention delegates was completed, Humphrey had swamped his opponent, winning 1,760 votes to McCarthy's 601. That Humphrey had such an easy time of it is explained by the fact that a majority of convention delegates in 1968, as in nearly every previous election in this century, were chosen by either the caucus-convention or appointment method, both of which were firmly controlled by the party elites, most of whom had lined up solidly behind Humphrey in 1968.

McCarthy and Kennedy supporters were outraged and disillusioned. The Democratic Party had, in their judgment, chosen a nominee whose views on the Vietnam War were not notably different from those of the president he served. Moreover, in contrast to McCarthy and Kennedy, both of whom had taken their cases directly to the people in the primaries, Vice-President Humphrey had not entered a single one. Furthermore, the McCarthy forces charged that during the nominating process they had repeatedly been victimized by arbitrary rules and procedures in connection with the caucus-convention method of delegate selection, the method used to select most of the delegates. The upshot of all these complaints was the creation of the McGovern-Fraser Commission (1969–1970), which was charged with examining how delegates were chosen and, where appropriate, making recommendations for change.

Confirming most of the charges leveled by the McCarthy forces, the McGovern-Fraser Commission called for sweeping reforms in the delegate selection process. These changes may be broadly characterized as follows: (1) the establishment of uniform and detailed procedures for selecting delegates by caucus-convention; (2) a significant reduction in the number of delegates who could be chosen by the appointment method, and a prohibition against reserving certain delegate slots for party and public officials; and (3) the requirement that states take immediate steps to increase the number of blacks, women, and young people in their state delegations. Taking its cue from the Democrats, the Republicans also decided to incorporate most of these reforms but declined to go beyond encouraging their state parties to include more blacks, women, and young people in their delegations. Although some of these reforms would be modified and others added in subsequent years, one overriding reality would remain: Party leaders no longer exercised the strong control over the presidential nominating process that they had enjoyed prior to 1972.

Just as the Democratic and Republican Party reforms served to reduce the influence of the party elites, so too did another equally important development—the proliferation of primaries. Although neither the McGovern-Fraser Commission nor any subsequent reform commissions specifically called for more primaries, since 1968 they have become the vehicle for choosing a majority of the delegates to our parties' national conventions. Several factors appear to have contributed to this change. Some states thought the complexity of the McGovern-Fraser Commission reforms could be implemented more easily in a primary than in a caucus-convention system. In addition, with the growing amount of media attention being given to primaries, states saw an opportunity to enhance their visibility and derive some financial benefit by switching. Further, it seems likely that some states, perceiving the broad-based support for expanding participation in the presidential selection process, understandably saw the primary as the best means for achieving this end.

Though the level of participation in the primaries has hardly been what one might have hoped for—the average turnout is around 30 percent—the fact remains that there are far more people participating in the president-by-primary process than ever took part in the nominating process prior to 1968.

Initiative, Referendum, and Recall

The power of the voters to preempt or overrule the actions of elected officials, and even revoke their election to office, is a very considerable power indeed and, as one might imagine, rooted in the belief that our elected representatives may on occasion not be acting in the public interest. The Founding Fathers, believing it prudent to create a certain constitutional distance between the elected representative and the voter, declined to give the citizenry any such power over public officials apart from electing them, and even here the power to directly elect extended only to members of the U.S. House of Representatives.

Many states, in contrast, have in fact seen fit to accord their citizens such power through the use of the *initiative, referendum,* and *recall.* The initiative allows both statutes and constitutional amendments to be presented directly to the voters for approval, thereby bypassing the legislative process, provided a requisite number of voter signatures is secured by petition. A variant of this procedure, the *indirect initiative,* allows statutes to be proposed by petition and then presented to the legislature for action. If the legislature fails to act or unacceptably alters the original proposal, then supporters may gather additional signatures and present the proposal to the voters for acceptance or rejection. The referendum enables voters to accept or reject laws passed by the legislature when those laws are placed on the ballot, a sufficient number of petition signatures again being necessary in order to do so. The recall empowers voters, after having secured the required number of signatures on a petition (typically 25 percent), to remove or discharge a public official from office, after which a special election is held (Cronin 1989, 2). As of 2000, twenty-five states allowed for some form of initiative, and twenty-four allowed for a referendum process. Twenty-one states permit both. With respect to recall, eighteen states provide for this process, with some applying it to all elected officials, others to all elected officials except judges, and one (Montana) to all elected and some appointed officials (Magleby 1984, 36; Cronin 1989, 126–127).

The impetus behind these rather stern measures dates back to the latter part of the nineteenth century, when state legislatures were seen by farmers, miners, and other members of the working class as being in the grips of financial and manufacturing interests. Accordingly, when the Populists convened in Omaha, Nebraska, for their first party convention, the party platform included a call for instituting the initiative and referendum—mechanisms seen as enabling the average citizen, including farmers, debtors, and laborers, to adopt laws that benefited them while undoing laws that did not. Other groups who saw themselves as outside the political process looking in, including a number of women's suffrage organizations, socialists, prohibitionists, and temperance groups, also jumped on the initiative/referendum train (Cronin 1989, 50, 51). South Dakota became the first state to adopt the initiative and referendum, with Utah (1900) and Oregon (1902) following not long after, the latter also becoming the first state to institute the recall procedure, in 1908.

The movement on behalf of the initiative and referendum also received the imprimatur of the Progressives. Upset with the quality of people being recruited to state legislatures by corrupt political machines, convinced that legislative bodies were in the stranglehold of special interests, and desirous of greater citizen participation in the political process, Progressives understandably saw great appeal in both of these procedures. The largest number of states signed on to the initiative and/or referendum between 1910 and 1920. Following a long hiatus, five more states (Alaska, Wyoming, Illinois, Montana, Florida) plus the District of Columbia adopted one or the other, or both, between 1959 and 1978 (Magleby 1984, 38, 39).

The initiative and referendum procedures achieved renewed visibility in 1978 when two senior citizens (Howard Jarvis and Paul Gann), exasperated by what they saw as ever-increasing property taxes in their state (California), launched a tax revolt that culminated in an initiative known as Proposition 13—a proposal that called for placing a cap on property taxes. Following a strongly contested campaign in which the governor (Jerry Brown) came out squarely against the proposal, Jarvis and his allies managed to secure enough petition signatures to place Proposition 13 on the ballot, where it achieved an easy victory with 65 percent of the vote. Although the wisdom of both Proposition 13 and the initiative process itself continued to be debated, this high-profile campaign was followed by an increased use of the initiative in the twenty-four states that allow it. In 1998, for example, voters in various states across the country invoked the initiative for the purpose of passing laws and amending their constitutions: "They ended affirmative action, raised the minimum wage, banned billboards, decriminalized a wide range of hard drugs, and permitted thousands of patients to obtain prescriptions for marijuana, restricted campaign spending and contributions, expanded casino gambling, banned many forms of hunting, prohibited some forms of abortions, and allowed adopted children to obtain the names of their biological parents" (Broder 2000, 3, 4).

Although most other democracies allow for *national* referenda by their citizens, efforts to institute such a process in the United States have never really caught fire. One of the leading figures in the Progressive movement, Robert LaFollette (D-WI), introduced legislation in 1916 calling for the establishment of an advisory referendum, but it never gained much traction. The high-water mark of support for such an idea came in the 1930s when Senator Robert Ludlow (D-IN) called for a constitutional amendment requiring a national referendum on the decision to go to war. The proposal initially attracted considerable support among members of Congress, opinion leaders, educators, and the general public, but it soon dissipated after opponents weighed in, including President Franklin Roosevelt, former president Herbert Hoover, and eminent members of the journalism community. In the 1970s, Congress held hearings on a proposal authored by two of its members calling for the creation of a national initiative, but the plan was never reported out of committee (Cronin 1989, 159–170).

Term Limits

Thus far in this section we have considered expansions in the opportunities to vote, be it for officeholders or policies. There have also been instances, however, where those opportunities have been narrowed rather than broadened at both the national and state/local levels.

The Founding Fathers rejected placing limits on how long an individual could serve in federal office, believing that a commendable record of service ought to be rewarded, and that the option of being able to run again would render officeholders more accountable. The American people saw fit, however, to alter the Founders' design on terms of office in one important respect. A Republican Congress, distressed by Franklin Roosevelt's decision not to abide by the tradition of presidents serving only two terms—he was elected to four—proposed an amendment to the Constitution limiting a president to two terms, unless he served two years of an unexpired term, in which case he could serve up to ten years. The Twenty-second Amendment was ratified in 1951 and has since been opposed by nearly every president on the ground that it makes him a "lame duck." To the extent that it limits the public's choices for president, it may be argued that it is to some degree antidemocratic as well.

Although a few groups and organizations have for some time advocated applying term limits to all individuals in federal elective office (see, for example, the Foundation for the Study of Presidential and Congressional Terms), it was not until the 1990s that this idea began to pick up some steam. Republicans in Congress proposed as part of their "Contract with America" to pass the Citizen Legislature Act, limiting members of Congress to a certain number of years (not specified in the proposal) in office (Wilcox 1995, 71). With incumbents enjoying such overwhelming advantages over challengers in seeking reelection, term limits were seen by some as the only way to infuse the legislative process with new blood while increasing the likelihood that term-limited legislators would eschew special interests and vote with the public interest in mind. Opponents argued that this ill-considered proposal not only would be taking the decision of whom to elect out of the hands of voters but also would terminate legislators just when they were developing expertise on policy issues, thereby forcing their successors to become overly dependent on the expertise of congressional staffs and bureaucrats. It should come as no surprise that term limits legislation never managed to pass Congress. After Republicans gained control of the Congress in 1994—the first time in forty years—the need to limit members of Congress suddenly seemed less urgent (Wilcox 1995, 55). Moreover, when the state of Arkansas, through amending its constitution, attempted to limit its representatives to three terms in the U.S. House and two terms in the U.S. Senate, the U.S. Supreme Court responded in 1995 (*U.S. Term Limits v. Thornton*), declaring state-imposed limits unconstitutional on the grounds that they abrogated the right of the people to vote for whomever they wished.

Term limitations for state and local offices have been quite another matter. Currently, seventeen states place term limits on service in state legislatures—with most setting the limit from eight to twelve years (United States Term Limits 2002, 8). Not coincidentally, these restrictions were imposed during the 1990s, when term limits were also being debated at the national level. Thirty-six states now also limit service in the governorship, with most restricting it to two consecutive terms. There are restrictions at the local level as well, not all of which are of recent vintage—indeed, some go back to the 1850s: "Eight of the ten largest cities in the United States have municipal term limits. . . . Nearly 3,000 cities have placed limits on the service terms of mayors and members of their city councils" (United States Term Limits 2002, 51).

Conclusion

A franchise that started out being limited to white males twenty-one and older, who owned property and, in some states, were of a particular religious persuasion, evolved into one that allowed any citizen eighteen years of age or older, of any race, sex, creed, or color, to vote. The forces that came to bear in achieving an inclusive electorate were many and complex, operating at times alone and at others in combination. They included, of course, the steadfast insistence of the excluded group that elemental fairness required their inclusion; allies who came to their cause echoing this view and exhibiting equal determination; others who may not have been primarily motivated by conscience but were supportive nevertheless, because they thought these new voters would see the world as they did; and still others who ultimately came on board only because a particular expansion of the suffrage seemed inevitable; the press of events, particularly westward expansion and wars; and the courts that over time came to see the guarantee and protection of the franchise as a federal responsibility.

The right to vote is, of course, meaningless without the opportunity to exercise it. When the constitutional design of 1787 went into effect, the limited number of eligible voters also had a very limited opportunity to use the franchise. Indeed, only their representative to the House was subject to direct election. As the spirit of Jacksonian democracy took hold, however, it seemed more and more appropriate to have voters choose presidential electors, and thus state legislatures ceded to them that responsibility. At the end of the nineteenth century there rose another spirited call for more democracy that found its voice in both the Populist and Progressive movements, with voters finally winning the right to directly elect their senators and, through primaries, to have a say in what choices they would be faced with on election day. These same movements also insisted that voters must be able to express their views about policies as well as people, and so came the initiative and referendum.

Whereas voters in European democracies are called upon to vote on average every forty-two months, Americans at the federal level are asked to go to the polls every two years. Add to this the fact that unlike their European counterparts, they are also asked to vote in primaries held for elective positions at both the federal and state levels. Consider further that many municipalities, seeking to insulate their elections from the politics of national and state contests, have over the years moved their local elections to different years. Thus, not only do Americans have unmatched opportunities to exercise the franchise, but their willingness to do so on each and every occasion requires a very high level of commitment indeed.

References

Beard, Charles A. 1913. *An Economic Interpretation of the Constitution.* New York: Macmillan.

Benson, George C. S. 1978. *Political Corruption in America.* Lexington, MA: Lexington Books.

Berke, Richard. 2001. "Lieberman Put Democrats in Retreat on Military Vote." *New York Times* (July 15): A15.

Brauer, Carl M. 1977. *John F. Kennedy and the Second Reconstruction.* New York: Columbia University Press.

Broder, David S. 2000. *Democracy Derailed: Initiative Campaigns and the Power of Money.* New York: Harcourt.

Brown, Robert E. 1956. *Charles Beard and the Constitution.* Princeton: Princeton University Press.

Burns, James MacGregor. 1982. *The Vineyard of Liberty.* New York: Alfred A. Knopf.

Cain, Bruce E., and David Butler. 1997. "Redrawing District Lines: What's Going on and What's at Stake?" *American Enterprise* 2 (July/August).

Collins, Gail. 2002. "Women's Suffrage: How Febb Burn and Her Son, Harry, Saved the Day." *New York Times* (July 28): 12.

Converse, Philip. 1972. "Change in the American Electorate," in Angus Campbell and Philip Converse, eds., *The Human Meaning of Social Change.* New York: Russell Sage Foundation.

Cronin, Thomas. 1989. *Direct Democracy: The Politics of Initiative, Referendum, and Recall.* Cambridge: Harvard University Press.

Crotty, William J. 1977. *Political Reform and the American Experiment.* New York: Thomas Y. Crowell.

Dershowitz, Alan. 2001. *Supreme Injustice: How the High Court Highjacked Election 2000.* New York: Oxford University Press.

Diamond, Martin. 1966. "Democracy and *The Federalist:* A Reconsideration of the Framers' Intent." In Willmoore Kendall and George Carey, eds., *Liberalism Versus Conservativism,* 10–24. Princeton: C. Van Nostrand.

———. 1977. *The Electoral College and the American Idea of Democracy.* Washington, DC: American Enterprise Institute.

DiClerico, Robert, and James W. Davis. 2000. *Choosing Our Choices: Debating the Presidential Nominating Process.* Lanham, MD: Rowman and Littlefield.

Dudley, Robert L., and Alan R. Gitelson. 2002. *American Elections: The Rules Matter.* New York: Longman.

Franklin, John Hope. 1967. *From Slavery to Freedom,* 3rd ed. New York: Alfred A. Knopf.

Keating, Dan, and Madonna Lebling. 2001. "Florida Election Showed Lack of Leadership." *New York Times* (June 1): A20.

Kelly, Alfred H., and Winfred A. Harbison. 1963. *The American Constitution,* 3rd ed. New York: W. W. Norton.

Key, V. O., Jr. 1949. *Southern Politics.* New York: Alfred A. Knopf.

Keyssar, Alexander. 2000. *The Right to Vote: The Contested History of Democracy in the United States.* New York: Basic Books.

Kleppner, Paul. 1982. *Who Voted? The Dynamics of Electoral Turnout, 1870–1980.* New York: Praeger.

Kyvig, David E. 1996. *Explicit and Authentic Acts: Amending the U.S. Constitution, 1776–1995.* Lawrence: University Press of Kansas.

Magleby, David B. 1984. *Direct Legislation: Voting on Ballot Propositions in the United States.* Baltimore: Johns Hopkins University Press.

Maisel, L. Sandy. 2002. *Parties and Elections in America.* Lanham, MD: Rowman and Littlefield.

Maltz, Earl M. 1990. *Civil Rights, the Constitution, and Congress, 1863–1869.* Lawrence: University Press of Kansas.

Mowry, George E. 1958. *The Era of Theodore Roosevelt and the Birth of Modern America, 1900–1912.* New York: Harper and Row.

National Commission on Federal Election Reform. 2001. *To Assure Pride and Confidence in the Electoral Process.* Charlottesville, VA: Miller Center of Public Affairs.

New York Times. 2001a. "Advancing Electoral Reform." July 8, A10.

————. 2001b. "Florida's Flawed Ballots." July 16, A18.

Padover, Saul. 1962. *To Secure These Blessings.* New York: Washington Square Press/Ridge Square Press.

Peterson, Merrill D., ed. 1966. *Democracy, Liberty, and Property: The State Constitutional Conventions of the 1820s.* Indianapolis: Bobbs-Merrill.

Piven, Francis Fox, and Richard A. Cloward. 2000. *Why Americans Still Don't Vote.* Boston: Beacon Press.

Rapoport, Miles. 2001a. "Democracy's Moment." *The American Prospect,* March 12–26.

————. 2001b. "Restoring the Vote." *The American Prospect,* August 13.

Sabato, Larry J. 2002. *Overtime: The Election 2000 Thriller.* New York: Longman.

Seeyle, Catherine Q. 2001. "Study Says 2000 Election Missed Millions of Votes." *New York Times* (July 17): A17.

Smith, Rogers M. 1997. *Civic Ideals: Conflicting Visions of U.S. Citizenship in U.S. History.* New Haven, CT: Yale University Press.

United States Term Limits. "State Legislative Term Limits." http:// www.termlimits.org/Current_Info/State_TL/index.html (accessed August 17, 2002).

Walsh, Edward. 2001. "Most Vote Machinery Worked, GAO Says." *Washington Post* (October 17): A4.

Washington Post. 2001. "No Quick Fixes Seen for Balloting Woes." March 8, A7.

Wilcox, Clyde. 1995. *The Latest American Revolution?* New York: St. Martin's.

Williamson, Chilton. 1960. *American Suffrage from Property to Democracy.* Princeton: Princeton University Press.

Wolfinger, Raymond E., and Steven J. Rosenstone. 1980. *Who Votes?* New Haven, CT: Yale University Press.

Wood, Gordon. 1969. *The Creation of the American Republic, 1776–1787.* Chapel Hill: University of North Carolina Press.

Cases Cited

Badham v. Eu 488 U.S. 1024 (1989)
Baker v. Carr 369 U.S. 186 (1962)
Colgrove v. Green 328 U.S. 549 (1946)
Davis v. Bandemer 478 U.S. 109 (1986)
Dred Scott v. Sandford 60 U.S. 393 (1857)

Dunn v. Blumstein 405 U.S. 330 (1972)
Gomillion v. Lightfoot 384 U.S. 339 (1960)
Grovey v. Townsend 295 U.S. 45 (1935)
Harper et al. v. Virginia Board of Elections 383 U.S. 663 (1966)
Hunt v. Cromartie 526 U.S. 541 (1999)
Kirkpatrick v. Preisler 395 U.S. 917 (1969)
Oregon v. Mitchell 400 U.S. 112 (1970)
Reynolds v. Sims 377 U.S. 533 (1964)
Schnell v. Davis 336 U.S. 933 (1949)
Shaw v. Hunt 519 U.S. 804 (1996)
Smith v. Allwright 321 U.S. 649 (1944)
U.S. Term Limits v. Thornton 514 U.S. 779 (1995)
United States v. Cruikshank 92 U.S. 542 (1876)
United States v. Reese 92 U.S. 214 (1876)
Wesberry v. Sanders 376 U.S. 1 (1964)
Williams v. Mississippi 170 U.S. 213 (1898)

2

Problems, Controversies, and Solutions

Although the United States has achieved a fully inclusive electorate, relatively unimpeded in its access to the ballot box, this state of affairs does not necessarily mean that all is well with how elections function in the country. On the contrary, it is argued in some quarters that the right to vote is compromised by a host of different circumstances and procedures that have as their effect one or more of the following consequences: limiting whom we can vote for, deciding elections with an unrepresentative majority, and thwarting the will of the majority. Others, meanwhile, are concerned that Americans are being asked to vote on too many matters better left to elected officials.

In this chapter we consider these complaints and the proposals to correct them, as well as differing assessments regarding the merits of both the complaints themselves and the remedies proposed.

Two-Party Monopoly

When Saddam Hussein, the now deposed president of Iraq, was reelected in 2002, he received 100 percent (11.4 million) of the vote—a percentage far exceeding any popular vote margin ever attained by a president of the United States, or for that matter, the leader of any Western democracy (Oppell 2002). There is, of course, a ready explanation for Saddam's unanimous election victory—he was the only candidate on the ballot! The absence of any other candidates was, it is safe to say, not a consequence of

51

overwhelming satisfaction with Saddam's rule but rather considerable fear of what fate might await anyone daring to make such a challenge. All of which is to suggest that the right to vote, no matter how extensive, is essentially meaningless unless those who are not part of the government have the opportunity to pose a ballot challenge to those who are.

Since 1854, the American political process has been dominated by two political parties—the Republican and Democratic. There have, of course, been third parties and independent candidates who have offered themselves as alternatives to the two major parties—since the early 1800s some two hundred third parties have appeared at one time or another on the political stage, with 117 active as of 2000 (Sifry 2002, 279). None, however, has come remotely close to winning the reins of power. The most successful third-party effort in our history was by the Progressive Party in the 1912 presidential election, led by Theodore Roosevelt, who managed to garner 27.5 percent of the popular vote and eighty-eight electoral votes. Since that time the most successful nonmajor party candidate has been George Wallace, who in 1968 ran as an independent, receiving 13.5 percent of the popular vote and forty-six electoral votes. In 1992, candidate Ross Perot, while succeeding in mustering a larger percentage of the popular vote (18.6 percent) than any nonmajor party candidate since Theodore Roosevelt, was nevertheless unable to convert it into even a single electoral vote; and as the presidential nominee of the Reform Party four years later, he did no better than 8.5 percent. The inheritor of the Reform Party label, presidential candidate Patrick Buchanan, failed even to reach 1 percent of the vote in the 2000 election, and Green Party candidate Ralph Nader finished with only 2.7 percent. Their finishes, it should be noted, were the best of any third-party candidates appearing on the ballot that year.

The inability of third parties to gain a more secure foothold in American politics is the result of numerous factors—some legal, some political, and some constitutional. Third parties have long complained of the legal hurdles they must jump to gain a place on the ballot. Prior to 1890, ballot access was not a problem because each party printed its own ballots. With the adoption of the Australian ballot, however, prepared by each state and cast in secret, states now had the authority to regulate who had access to the ballot. Not surprisingly, the major parties, which controlled the state legislatures, were not inclined to have their own control challenged by other parties. Accordingly, they established laws making it difficult for third parties to get on the ballot. Twenty states, for example, outlaw fusion parties—minor parties that endorse candidates in another party. Nine states have a "sore loser" law prohibiting candidates who run and lose in a state's primary from then running as a third-party candidate in the general election. Four states prohibit their voters from voting in a state's primary if they signed a third-party petition to gain access to the ballot. Finally, the petition process carries with it numerous regulations that third parties view as onerous. More precisely, the filing deadlines for petitions vary by state, thereby making it difficult to wage a coordinated national petition campaign, to say nothing of the fact that some states require many more petition signatures than others. In the 2000 presidential election, for example, Ralph Nader needed some 600,000 signatures to get on the ballot in all the states and the District of Columbia. Actually, it was more than that, for candidates also need about a third more signatures than are required in order to protect against challenges (Flood and Mayer 1996, 292). Thus, the actual number of signatures needed is closer to 800,000. Despite this hurdle, Nader ultimately won ballot status in forty-three states. A third party's problems do not necessarily end here, however, for states typically charge them to validate signatures—Florida, for example, charges ten cents per signature. Moreover, even if a third party is ultimately successful in getting on the ballot, it is not guaranteed ballot access for the next election unless it received a certain percentage of the vote.

Despite these hurdles, the independent candidacies of George Wallace (1968), John Anderson (1980), and Ross Perot (1992) managed to gain ballot access in all fifty states, and in the 1996 presidential election the Libertarian and Reform parties did likewise, while the Natural Law Party made it in forty-four states and the Taxpayers Party in thirty-nine. The willingness of third parties to challenge some of the state-imposed requirements in court—number of signatures required, where in a state they must be collected, percentage of the vote needed to retain ballot access—has made the road easier for third parties. The fact remains, however, that the money expended on court challenges and otherwise meeting ballot requirements drains away a precious resource that could be used by third parties to get out their message. These funds, moreover, are particularly crucial for third parties because federal campaign finance regulations allow them to qualify for public funds to help finance their election campaigns only if they appeared on the ballot in at least ten states in the *previous* presidential election and received at least 5 percent of the vote. (Ross Perot, having received 19 percent of the popular vote in 1992, was entitled to $29.2 million in public funds for 1996; see Herrnson and Green 1997, 26.) Add to this the fact that third parties rarely achieve the quantity of *free* media coverage accorded the major parties on evening news programs, largely because they are peripheral to where the action is and thus not deemed especially newsworthy. Nor are they guaranteed inclusion in what has become the major media event of the general election campaign—televised presidential debates. Ross Perot was allowed to participate in the 1992 debates because the Presidential Debates Commission decided not to strictly enforce its criterion that a candidate must achieve 10 percent support in the polls, and because Bill Clinton and President George Bush each saw political advantage in including him (Just 1997, 88, 90; Arterton 1993, 95). In 1996, however, the commission decided to enforce the 10 percent threshold, thereby denying Perot the right to participate. On the same grounds, Reform Party nominee Patrick Buchanan was also excluded from the presidential debates in 2000.

The difficulties that third-party and independent candidates face in the U.S. political system, however, go well beyond intentional legal and political hurdles placed in their path. The fact that the United States has winner-take-all single-member elections to Congress and state offices means that third parties have little chance of gaining representation in these elected bodies, which, in turn, greatly limits their recruitment base for higher office. This reality means that third parties are left with nominees lacking in national stature, and thus also voter appeal.

The winner-take-all feature of the Electoral College, whereby the winner of the popular vote in a state receives all of that state's electoral votes (Maine and Nebraska being the sole exceptions), disadvantages third-party and independent presidential candidates as well. Some voters who are inclined to support third-party or independent presidential candidates may nevertheless view casting a vote for them as a wasted vote, and thus ultimately end up voting for one of the major party candidates. In 1980, for example, 43 percent of those voters who ranked John Anderson as their first choice for president ended up voting for Jimmy Carter or Ronald Reagan, and in the 1992 presidential election Ross Perot saw 21 percent of his supporters cast their votes for the major party candidates (Bibby and Maisel 1998, 66).

Finally, there might be a greater incentive for dissident groups within the population to turn to third parties if the major parties made it more difficult for them to work within the two-party framework, but the fact of the matter is that the major parties are highly permeable institutions. There are no bars to becoming a member of either party, and with the advent of the direct primary, if you want to run for office on the Democratic or Republican Party label, you are pretty much free to do so. Given this degree of openness, factional groups within the party find it easier to work within the major party framework than to pick up their marbles and go elsewhere.

Whether we would be better off with a vigorous multiparty system as exists in a number of other democracies (e.g., England, Canada, Italy, Germany, the Netherlands, and Israel) is a matter of some debate. Some believe that our major parties have dominated for so long that they have atrophied and are unable to infuse the political process with new ideas (Lowi 1998, 8). Moreover, in an effort to appeal to the broad middle in American politics, the two major parties leave marginalized groups in the population with little leverage as their interests become homogenized with a host of others—all in an attempt by each party to create a majority coalition. More parties, it is argued, would provide more choice for more voters, force parties to define themselves in less ambiguous terms, give women and minorities greater leverage over the political system, and significantly increase election turnout (Richie and Hill 2001, 6–20; Fresia 1986).

Others remain decidedly less sanguine about the benefits to be derived from more parties. Fostering an environment most conducive to their development would require replacing our winner-take-all system of allocating electoral votes in presidential elections with a proportional system, and also replacing the single-member district system of electing legislators with a proportional system whereby the seats won by a party in the legislative branch would be proportionate to its share of the popular vote. Both the winner-take-all and single-member district systems have done a good job of marginalizing extreme elements within the society by preventing them from gaining a foothold in government. Moreover, a legislature populated with several parties would only increase the prospects of government by gridlock and further complicate the voter's task of deciding whom in government to hold accountable for the actions it takes (Romance 1998, 34, 38). Finally, the fact that third parties have not proven successful in gaining a foothold in our national government does not necessarily mean that they have been without influence. When third-party or independent candidates have advocated positions that captured the support of significant parts of the voting population, the major parties often have either co-opted that support by adopting the issue as their own or else moved toward that issue position (Mazmanian 1974, 149).

Primaries, Caucuses, and the Problem of Frontloading

The presidential selection process occurs in two stages—the nomination of candidates, followed by the general election. To the extent that the nominating stage structures the choices we will ultimately be faced with on election day, it is arguably the most important part of this two-stage process, a point not lost on the notorious Boss Tweed of New York City's Tammany Hall: "I don't care who does the electin' so long as I do the nominatin'."

The way candidates for president are nominated has not been free of criticism, and in the previous three presidential elections a phenomenon known as "frontloading" has attracted particular attention from scholars and political observers. Frontloading is the result of more and more states moving their primaries and caucuses up to the front end of the nomination calendar. The factors responsible for this development are varied and interconnected.

When the Democratic Party in the 1970s decided to reform the procedures by which delegates to its national convention were selected, the effect of some of these changes was to make clearer who the winners and losers were in the primaries and caucuses. Prior to the reforms a state selecting delegates by the caucus-convention system was not required to hold its first-stage precinct caucuses on the same day at uniform times. Reforms in both parties required precinct caucuses throughout a state to do so. In addition, whether chosen in primaries or caucuses, delegates were often chosen first and stated their presidential preference later, making it difficult immediately following a given primary or caucus to determine how much delegate support a candidate had. Subsequent to the reforms, individuals running for delegate were required to express a preference, including uncommitted (Kamarck 1990, 163–168). To the extent that some of these changes applied to primaries and required action by state legislatures, they affected Republican primaries as well, since most state legislatures at that time were controlled by the Democrats. At any rate, with nomination contests now more readily interpretable in terms of winners and losers, the media saw them as more newsworthy and thus deserving of greater coverage. The states of Iowa and New Hampshire benefited from all this and more, because the former was traditionally allowed to hold its caucus before any other state caucus, and New Hampshire likewise was permitted to run its primary before any other state primary. Thus, as *the first* and *the only* contest of its kind on a given day, each captured all of the media attention, which caused both the Iowa caucus and New Hampshire primary to grow in importance. Indeed, the amount of network attention afforded these two opening contests dwarfed that received by other states (Robinson and Sheehan 1980, 76; Lichter, Amundson, and Noyes 1988, 14). If a candidate could finish ahead of the field in both Iowa and New Hampshire (assuming he was not from one of those states) as Jimmy Carter did in 1976, then he could build up a head of steam that would make him very difficult to stop. By the same token, candidates who lost or failed to meet expectations in both states found themselves frozen out of media coverage and the victims of suddenly dwindling financial support, making it almost impossible for them to recover (Patterson 1980, 43–53; Moore 1984, 57; Adams 1984, 10–13). For those who won or met expectations in one or the other of these two opening contests, their tickets were punched for the next round of contests.

Thus, Iowa and New Hampshire had the effect of greatly narrowing the field of presidential contenders, a role that came in for a good deal of criticism in some quarters because neither state could be said to represent a microcosm of the nation as a whole, or even the rank and file in each party. New Hampshire, particularly, has only 0.4 percent of the nation's population, few urban areas, low union membership, and scarcely any blacks or Hispanics within its borders. As some have suggested, however, allowing Iowa and New Hampshire to open the nominating contest is not without its benefits. Because they are relatively small states, candidates of limited funds can compete against more moneyed opponents, and voters have an opportunity to observe presidential contenders "up close and personal." Add to this the fact that New Hampshire voters appear to be more informed than the average citizen, pay attention to the campaign and learn from it, and are in general less susceptible to the horse-race coverage that permeates media reporting (Buhr 2000, 224, 228, 299, 232, 233).

In an effort to have an impact on this now crucially important early part of the nominating process, and to dilute the influence of Iowa and New Hampshire, more and more states began to move their contests forward. The effect of this rush to the front end of the process has been to decide the outcome of the nomination race earlier and earlier. In 1980, Jimmy Carter and Ronald Reagan had not accumulated enough delegates to win the nomination until May and June, respectively. By 1996, however, both Bill Clinton and Bob Dole had enough delegates to win their party's nomination by March and April, respectively, and in 2000 both George W. Bush and Al Gore reached the magic number in March. In short, by 2000 a nominating process "that once ran from January to June had shrunk to one in which nearly three quarters of the elected delegates to both conventions were chosen during the first three Tuesdays in March, and both nominations were decided on the first Tuesday" (Plissner 2002, 4).

From the perspective of party leaders, a battle for the nomination that concludes sooner rather than later is not an unwelcome result, for the longer the contest drags on, the more divided the party becomes, thereby making it increasingly difficult to present a united front as the party moves into the general election (Barnes 2001, 3699). Whether such an abbreviated nominating contest is best for the voters and candidates, however, is certainly open to question. A process in which the contests are bunched at the front is likely to disadvantage the lesser-known candidate who lacks the resources to organize simultaneously in a whole series of states. Even more important, we run the risk of a rush to judgment whereby the presidential nomination is decided in a matter of weeks, not months, providing voters with little opportunity to digest how the candidates are performing, and on that basis, perhaps reconsider or reconfirm an initial impression.

There has been no shortage of proposals to correct or alleviate frontloading. One, a *national primary*, although predating frontloading by many years, is nevertheless deemed pertinent to solving this particular problem. Under this plan, candidates would campaign from January to May or June, at which time voters in each party would go to the polls and vote for their nominee. There are several alluring aspects to such a procedure. For one thing, all voters in a party would be presented with the same choice of candidates, unlike the current system where candidates drop out at various points in the process. Voters would also have an extended period of time during which to observe the candidates, and the inordinate amount of influence that Iowa and New Hampshire exert over the process would be ended. The advantages end here, however. A national primary would be exceedingly expensive, giving a distinct advantage to the candidate who is already well known and well financed. Moreover, the current process, for all its shortcomings, does provide lesser-known candidates some opportunity to demonstrate their viability by doing well in one of the opening contests—something that would be lost in a one-shot national primary occurring in May or June. And for those who believe that the party organization already exerts too little influence over the reformed nominating process, a national primary would take them out of the picture altogether, relegating national conventions to arguing over party platforms and the selection of a vice presidential nominee. Finally, with a one-shot primary in which the field of candidates would not have been narrowed down, the vote could well be divided among eight to ten candidates, with the victor garnering, for example, no more than 25 percent of the vote. It would hardly seem advisable to send a candidate with such limited support into a general election. Of course, each party could hold a runoff election among the top two finishers, but this would add to the expense as well as severely test the attention span of the average voter and the physical endurance of the candidates. The two runoff candidates, moreover, while they might be the first choice of a plurality of voters in their party, could very well be the *least* popular choices for the majority of the party's voters.

Thomas Cronin and Robert Loevy have proposed a combination of a national convention and presidential primary. The convention, composed exclusively of party officials, would choose two or three candidates to be presented to the voters in a national primary. This plan would retain the advantages of a national primary while also giving an important role to the parties, eliminating the necessity for a runoff, and freeing the voters from having to sort through a wide field of candidates—a task best left to party activists more knowledgeable about the candidates' competence and electability (Cronin and Loevy 1983, 50–53).

At its national convention in 1996, the Republican Party attempted to address frontloading by establishing a *bonus award system* for the selection of convention delegates in the 2000 nomination campaign. Those states holding off the selection of delegates until March 15 had their state delegations increased by 5 percent. The bonus grew to 7.5 percent for states waiting until April 15, and 10 percent for those that deferred until May 15 or later. Despite these enticements, however, the plan was less than a resounding success, for California and Ohio decided to move their contests forward three weeks to March 7, while Michigan, Washington, and Virginia jumped from March into February.

The Republican Party also established the Brock Commission, which was charged with reporting to its 2000 national convention further recommendations on primary reform that were slated to be implemented in 2004. The commission called for primaries to occur in waves starting with the first Tuesday in March and going through the first Tuesday in June, beginning with the states having the smallest populations and working up to those having the largest population. The percentage of delegates to be chosen in each wave was as follows: March (12 percent), April (18 percent), May (23 percent), and June (47 percent). With small states starting the process, candidates who were less known and less well heeled would have an opportunity to demonstrate their viability. This plan, moreover, would discourage a rush to judgment since the largest block of delegates (47 percent) would not be chosen until the final month. Although the Republican National Committee approved the plan by a vote of 92 to 55, the Bush campaign prevented it from coming to the floor of the 2000 convention for a vote, believing that it would be a divisive issue particularly unpopular with large states that, under the plan, could not hold their contests until the final month.

In 1999, the National Association of Secretaries of State also offered up a plan of its own—this one organized around *regional primaries*. Beginning in rotation with the eastern region, followed by the southern, midwestern, and western regions, it proposed that primaries be held on the first Tuesday in March, April, May, and June. (Four years later, the eastern region would move to the end of the line). Thus, there would be a month interval between each region, thereby allowing candidates an opportunity to catch their breath and voters a chance to digest the results. Under this plan, an exception would continue to be made for Iowa and New Hampshire, which would hold their contests first because their relatively small size fosters an "up close and personal" form of campaigning. Although this proposal may represent an improvement over the frontloaded primary process, some would surely argue that the candidate(s) from the region going first could well enjoy a decided advantage over his or her opponents.

Money and Elections

Apart from candidates' own time and talents, the volunteers they are able to attract, and whatever free media coverage comes their way, virtually everything else associated with their run for federal or state office requires money—staff, consultants, travel, lodging, headquarters, TV ads, fundraising, polls, speaker systems, buttons, signs, and bumper stickers. Money is, in short, the fuel that drives the engine of election campaigns.

There have been three long-standing complaints against the role of money in elections, namely, that it influences (1) access to the electoral process, (2) election outcomes, and (3) decisions on public policy. It is these concerns that have animated repeated efforts to regulate its use, with the first modest attempt dating back to 1867, when Congress passed a naval appropriations bill stipulating that no naval officer or federal employee could solicit contributions in the navy yards. The next hundred years were punctuated by more legislation intended in one way or another to curb the influence of money in elections, including limitations on individual contributions and outright prohibitions against contributions by banks, corporations, and labor unions. The seriousness of these efforts is certainly open to question, however, for not only were the enforcement mechanisms extremely weak, but the restrictions themselves left open numerous ways by which resourceful presidential candidates, private citizens, and organizations could circumvent the letter and spirit of the laws. Not until the 1970s did Congress pass legislation that seriously addressed the problem of money in presidential elections. These regulations came in the form of the Revenue Act and the Federal Election Campaign Act (FECA), both passed into law in 1971. In response to the scandals of Watergate, there followed a series of amendments to FECA in 1974. Taken together these statutes:

1. Limited contributions by individuals and groups to candidates running for federal office

2. Established overall spending limits for candidates running for federal office
3. For presidential candidates only, provided optional partial public funding of their nomination campaigns and full funding for their general election campaigns
4. Established an enforcement mechanism (Federal Election Commission) to monitor compliance, including the public disclosure of all contributions of $200 or more

Thus, these reforms were seen as enhancing candidate accountability by public disclosure of campaign contributions to the Federal Election Commission, limiting the potential of influence-buying through the imposition of contribution limits, and creating a more level electoral playing field by instituting campaign spending limits. They also afforded presidential candidates the option of securing partial public funding of their campaign for the nomination and, if successful, full funding of their general election campaign.

Although these reforms certainly represented progress, some would argue that a number of subsequent developments served to dilute their impact. Opponents of the reforms, believing that they violated the First Amendment, took their objections all the way to the Supreme Court. In a landmark decision (*Buckley v. Valeo*) handed down by the Court in 1976, the justices upheld the individual contribution limit ($1,000), arguing that a contribution did not itself constitute speech but rather was money being given so that someone else (i.e., a candidate) could exercise speech. The Court also upheld campaign spending limits for presidential candidates agreeing to accept public funding of their campaigns. What the Court could not accept, however, was the provision limiting individuals and groups to spending no more than $1,000 *on behalf of* a candidate. This prohibition, in the Court's judgment, did constitute a violation of the right to free speech.

As a consequence of this decision, individuals and groups were now free to spend unlimited amounts of money on behalf of candidates. Although the Court stipulated that there could be no collusion between those doing the spending and members of a candidate's campaign, such a prohibition is exceedingly difficult to enforce. Moreover, even in the absence of collusion, candidates will surely know who is spending significant sums of money on their behalf, which reintroduces the possibility of influence-buying.

A second development diluting the impact of the campaign finance reforms grew out of a concern voiced by scholars and politicians that the 1976 presidential election campaign was devoid of the party-building activities—buttons, bumper stickers, get-out-the-vote campaigns, recruiting volunteers—that had characterized previous presidential election campaigns. The culprit, it was argued, was the limit that campaign finance laws had placed on how much state and local parties could spend in connection with presidential election campaigns. Accordingly, in 1979 Congress decided to allow individuals and groups (including banks, labor organizations, and corporations, which have long been prohibited from making contributions directly to candidates) to give *unlimited* sums of money to state and local parties for purposes of "party-building" activities. Known as "soft money," this congressionally created exception released a waterfall of pent-up giving—the amount of "soft money" growing with each passing presidential election, and in the 2000 election cycle reaching a combined total of $438 million for both parties (*Washington Post* 2002a, A24). For those concerned about the potential for contributions to buy access and influence, the proliferation of soft money giving was not reassuring, for it is highly unlikely that candidates will remain unaware of who is making huge contributions to their party. In the 2000 election cycle, for example, the biggest soft money contributions by an individual, corporation, labor union, and issue group were, respectively, $1,493,000 (Daniel and Ewa Abraham), $3,626,230 (AT&T), $5,914,000 (American Federation of State, County, and Municipal employees), and $1,489,872 (National Rifle Association) (*Washington Post* 2002a, A25).

The contribution limits imposed by the campaign finance reforms also came in for criticism. Unlike the spending limits, which under the law were adjusted every four years for inflation, no such provision was made for contribution limits, leaving $1,000 in the year 2000 worth under $500 in real dollars. Not surprisingly, presidential candidates complained of having to spend more and more of their time to raise less and less money.

After several unsuccessful attempts, Congress in 2002 finally passed new campaign reform legislation. The Bipartisan Campaign Reform Act, more commonly known as the McCain-Feingold bill, prohibited national parties from accepting any soft money contributions, while allowing state and local parties to accept up to $10,000 in soft money each year per individual for get-out-the-vote and voter registration efforts in federal elections. In addition, unions, corporations, and nonprofit groups are prohibited from paying for broadcast advertisements from their treasuries if the ads refer to a specific candidate and run within thirty days of a primary or sixty days of the general election. Finally, the bill also raises the individual contribution limit from $1,000 to $2,000 and indexes it to the rate of inflation.

Critics of this legislation fear that what was given as soft money contributions to political parties will now be diverted to independent spending by groups and individuals *on behalf of candidates.* Thus, the accountability that existed by having the money flow directly to the national political parties will now be lost, for individuals and groups spending on behalf of candidates are likely to feel less constrained than parties in what they say about a candidate. Others argue that the soft money prohibitions abridge freedom of speech—a view shared by a federal appeals court, which in May 2003 ruled the soft money provisions of the act unconstitutional. That ruling was appealed to the U.S. Supreme Court, which upheld both the ban on soft money and the restrictions on campaign advertisements (*McConnell v. Federal Election Commission*).

Even with McCain-Feingold now in place, the more deeply skeptical will continue to believe that resourceful candidates and their lawyers can always find creative ways to circumvent *any* campaign finance restrictions. Thus, in their view, the most realistic approach is to do away with all restrictions on contributions and spending, insist on full and complete public disclosure of all contributions and expenditures, and let the voters draw whatever conclusions they wish.

Voter Turnout in Presidential Elections

It has become a ritual in American politics following each presidential election to bemoan the number of Americans who fail to avail themselves of the opportunity to vote, and to compare the United States disparagingly to other democracies that have decidedly higher turnouts.

When John F. Kennedy was elected president in 1960, voter turnout was 63 percent. The U.S. Census recorded a continuous drop over the next five presidential elections, with turnout reaching a low of 52 percent by 1980. There was a small increase (to

53.4 percent) in 1984 and a significant five-point spike in 1992, more than likely due to the interest generated by the independent candidacy of Ross Perot. The election of 1996 saw a further drop, to 49 percent—the lowest turnout figure since 1924, and the biggest single four-year decline since 1920, manifesting itself in every one of the fifty states (Knack 1999, 237). In 2000, it went up slightly, to 51.2 percent—a figure that put the United States nearly ten points below average voter turnout rates in Japan, Canada, and England; twenty points below France, Austria, and Italy; and twenty-five points below Denmark and Germany (Patterson 2003, 201).

The turnout problem in presidential elections may, however, not be quite as bad as the above statistics would appear to suggest. For one thing, Census statistics calculate turnout on the basis of the vote *for president* cast by all those in the United States who are of *voting age*. There are, however, people who come out to vote but simply choose to leave the presidency portion of the ballot blank (roughly 100,000 in the 2000 election) (CalTech/MIT Voting Technology Project 2001, Part I, 6). More important, roughly 2 percent of all ballots cast in presidential elections (two million in the 2000 election) are disqualified for one reason or another. Of greatest significance, however, is the fact that calculating turnout on the basis of the voting-age population includes certain individuals who are not, in fact, eligible to vote, most notably *legal aliens, convicted felons,* and *the incompetent.* According to one recent study, the ineligible portion of our population has since 1972 been increasing at a faster rate than the eligible. Once these ineligible voters are subtracted from the pool of potential voters, there is no decline in turnout after 1972, and in the southern region of the country there is actually a slight increase (McDonald and Popkin 2001, 963–971).

Nor is it entirely fair to compare turnout in the United States to other Western democracies. Many of them assume the responsibility for registering their population to vote rather than leaving it to the initiative of the individual, as is done in the United States. Moreover, these countries calculate turnout on the basis of registered voters, not eligible voters as is done here (McDonald and Popkin 2001, 964). Countries such as Australia and Italy, moreover, also require their population to vote under penalty of fine. There are constitutional differences to consider as well. Unlike a number of European countries that employ a proportional system of representation, in the U.S., elections are run on a winner-take-all basis, which discourages turnout in states where one party dominates. Some members of the dominant party may not go to the polls because they don't think their vote is needed, and those in the weaker party stay home because they conclude there is no way their party can win. Under our constitutional system, voters are also asked to elect members of Congress every two years and elect a president every four. No other democracy schedules its national elections with such frequency (Crewe 1981, 251–253). Add to this the fact that four-fifths of the states have moved their gubernatorial elections to nonpresidential years, and 60 percent of our municipal elections have been moved to nongubernatorial years—all in an attempt to insulate these contests from national and state political influences, respectively (Boyd 1981, 142). Consider finally that unlike any other democracy in the world, the United States holds primary as well as general elections, thereby calling upon Americans to vote twice to fill an office (Ranney 2001, 79; Bennett and Resnick 1990, 779). The consequence of all this is that Americans are asked to go to the polls with very great frequency indeed, thereby causing them to attach less importance to voting in any given election.

Of course, even if turnout in the United States is several points higher than the 51.2 percent U.S. Census figures record for the 2000 presidential election, should we not be concerned that more than 40 percent of the eligible electorate are staying home on election day? Isn't such abstention from voting an indication of alienation from the political system, and might it not lead to the election of a president who would not have won had more people voted? To both questions the answer is "not necessarily." As surprising as it may appear, levels of alienation are not a very good predictor of whether people vote (Ranney 2001, 79; Bennett and Resnick 1990, 779). The alienated are not any less likely to come out to the polls than the nonalienated. Moreover, there is considerable evidence to suggest that the policy views of nonvoters do not differ significantly from voters', and consequently, past election results would in all likelihood not have been altered had nonvoters voted (Wolfinger and Rosenstone 1980; Teixeira 1992, 96–97; Kagay 2000; Bennett and Resnick 1990, 795). Some might also add that we are all better off without the nonvoters. After all, if they are not voting, it is probably because they are not interested in, and do not care enough about, the outcome. Thus, were they to come to the polls they would in all likelihood be contaminating the election with an uninformed vote (Doppelt and Shearer 1999, 10).

Concerns about low turnout cannot be dismissed quite so easily, however. Not only does the act of voting carry with it an intrinsic sense of satisfaction with having fulfilled one's obligation as a citizen, but there is evidence to indicate that voting also encourages other kinds of action associated with good citizenship (Patterson 2002, 14). Moreover, to the extent that a disproportionate number of nonvoters falls at the lower end of the socioeconomic spectrum—individuals for whom the vote may be the only political resource they have—using it should be even more essential. For it is not unreasonable to assume that politicians will be less attentive to groups that consistently fail to turn up at the polls—a point put well by two political scientists who have studied political participation in the United States: "The idle go unheard: They do not speak up, define the agenda, frame the issues, or affect the choices leaders make" (Rosenstone and Hansen 1993, 247; cited in Patterson 2002, 13).

It has long been argued that the best predictor of whether someone will vote is whether or not they are registered to vote (Erickson 1981, 259–276; Jackson and Wright 1998, 259–281). Accordingly, scholars and political reformers have focused considerable attention on reducing the legal barriers to registration. Many European countries, as noted earlier, assume the responsibility for registering their populations—a practice that, if adopted in the United States, would increase voting turnout by roughly 14 percentage points (Powell 1986, 17–44). In our decidedly more *individualistic* culture, that obligation has been placed squarely on the shoulders of each American citizen. All citizens have not, however, had to jump the same number of hurdles in meeting that obligation. Some states have closed off registration closer to election day than others; some states require registration at one location, while others permit it in neighborhoods, libraries, or firehouses; registration offices are open only during normal business hours in some states, but others remain open in evenings and on weekends; some, but not others, authorize deputy registrars who may visit homes or set up a booth at shopping malls; and some states have purged nonvoters from their voting rosters sooner than others (Wolfinger and Rosenstone 1980, 64).

In 1996, those who had long advocated more "voter-friendly" registration procedures finally secured passage of the National Voter Registration Act, which requires that citizens be allowed to register while applying for or renewing their driver's license, in state offices that provide welfare and disability assistance, and by mail with the use of a standardized form. The act also prohibited states from purging their voting rolls except for change of residence. To date, this landmark piece of legislation has been both a success and a failure. Although an estimated ten million voters had been registered by the time of the 2000 presidential election, there was no equivalent increase in voter turnout. On the contrary, there was a six-point drop in turnout between 1992 (55 percent) and 1996 (49 percent), with only a slight increase to 51.7 percent in 2000. Quite obviously, there are factors at work in reducing turnout apart from those related to the mechanics of registration. Possible explanations range from the diminished importance of party, decline in political efficacy, and reduced campaign involvement, to electoral reforms and the way our campaigns are waged and covered (Teixeira 1992, 107, 108; Patterson 2002, 21, 22).

Other reforms are being floated to increase turnout. One eminent scholar has proposed that the United States adopt compulsory voting, as is done in countries such as Australia, Italy, Greece, and Belgium. This reform, it is argued, would not only reduce the gap between rich and poor by equalizing participation but also deal a body blow to negative campaign ads, the goal of which is to lower the vote of one's opponent (Lijphart 1996, B3, B4). Others see great promise in remote Internet voting, which would allow voters to cast their ballots from their homes or offices (Matthews 2000, 1–6; Simon, Corrales, and Wolfensberger 2002, 34). Neither of these proposals, however, is free of problems. Compulsory voting would have to overcome the deep aversion in our highly individualistic culture to laws that would reduce our autonomy over the decision to vote; add to this the certain opposition of some partisan political groups who believe they would have much to lose and little to gain by bringing a host of new voters to the polls. Not only would this very same concern greet the prospect of Internet voting, but more dispassionate observers might object as well, arguing that it would make access to the ballot box too easy, thereby attracting uninformed, manipulable voters whose lack of interest might be sufficient to deter them from driving to a polling place but not from casually pushing a button or two in their own home. Moreover, securing the Internet voting process against fraud—in this case fraud that could be perpetrated from abroad as well as at home—constitutes a formidable practical problem that has yet to be resolved.

Writing a quarter century ago, one thoughtful student of voting characterized declining turnout as a "puzzle" (Brody 1978, 287–324). He did so because turnout continued to decline despite increasing levels of education, the elimination of poll taxes and literacy tests, and the establishment of a thirty-day residency requirement in federal elections—all factors that should have led to an increase in turnout. In the time that has passed since that assessment, education levels have continued to rise, more and more states have lowered barriers to registration, and Congress has passed legislation greatly facilitating the opportunities to register. And yet, there has still been no significant increase in the number of people going to the polls. Thus, what was a puzzle twenty-five years ago remains a puzzle today.

The Electoral College

Of all the issues that the Founding Fathers had to confront at the Constitutional Convention, none confounded them as much as how the president should be chosen. James Wilson, arguably the most influential Founding Father after James Madison, told the members of the Pennsylvania ratifying convention: "The Convention, sir, were perplexed with no part of this plan so much as with the mode of choosing the President of the United States" (Elliot 1861, 511). They started talking about it in the early part of the convention and couldn't reach agreement until near the end, and then only because they fastened together an odd mechanism that had in it something that would appeal to every faction at the Convention: big states, small states, southern states, pro-executive, pro-legislature, pro-states, pro–national government. We refer to it as the Electoral College, although it is not a term the Founding Fathers used.

Alexander Hamilton in *Federalist Paper* No. 68 defended the proposed method of choosing the president, noting that "if the manner be not perfect, it is at least excellent" (Cooke 1961, 458). There are a considerable number of people who would argue that it is neither, for not only did this peculiar process visit upon us for the fourth time in history its greatest drawback—a president elected with a minority of the popular vote—but it also failed to provide one of its greatest alleged benefits—converting an ambiguous popular vote mandate into an unambiguous electoral vote mandate. More specifically, in 2000 George W. Bush lost the popular vote by over half-a-million votes and just barely eked out an electoral vote victory, defeating Gore 271 to 266. No unambiguous electoral mandate there. And bear in mind that had neither Gore nor Bush won a majority of the electoral vote outright, the election would have been forced into the House of Representatives, where each state would have had one vote to cast. (This provision was incorporated into the plan by the Founding Fathers to secure the support of convention delegates from less populous states.) Thus, for example, seven states having just one representative each (Alaska, Delaware, Montana, North Dakota, South Dakota, Vermont, and Wyoming) and together representing four million people would be able to outvote 177 congressmen and -women from the six most populous states, representing more than one hundred million people.

Shifts of just a few thousand votes also would have given us a minority president in 1988 and 1976, and a change of 1.5 percent of the vote or less would have forced the elections of 1948, 1960, and 1968 into the House of Representatives (Abbott and Levine 1991, 21–41). Nor do the problems with the Electoral College end here. Presidential electors are not constitutionally bound to vote for the presidential candidate who carried their state—the "faithless elector" problem—and even though the occasional faithless elector has never determined the outcome of an election, it creates the potential for mischief in a very close electoral vote contest such as was experienced in 2000. On the afternoon of election day, operatives in both the Gore and Bush camps believed there was a real possibility that Bush would win the popular vote and Gore, the electoral vote. Thus, Gore's people were making elaborate plans to keep "weak" Democratic presidential electors from defecting to Bush in the event that the Texan won the popular vote; and the Bush people were just as intently shopping around for those same "weak" Democratic presidential electors in the event Bush won the popular vote and lost in the electoral vote. After the election, the Democrats, having won the popular vote, were now shopping around for "weak" *Republican* electors even as the Bush side now expressed its outrage that the Democrats would stoop to such a tactic (Sabato 2002, 100, 101)!

The winner-take-all allocation of electoral votes also draws criticism on the grounds that it discourages turnout and essentially disenfranchises those in a state who voted for the losing candidate. Moreover, given the fact that the decennial census determines how many seats a state has in the House of Representatives, and thus how many electoral votes it has in addition to the two each state receives for its U.S. senators, some states may end up having fewer or more electoral votes than they deserve. This is due to the lag time that exists between population shifts and the taking of the census every ten years. Based upon the 1980 census, for example, California was entitled to 47 electoral votes, but by 1984 its population had increased enough to merit 54, a change that would not be reflected until 1992, following the 1990 census.

Although it is not difficult to identify shortcomings in the Electoral College, it also has to be said that finding workable alternatives is not an easy task either. The *automatic plan*, which merely does away with presidential electors—and thus the potential problem of "faithless electors"—but retains electoral votes, does not solve the preeminent problem of electing a president with a minority of the popular vote. The *proportional plan*, which would allocate a state's electoral votes in proportion to a candidate's popular vote, would not prevent a minority president either. Indeed, had the 2000 election been held under this plan, it would have produced an even closer result, making Bush president "with neither a majority nor a plurality of the popular vote" (Pomper 2001, 150). The *district plan*, which calls for allocating electoral votes by congressional district, likewise fails to guarantee a popular vote winner and would only compound the political machinations that already envelop the periodic redrawing of congressional districts (Longley and Braun 1972, 80).

Only *direct election* of the president guarantees that the winner will have more votes than his or her opponent. This proposal also includes the proviso that if no candidate receives at least 40 percent of the vote, then a runoff will be held between the top two vote-getters. As with the other proposed reforms, however, direct election is not free of drawbacks either, the most formidable of which may well be the problem of a national recount in a close election. The contested 2000 election results in Florida would probably be multiplied fifty times as candidates trolled for votes anywhere they could find them, whether they had won or lost a state, and regardless of the margin, for in a direct popular election state boundaries become essentially meaningless.

There is also the fear that direct popular election would encourage third-party and independent candidates to run—a prospect, incidentally, that also attends the proportional and district plans and is greatly discouraged under the current winner-take-all Electoral College system. Thus, with a wide field of candidates, runoffs could be frequent, and some might even use the threat of running as leverage over the two major party candidates (Schlesinger 2002, 27). As a way around this problem, the Twentieth Century Fund Task Force on Reform of the Presidential Election Process proposes a *national bonus plan,* which would retain the Electoral College but award the popular vote winner a bonus of 102 electoral votes, thereby insuring that the popular vote and electoral vote winners are one and the same (Twentieth Century Fund 1978, 205) and eliminating any possibility of having the election forced into the House. Once again, however, the prospect of endless recounts in close elections rears its head, to say nothing of the unlikelihood of securing a constitutional amendment to achieve this change. Such a proposal, it must be remembered, would first have to clear the Congress with a two-thirds vote in each house. Given the fact that the Electoral College accords less populous states more influence than they would have under direct election, it seems highly unlikely that direct election plus the bonus would ever make it through the U.S. Senate, let alone the thirty-eight state legislatures needed to ratify, and where just thirteen of ninety-nine legislative chambers could kill it.

After considering the alternatives, the Electoral College seems less objectionable, and that indeed is the view of a majority of thirty-seven political scientists who, in the aftermath of the 2000 presidential election, systematically addressed the workings of the Electoral College, its impact, and alternatives to it: "We do not regard any alternatives as offering such significant gains as to be worth the risks that would accompany wholesale changes in our electoral system" (Schumaker and Loomis 2002, 205). For all its limitations, the Electoral College reinforces the principle of federalism by making states the focal point in the process, marginalizes extreme candidates, and discourages third parties, thereby making the task of governing easier with the dominance of two stable political parties (Schumaker and Loomis 2002, 183–185); and, if the 2000 election and its aftermath are any indication, the fact that the Electoral College may on rare occasions send individuals into the presidency with a minority of the popular vote does not necessarily mean that they will be unable to govern effectively.

Direct Legislation: Initiatives and Referenda

In the 2002 midterm election, there were some 202 measures appearing on the ballot in various states, 149 of which (referendums) were being referred to the voters by state legislatures, while the remaining 53 (initiatives) were placed on the ballot at the initiative of the citizens in those states (Reid 2002). Voters were, for example, being asked to approve after-school programs (California), the termination of bilingual education (Massachusetts), decriminalization of marijuana for personal use (Nevada), comprehensive health care, labeling of genetically engineered foods, raising the minimum wage (Oregon), a ban on the confinement of pregnant pigs (Florida), a ban on cockfighting (Oklahoma), and the reimbursement of student loans (North Dakota). Arizona and New Mexico tied for having the largest number of measures on the ballot—fourteen (Marquis 2002; Jacobson 2002, 2879).

An offspring of the Populist movement, the initiative and referendum were seen by farmers, laborers, and miners of the late nineteenth century as a means of correcting the actions or inactions of legislatures judged to be in the clutches of manufacturing and financial interests. The Progressives, displeased with control exerted by corrupt political machines over state legislatures, also took up the cause of citizen initiatives, as did other groups (e.g., suffragettes, socialists, prohibitionists) who saw their leverage over the political process as highly limited. The cause received a further boost from no less a figure than Woodrow Wilson, himself a distinguished scholar of the political process: "It must be remembered that we are contrasting the operation of the initiative and referendum, not with the representative government which we possess in theory . . . but with the actual state of affairs, with legislative processes that are carried on in secret, responding to the impulse of subsidized machines and carried through by men whose unhappiness is to realize that they are not their own masters, but puppets in a game" (cited in Cronin 1989, 54).

It was by using the initiative that a number of social changes were realized in some states well before they became national policy, including women's suffrage, reapportionment, abolition of poll taxes, primaries, restrictions on child labor, and prohibition of liquor sales. Initiative use reached a peak in the early 1910s (when the aforementioned changes were adopted),

declined somewhat in the 1920s and 1930s, and declined significantly over the next forty years, only to achieve renewed use in
the 1980s and 1990s (Ernst 2001, 7, 22). Its newfound popularity
has been greeted with considerable concern by some scholars,
political observers, and practitioners. They warn that a process
originally intended to provide the citizenry with a procedural
protection against unresponsive legislative bodies captured by
special interests has itself become the plaything of those interests
(Broder 2000; Ellis 2002; Smith 2001, 71–89). In the words of
David Broder, dean of American political journalists, "this
method of lawmaking has become the favored tools of million-
aires and interest groups that use their wealth to achieve their
own policy goals—a lucrative business for a new set of political
entrepreneurs" (Broder 2000, 1). Gone are the days of citizen activists who, strongly committed to a cause, went tirelessly from
house to house trying to convince voters to sign a petition to get
an issue on the ballot. Today, critics argue, there are professional
signature-gatherers for hire, with no commitment to the petitions they are promoting, who sometimes even show up on
doorsteps flogging several different petitions at once (Ayoub
2002). Consultants are hired to draft the initiative or identify its
flaws, as the case may be, run focus groups, do opinion polling,
and wage a massive advertising campaign to persuade often un-
suspecting voters to support or oppose a particular initiative
(Broder 2000, 52). Indeed, there has grown up what two scholars
describe as a virtual "initiative industrial complex" to manage
and promote the campaign of placing issues on the ballot (Donovan, Bowler, and McCuan 2001, 101). To access these resources
requires a considerable amount of money that, Broder suggests,
gives the well-heeled a great advantage in initiative politics. He
chronicles the efforts of one millionaire (Ron Unz) to secure passage of an initiative to end bilingual education in the California
schools—a policy change that the legislature had declined to
support. Unz put up $650,000 of the $976,632 ultimately spent in
a successful campaign to win voter approval. Billionaire Paul
Allen, owner of the Seattle Sea Hawks, wanted a new football
stadium ($425,000,000) with taxpayers footing part of the bill for
its construction. To this end, he put up $6.3 million to get it on
the ballot and pay for the media campaign. He even paid the
nearly $4 million it cost for the special election held to approve
it. The voters gave him his stadium. Believing that current drug
laws were wrongheaded, billionaire financier George Soros

joined forces with two other wealthy businessmen to legalize the use of marijuana for medicinal purposes. They campaigned for ballot initiatives in Alaska, Colorado, Nevada, Oregon, and Washington, vastly outspending their opponents, and ultimately carrying the day in all five (Broder 2000, 168–171, 191–197).

To fears that initiative politics now allow the very wealthy to gain access to the ballot must be added more long-standing concerns about making public policy at the ballot box rather than in a legislative body, with a second look given to it by the governor. When a proposal is presented to a legislature, it must typically pass through several screening processes before becoming law, during which time there is an opportunity to fine-tune, consider, and perhaps take into account views of the opposing side. In the words of one state legislator, "In the legislative process you learn a lot as you go along. It's a deliberative process. You can amend and improve a bill" (Broder 2000, 206). Moreover, in determining how to vote, legislators will likely be seeking to balance a variety of competing interests, if only because their reelection will be significantly influenced by their voting record. They are, in short, accountable for their actions. The initiative process, critics argue, is something quite different. Private groups and their attorneys draw up the initiative with no input from the opposing side, and once it is presented for petition signatures it may not be changed. The voters, meanwhile, are presented with an up or down vote on the issue; they are not required to consider any interest other than their own, thus granting approval to initiatives such as mandatory tax and spending limits that may seem highly appealing in the short run but not particularly prudent policy over the long haul. Add further that they have to fathom the often complex wording in ballot measures and are not accountable to anyone for how they vote. A simple majority decides, and particularly in off-year elections, that majority may be a very small proportion of the total electorate. Finally, in the face of initiative majorities, permanent minorities may find themselves at a very considerable disadvantage (Cain and Miller 2001, 43–52).

Although defenders of the initiative would readily agree that it is not free of problems, there are also grounds for concluding that some are overstated. It is not clear, for example, that the initiative is employed primarily by special interests to pursue their own narrow economic issues as opposed to other groups using it for more broad-based purposes (Jacob 2001, 95). Moreover, the evidence over an extended period of time indicates quite clearly that "narrow-based issues" have a far lower success rate (28.1 percent) than the more broad-based issues (60.7 percent). Furthermore, ballot initiatives that receive their funding from "citizen interests" as opposed to more narrow "economic interests" have a much higher success rate—60 percent as opposed to 22 percent (Ernst 2001, 23, 24; Jacob 2001, 96).

The notion that voter attitudes can be shaped and manipulated by media blitz campaigns is probably overstated as well. Those who vote appear to be a rather cautious lot, inclined to vote "no" when in doubt, even in the face of massive campaigns for the affirmative side; and they turn to newspapers and ballot summaries for their information, not campaign advertisements (Cronin 1989, 85–89; Magleby 1984, 165; Donovan, Bowler, and McCuan 2001, 112). As for how the interests of minorities fare in initiative politics, the evidence to date is mixed, but voters' judgments are probably more balanced than some skeptics might have expected (Wenzel, Donovan, and Bowler 2002, 241; Cronin 1989, 123, 229).

If the initiative process operates with greater effectiveness than some have suggested, there is nevertheless room for considerable improvement—improvements intended to increase voter awareness and knowledge while at the same time avoiding constitutional challenges. Knowing who is putting up the money to bankroll initiative campaigns is an important datum for voters to consider in deciding whether to support a given initiative. To this end, it has been suggested that such individuals and groups be required to form a campaign committee and register with the secretary of state's office, and provide disclosures of contributions made. In the interest of creating a more level playing field for who gets heard, it might also be helpful to provide some campaign subsidies and free airtime to initiative campaigns that are not adequately funded—defined as falling below 20 percent of the total amount of spending in an initiative campaign. This goal could also be further reinforced with the use of public hearings, and even initiative debates, much as we have debates among candidates in campaigns—both of which would gain substantial coverage by the press. Finally, greater attention should be given to the quality of state-published voter guides made available during initiative campaigns. California is a model in this regard. These are sent to all voters in the state, complete with a legislative assessment compiled by the office of secretary of state on how the initiative will affect the state economy, and with arguments made by the affirmative and negative sides of the initiative. Finally, it has also been suggested that states limit the number of initiatives that can be placed on the ballot in a given year. Asking voters to digest twelve or more initiatives at one time, as has been the case in some states, taxes the patience of even the most civic-minded of our citizens (Sabato, Ernst, and Larson 2001, 185–189).

Conclusion

The issues raised in this chapter relate to the *value* of the vote as opposed to the *right* to vote, the latter having now been firmly secured in our political system. They are controversial because there is disagreement over the extent to which they are seen as a serious problem, and if so, whether and how they should be addressed.

For some, the value of the vote is diminished by the lack of meaningful choices on the ballot—the result, according to some, of the monopoly over the political process enjoyed by the Republican and Democratic parties. But where these critics see monopoly, others see a healthy stability, which protects against extreme elements gaining any traction in the electoral process, a safeguard that would be lost with a proposed shift to proportional representation.

There are also concerns that the value of our vote may be compromised in the crucially important presidential nominating process as the frontloading of primaries risks a rush to judgment, forcing a decision on some voters too quickly while leaving others in later primaries with essentially nothing left to decide. The party organizations see it differently, however, believing that the sooner the decision is made, the more quickly the internal fighting ends and the more time they have to present a united front against the nominee of the other party.

In contrast to the two-party monopoly and frontloading, there is a greater consensus, but not unanimous agreement, that the role of money in campaigns is a problem that for many years has compromised both the nominating and general election stages, allowing some candidates' voices to be heard more than others, and after the election, providing special access to those who bankrolled the candidates rather than those who merely voted for them (Clawson, Neustadtl, and Weller 1998; Drew 1983; Gais 1998; Lewis 1996; Phillips 2003). There are some who suggest that the influence of money is overblown (Smith 1998; Brubaker 1988). But if most observers are inclined to acknowledge the potential contaminating effect of money, there is far less agreement on the nature of the cure. Some believe we can and should curb the flow of money into campaigns, while others contend that such efforts rub up against the First Amendment and/or are likely to be futile in any event, since creative lawyers always find creative ways around any regulations.

As with money, the disagreement over the Electoral College is rooted primarily in solutions. Scarcely anyone argues that electing a president without a popular majority is a desirable outcome, but the consensus breaks down over what to do about it. Direct election, while strongly favored by the American people and a number of scholars, is seen by others as creating more problems than it solves, including providing extremist elements with political leverage they do not deserve, and bogging us down in interminable election recounts.

In contrast to money and the Electoral College, the controversies over voter turnout and direct legislation turn more on the extent to which they are seen as a problem than on potential solutions. Some contend that the growing number of nonvoters leads to officials being chosen by unrepresentative majorities. Others, however, question whether the numbers are in fact growing and claim that more voters probably would not alter election outcomes in any event. Likewise, defenders of the initiative, while acknowledging room for improvement in the process, reject as overstated claims that the process has become the plaything of the well-heeled, who take advantage of manipulable voters to advance their own narrow economic interests.

References

Abbott, David W., and James P. Levine. 1991. *Wrong Winner: The Coming Debacle in the Electoral College.* New York: Praeger.

Adams, William. 1984. "Media Coverage of Campaign '84: A Preliminary Report." *Public Opinion* 7 (April/May): 10–13.

Arterton, Christopher. 1993. "Campaign '92: Strategies and Tactics of the Candidates." In Gerald M. Pomper et al., *The Election of 1992,* 39–73. Chatham, NJ: Chatham House Publishers.

Ayoub, Nina C. *The Chronicle of Higher Education.* 2002. "New Scholarly Books." (February 22): a18.

Barnes, James. 2001. "Democrats Compressing 2004 Calendar." *National Journal* (December 1): 3698–3699.

Bennett, Stephen Earl, and David Resnick. 1990. "The Implications of Nonvoting for Democracy in the United States." *American Journal of Political Science* 43 (August): 771–802.

Bibby, John F., and L. Sandy Maisel. 1998. *Two Parties—or More?* Boulder, CO: Westview Press.

Boyd, Richard. 1981. "Decline of U.S. Voter Turnout." *American Politics Quarterly* 9 (April): 123–159.

Broder, David S. 2000. *Democracy Derailed: Initiative Campaigns and the Power of Money.* New York: Harcourt.

Brody, Richard A. 1978. "The Puzzle of Political Participation in America." In Anthony King, ed., *The New American Political System,* 287–324. Washington, DC: American Enterprise Institute.

Brubaker, Stanley C. 1988. "The Limits of Campaign Spending Limits." *The Public Interest* 133 (Fall): 33–54.

Buhr, Tami. 2000. "What Voters Know about the Candidates and How They Learn It: The 1996 New Hampshire Republican Primary as a Case Study." In William G. Mayer, ed., *In Pursuit of the White House 2000: How We Choose Our Presidential Nominees,* 203–254. New York: Chatham House.

Cain, Bruce E., and Kenneth P. Miller. 2001. "The Populist Legacy: Initiatives and the Undermining of Representative Government." In Larry J. Sabato, Howard R. Ernst, and Bruce A. Larson, eds., *Dangerous Democracy? The Battle over Ballot Initiatives in the United States,* 43–52. Lanham, MD: Rowman and Littlefield.

CalTech/MIT Voting Technology Project. 2001. *Voting: What Is, What Could Be.* Pasadena and Cambridge: California Institute of Technology and Massachusetts Institute of Technology.

Clawson, Dan, Alan Neustadtl, and Mark Weller. 1998. *Dollars and Votes: How Business Campaign Contributions Subvert Democracy.* Philadelphia: Temple University Press.

Cooke, Jacob E., ed. 1961. *The Federalist.* Cleveland: World Publishing.

Crewe, Ivor. 1981. "Electoral Participation." In David Butler, Howard Penniman, and Austin Ranney, eds., *Democracy at the Polls,* 251–253. Washington, DC: American Enterprise Institute.

Cronin, Thomas E. 1989. *Direct Democracy: The Politics of Initiative, Referendum, and Recall.* Cambridge, MA: Harvard University Press.

Cronin, Thomas, and Robert Loevy. 1983. "The Case for a National Pre-Primary Convention Plan." *Public Opinion* (December/January): 50–53.

Donovan, Todd, Shaun Bowler, and David McCuan. 2001. "Political Consultants and the Initiative Industrial Complex." In Larry J. Sabato,

Howard R. Ernst, and Bruce A. Larson, eds., *Dangerous Democracy?: The Battle over Ballot Initiatives in the United States*, 101–134. Lanham, MD: Rowman and Littlefield.

Doppelt, Jack C., and Ellen Shearer. 1999. *Nonvoters: America's No-Shows.* Thousand Oaks, CA: Sage.

Drew, Elizabeth. 1983. *Politics and Money: The New Road to Corruption.* New York: Macmillan.

Elliot, Johnathan, ed. 1861. *The Debates in the Several Conventions on the Adoption of the Federal Constitution*, Vol. 2. Philadelphia: Lippincott.

Ellis, Richard J. 2002. *Democratic Delusions: The Initiative Process in America.* Lawrence: University Press of Kansas.

Erickson, Robert. 1981. "Why Do People Vote? Because They Are Registered." *American Politics Quarterly* 9 (July): 259–276.

Ernst, Howard R. 2001. "The Historical Role of Narrow-Material Interests in Initiative Politics." In Larry J. Sabato, Howard R. Ernst, and Bruce A. Larson, eds., *Dangerous Democracy?: The Battle over Ballot Initiatives in the United States*, 1–32. Lanham, MD: Rowman and Littlefield.

Flood, Emmet T., and William G. Mayer. 1996. "Third-Party and Independent Candidates: How They Get on the Ballot, How They Get Nominated." In William G. Mayer, ed., *In Pursuit of the White House: How We Choose Presidential Nominees*, 283–331. Chatham, NJ: Chatham House.

Fresia, Gerald John. 1986. *There Comes a Time: A Challenge to the Two-Party System.* New York: Praeger.

Gais, Thomas. 1998. *Improper Influence: Campaign Finance Law, Political Interest Groups, and the Problem of Equality.* Ann Arbor: University of Michigan Press.

Herrnson, Paul S., and John Green. 1997. "Two-Party Dominance and Minor Party Forays in American Politics." In Paul S. Herrnson and John Green, *Multiparty Politics in America*, 21–42. Lanham, MD: Rowman and Littlefield.

Jackson, Robert, Robert D. Brown, and Gerald D. Wright. 1998. "Registration, Turnout, and the Representativeness of U.S. State Electorates." *American Politics Quarterly* 26 (July): 259–281.

Jacob, Paul. 2001. "The Initiative Process: Where People Count." In Larry J. Sabato, Howard R. Ernst, and Bruce A. Larson, eds., *Dangerous Democracy? The Battle over Ballot Initiatives in the United States*, 94–99. Lanham, MD: Rowman and Littlefield.

Jacobson, Louis. 2002. "Ground-Level Democracy." *National Journal*, 2876–2882.

Just, Marion R. 1997. "Candidate Strategies and the Media Campaign." In Gerald M. Pomper et al., *The Election of 1996*, 77–106. Chatham, NJ: Chatham House.

Kagay, Michael R. 2000. "The Mystery of Nonvoters and Whether They Matter." *New York Times* (August 27): A1, A4.

Kamarck, Elaine. 1990. "Structure as Strategy: Presidential Nominating Politics in the Post-Reform Era." In L. Sandy Maisel, ed., *The Parties Respond: Changes in the American Party System*, 163–168. Boulder, CO: Westview Press.

Knack, Stephen. 1999. "Drivers Wanted: Motor Voter and the Election of 1996." *P.S.* 32 (June): 237–243.

Lewis, Charles L. 1996. *The Buying of the President*. New York: Avon.

Lichter, S. Robert, Daniel Amundson, and Richard Noyes. 1988. *Video Campaign: Network Coverage of the 1988 Primaries*. Washington, DC: American Enterprise Institute.

Lijphart, Arend. 1996. "Compulsory Voting Is the Best Way to Keep Democracy Strong." *Chronicle of Higher Education* (October 18): B3–B4.

Longley, Lawrence D., and Alan Braun. 1972. *The Politics of Electoral College Reform*. New Haven, CT: Yale University Press.

Lowi, Theodore. 1998. "Toward a More Responsible Three-Party System: Prospects and Obstacles." In Theodore J. Lowi and Joseph Romance, *Republic of Parties?: Debating the Two-Party System*, 3–30. Lanham, MD: Rowman and Littlefield.

Magleby, David B. 1984. *Direct Legislation: Voting on Ballot Propositions in the United States*. Baltimore: Johns Hopkins University Press.

Marquis, Christopher. 2002. "Voters to Consider Ballot Proposals on Marijuana Use, Bilingual Schools and Pigs." *New York Times* (November 3): 20.

Matthews, William. 2000. "Can the Net Revive the Vote?" http://www.few.com/few/articles/2000/0904/cov-vote-09-04-00.asp (accessed January 15, 2003).

Mazmanian, Daniel A. 1974. *Third Parties in Presidential Elections*. Washington, DC: Brookings Institution.

McDonald, Michael P., and Samuel L. Popkin. 2001. "The Myth of the Vanishing Voter." *American Political Science Review* 95 (December): 963–971.

Moore, David. 1984. "The Death of Politics in New Hampshire." *Public Opinion Quarterly* 7 (February/March).

Oppell, Richard A., Jr. 2002. "Soft Money Rolls into Coffers While It Can." *New York Times* (October 17): A13.

Patterson, Thomas E. 1980. *The Mass Media Election.* New York: Praeger.

————. 2002. *The Vanishing Voter: Public Involvement in an Age of Uncertainty.* New York: Alfred A. Knopf.

————. 2003. *The American Democracy,* 6th ed. Boston: McGraw-Hill.

Phillips, Kevin. 2003. "How Wealth Defines Power: The Politics of the New Gilded Age." *American Prospect* (May 24): A10.

Plissner, Martin. 2002. "A Really Super Tuesday." *Public Perspective* (July/August): 4.

Pomper, Gerald M. 2001. "The Presidential Election." In Gerald M. Pomper et al., *The Election of 2000,* 125–154. New York: Chatham House.

Powell, G. Bingham, Jr. 1986. "Voter Turnout in Comparative Perspective." *American Political Science Review* 80 (March): 17–44.

Ranney, Austin. 1981. "Candidate Selection." In David Butler, Howard Penniman, and Austin Ranney, eds., *Democracy at the Polls,* 75–106. Washington, DC: American Enterprise Institute.

————. 2001. "Nonvoting Is Not a Social Disease." In Robert E. DiClerico and Allan S. Hammock, eds., *Points of View: Readings in American Government,* 78–84. Boston: McGraw-Hill.

Reid, T. R. 2002. "From Pigs to Pot: Voters' Concerns on Ballot." *Washington Post* (October 23): A1.

Richie, Robert, and Steven Hill. 2001. *Whose Vote Counts?* Boston: Beacon Press.

Robinson, Michael, and Margaret Sheehan. 1980. *Over the Wire and on TV.* New York: Russell Sage Foundation.

Romance, Joseph. 1998. "Gridlock and Reform at the End of the Twentieth Century." In Theodore J. Lowi and Joseph Romance, *Republic of Parties?: Debating the Two-Party System,* 31–74. Lanham, MD: Rowman and Littlefield.

Rosenstone, Steven, and John Mark Hansen. 1993. *Mobilization, Participation, and Democracy in America.* New York: Macmillan.

Sabato, Larry J. 2002. "The Perfect Storm: The Election of the Century." In Larry J. Sabato, ed., *Overtime: The Election 2000 Thriller,* 95–122. New York: Longman.

Sabato, Larry J., Howard R. Ernst, and Bruce A. Larson. 2001. "A Call for Change: Making the Best of Initiative Politics." In Larry J. Sabato, Howard R. Ernst, and Bruce A. Larson, eds., *Dangerous Democracy?: The Battle over Ballot Initiatives in the United States,* 185–189. Lanham, MD: Rowman and Littlefield.

Schlesinger, Arthur M., Jr. 2002. "Not the People's Choice: How to Democratize American Democracy." *American Prospect* (March 25): 23–27.

Schumaker, Paul D., and Burdett A. Loomis. 2002. "Reaching a Collective Judgment." In Paul D. Schumaker and Burdett A. Loomis, *Choosing a President: The Electoral College and Beyond,* 176–208. New York: Chatham House.

Sifry, Micah L. 2002. *Spoiling for a Fight.* New York: Routledge.

Simon, Leslie David, Javier Corrales, and Donald R. Wolfensberger. 2002. *Democracy and the Internet: Allies or Adversaries?* Washington, DC: Woodrow Wilson Center Press.

Smith, Bradley A. 1998. "Faulty Assumptions and Undemocratic Assumptions of Campaign Finance Reform." In Frederick G. Slabach, *The Constitution and Campaign Finance Reform,* 124–133. Durham, NC: Carolina Academic Press.

Smith, Daniel. 2001. "Campaign Financing of Ballot Initiatives in the United States." In Larry J. Sabato, Howard R. Ernst, and Bruce A. Larson, eds., *Dangerous Democracy?: The Battle over Ballot Initiatives in the United States,* 71–89. Lanham, MD: Rowman and Littlefield.

Teixeira, Ruy A. 1992. *The Disappearing American Voter.* Washington, DC: Brookings Institution.

Twentieth Century Fund. 1978. *Winner Take All: A Report of the Twentieth-Century Fund Task Force on Reform of the Presidential Election Process.* New York: Holmes and Meier.

Washington Post. 2002a. "The Power of Soft Money. The Big Givers." February 13, A25.

———. 2002b. "218 at Last." January 25, A24.

Wenzel, James, Todd Donovan, and Shaun Bowler. 2002. "Direct Democracy and Minorities: Changing Attitudes about Minorities Targeted by Initiatives." In Shaun Bowler, Todd Donovan, and Caroline J. Tolbert, eds., *Citizens as Legislators: Direct Democracy in the United States,* 228–248. Columbus: Ohio State University Press.

Wolfinger, Raymond E., and Steven J. Rosenstone. 1980. *Who Votes?* New Haven, CT: Yale University Press.

Cases Cited

Buckley v. Valeo 424 U.S. 1 (1976)
McConnell v. Federal Election Commission 124 S.Ct. 619 (2003)

3

Chronology

This chapter chronicles the events, people, circumstances, and government actions that influenced how the right to vote evolved over the course of American history. The path from a highly limited franchise to a highly inclusive one has been neither flat nor straight. The unpropertied, women, blacks, Native Americans, immigrants, and the illiterate had to scale the mountains of prejudice and economic self-interest in order to secure the right to vote; and even after doing so, the path at times—as with blacks and immigrants—circled back, making it deliberately more cumbersome, and even impossible, for them to exercise the franchise, and at other times structuring the voting environment (gerrymandering) so as to dilute the impact of the vote.

The expansion in the number of opportunities to vote, in contrast, has not been characterized by the detours and retrenchment associated with the right to vote. On the contrary, not only did the number of officeholders subject to election gradually increase over time as a result of constitutional and political changes, but so did our opportunities to determine the choices we would have for those offices.

1715	Connecticut establishes a property qualification for voting.
1734	Delaware establishes a property qualification for voting.
1762	Rhode Island establishes a property qualification for voting.

1776   Maryland and North Carolina establish a property qualification for voting applicable to white and free African American males.

New Jersey establishes a financial worth qualification for voting applicable to white males and females.

Pennsylvania establishes a taxpaying qualification for voting applicable to white and free African American males.

Virginia establishes a property qualification for voting applicable to white males.

1777   New York establishes a property qualification for voting applicable to white and free African American males.

Georgia establishes for white males a financial worth and taxpaying qualification for voting, or, in place of these requirements, "being of the mechanic trade."

1778   South Carolina establishes for white males a property or taxpaying qualification for voting.

1780   Massachusetts establishes for white and free African American males a property or financial worth qualification for voting.

1781   The Articles of Confederation are ratified, reserving to the states the authority to decide qualifications for voting (Article II).

1784   New Hampshire establishes for white males a poll tax as a qualification for voting.

1787   The Northwest Ordinance passes Congress (repasses in 1789). It provides for the governing of territory north of the Ohio River and west of New York to the Mississippi River. Among its other provisions are a property requirement (200 acres) as a condition of eligibility to serve as a representative, and 50 acres as a requirement for eligibility to vote.

The Founding Fathers sign the final draft of the U.S. Constitution on September 17. Given the great variation in the qualifications for voting among the several states, and the desire to avoid taking any action that might cause states not to ratify the final draft, the Founding Fathers decide to leave it up to each state to decide the qualifications for voting (Article I, Sec. 2). In addition, they allow the people to elect members of the U.S. House of Representatives (Article I, Sec. 2), while allowing each state legislature to select its two U.S. senators (Article I, Sec. 3). The states have the power to determine the times, places, and manners of election for senators and representatives, but Congress may at any time make or alter such regulations, except for the places for choosing senators (Article 1, Sec. 4). The president, meanwhile, is to be chosen by a group of presidential electors, with the number of electors from each state being determined by the number of members it has in the U.S. Congress. It is left to each state legislature to determine the manner in which that state's presidential electors will be chosen. Presidential electors are to vote for two candidates for president, one of whom must reside outside of the elector's state. The individual receiving a majority of the electoral votes cast shall be elected president, and the second highest number of votes, vice president. If there is a tie for the second highest number of votes, the Senate shall choose the vice-president. In the event that no candidate receives a majority of the electoral votes, the election is then decided by the House of Representatives, which chooses among the top five candidates. The Congress is given the power to determine the time for choosing presidential electors, and to establish a uniform election day throughout the United States (Article II, Sec. 1).

1788   By June 21, nine of the thirteen states have ratified the Constitution. On September 13, Congress by resolution fixes the date for the election of the president and the organization of the new government.

1789   Georgia establishes for white males a taxpaying qual-
            ification for voting.

1790   Pennsylvania establishes for white and free African
            American males a taxpaying qualification for voting
            but exempts those less than age twenty-two whose fa-
            thers are qualified voters.

1791   Vermont imposes on white and free African American
            males no property or taxpaying requirement as a con-
            dition for voting.

1792   Delaware rescinds property requirement for voting.

            New Hampshire eliminates taxpaying qualification
            for voting.

            New Hampshire is the first state to exclude pau-
            pers—those supported at the public expense—from
            voting.

            Kentucky is admitted to statehood with no property
            qualification for voting.

            South Carolina extends the franchise to white males
            only and requires either ownership of property or
            personal residence in a voting district and payment of
            three shillings in taxes.

            Congress passes the Act of 1792, stipulating that pres-
            idential electors must be chosen within thirty-four
            days preceding the first Wednesday in December
            every fourth year.

1796   Following George Washington's late announcement
            that he will not be running again in 1796, there is not
            much time for prospective candidates for the presi-
            dency to launch a campaign. Accordingly, two com-
            peting factions within Congress, the Federalists and
            the Democratic-Republicans, use their newly created
            caucuses in that body to nominate candidates, with
            the Federalists choosing John Adams, and Thomas

Pinckney as his running mate, while the Democratic-Republicans settle on Thomas Jefferson and running mate Aaron Burr. The congressional caucus will serve as the method for nominating presidential candidates through 1820.

1800   The constitutional requirement that presidential electors must vote for two candidates for president had already produced one political oddity in 1796—the election of a president (John Adams) and a vice president (Thomas Jefferson) from different political parties. It now leads to another. Republican Thomas Jefferson and his running mate, Aaron Burr, challenge Federalist president John Adams and his new running mate, General Charles Pinckney. Prior to the voting, the Jeffersonian Republicans neglect to instruct one of their electors not to vote for Burr. As a consequence, Jefferson and Burr tie with 73 votes each, followed by Adams (65), Pinckney (64), and John Jay (1). The election is forced into the House, which remains in continuous session for six days, failing to produce a winner (Jefferson) until the thirty-sixth ballot. To avoid a recurrence of these circumstances, Republicans push for and the states ultimately ratify the Twelfth Amendment to the Constitution (see 1804).

1801   Maryland drops property qualifications for state elections.

Massachusetts adopts a voter registration system.

1803   Ohio, admitted to statehood with a taxpaying requirement for voting, is also the first state to prohibit idiots and the insane from voting. Forty-four other states will ultimately do likewise.

1804   The Twelfth Amendment takes effect on September 25, changing the original Constitution in two important respects. First, presidential electors are now required to vote separately for president and vice president. In addition, should the election be forced into

1804 (cont.)	the House of Representatives, it must choose from among the three candidates with the highest number of electoral votes, rather than from the top five as stipulated in the original Constitution.
1810	Maryland drops its property qualification for all elections. South Carolina drops its taxpaying qualification for voting but retains a property requirement.
1812	Louisiana is admitted to statehood. Suffrage within this state is conditional upon having purchased land from the United States, or having paid taxes six months prior to voting.
1816	Indiana is admitted to statehood without any property qualification for voting.
1817	Connecticut rescinds its property requirement for voting. Mississippi is admitted to statehood; voters are required to pay state or county taxes or show proof of enlistment in the local militia.
1818	Illinois is admitted to statehood without any property qualification for voting.
1819	Alabama is admitted as a state with no property or taxpaying requirements as a condition of suffrage.
1820	Maine is admitted to statehood with no property qualification for voting. States that had allowed blacks to vote at independence (New Jersey, Maryland, and Connecticut) are by now limiting the franchise to whites only.
1821	Missouri is admitted to statehood with no property or taxpaying qualifications for voting.

New York drops its property qualification for voting for whites only.

Massachusetts drops its property qualification for voting.

1824   With the Federalist Party largely dissipated, the Jeffersonian Republicans have little incentive to suppress intraparty differences. Thus, six individuals are nominated for president—one by congressional caucus (Secretary of the Treasury William H. Crawford), and five by state legislatures, three of whom remain in the race—Andrew Jackson, John Quincy Adams, and Henry Clay.

Jackson finishes first with 99 electoral votes and 152,933 popular votes, while Adams pulls in 84 electoral votes and 115, 696 popular votes. Crawford and Clay, meanwhile, garner only 41 and 37 electoral votes, respectively, but do well enough to force the election into the House. Under the provisions of the Twelfth Amendment, the House is now required to choose from among the top three candidates—Jackson, Adams, and Crawford. Clay, having been eliminated, throws his support to Adams, who wins on the first ballot. The election leaves a bitter aftertaste, however. Not only does Adams proceed to make Clay his secretary of state, thereby fueling speculation that a deal had been struck for Clay's support, but the House chooses as president an individual who came in second to his opponent (Jackson) in both the popular and electoral votes.

1831   Derisively referred to as "King Caucus," the congressional caucus falls into disfavor as the method for nominating presidential candidates. State and local parties complain that the caucus process excludes them from playing any role in the selection of a nominee. Add to this the fact that limiting the selection only to party members in Congress seems increasingly inappropriate in the era of Jacksonian

1831 *(cont.)*	democracy. Accordingly, the parties adopt a new mechanism to nominate presidential candidates—national party conventions made up of delegates chosen by each state's political party.
	In *Cherokee Nation v. Georgia,* the U.S. Supreme Court rules that American Indians are dependent nations within the United States and fall directly under the sovereignty of the United States government. According to the U.S. attorney general, who renders an opinion proximate to the court's ruling, American Indians cannot become U.S. citizens through the normal procedures governing naturalization of foreigners. Why? Because they are not really foreigners since they are already "in our allegiance." This curious bit of reasoning means, according to the attorney general, that citizenship for Native Americans can be achieved only pursuant to a treaty or congressional action.
1832	All but one state legislature is now allowing its citizens to choose presidential electors. The exception is South Carolina, whose legislature continues to pick presidential electors until 1860.
1834	Tennessee drops its property qualification for voting.
1836	All states except South Carolina are casting their electoral votes as a block for the presidential candidate who wins the most votes in the state.
	Arkansas is admitted to statehood with no property qualification for voting.
1837	Michigan is admitted to statehood with no property or taxpaying qualifications for voting.
1838	Kentucky extends to propertied widows and unmarried women the right to vote in school elections.
1841	Laboring under one of the most onerous freehold requirements, nearly one-half of Rhode Island's white

male population cannot vote. Thomas Dorr takes up their cause, spearheading a move to draft a People's Constitution, which grants the vote to any white male residing in the state for a year. Conservatives answer with a less reformist document, but Dorr's wins popular approval. Rhode Island now finds itself with two governments, the original one and the new one led by the "people's governor," Thomas Dorr. When the old begins to arrest the new, Dorr retreats to New York, promising to return with hundreds of armed men. Only around two hundred manage to make an unsuccessful attack on the Providence Arsenal, and Dorr flees across the border. Dorr's Rebellion, however, is not completely for naught: Rhode Island's government eventually agrees to adopt a more liberal constitution.

1842   The Congressional Apportionment Act is passed, requiring states to use single-member districts for the election of members to the U.S. House of Representatives.

Rhode Island retains its property requirement for nonnative citizens and requires all voting males to either pay a tax of one dollar or at least serve a day in military service.

Connecticut, revising a voter registration law passed in 1839, now places the responsibility for registering voters on town officials.

1844   New Jersey drops its property and taxpaying qualifications for voting.

1845   Connecticut drops its property and taxpaying qualifications for voting.

Florida is admitted to statehood with no property or taxpaying qualifications for voting.

Texas is admitted to statehood with no property or taxpaying qualifications for voting.

1845 (cont.)	Congress decides that all states shall choose their presidential electors "on the Tuesday next, after the first Monday in November, in every fourth year."
1846	Iowa is admitted to statehood without any property qualification for voting.
	New York drops its taxpaying qualification for whites only.
1848	Wisconsin is admitted to statehood with no property or taxpaying qualifications for voting.
	Wisconsin is the first state to extend the right to vote to resident aliens who have lived in the United States for two years and filed papers stating their intention to become U.S. citizens (i.e., declarant aliens).
	The long march to secure the right of women to vote begins with a conference held in Seneca, New York, under the leadership of Elizabeth Cady Stanton and Lucretia Mott, the outcome of which is a Declaration of Sentiments stating that men and women are equal.
1850	California is admitted to statehood with no property or taxpaying qualification for voting.
	Virginia drops its property and taxpaying qualification for voting.
	The first National Women's Rights meeting is convened in Worcester, Massachusetts.
	Michigan allows declarant aliens the right to vote.
1851	Indiana allows declarant aliens the right to vote.
1853	Originally organized as a secret society, the "Know Nothings," so characterized by Horace Greeley because they refuse to divulge any information about themselves, harbor a special antipathy toward the growing number of foreigners—particularly Catho-

lics—entering the country. The group now decides to go public as the American Party, advocating among other things that immigrants be required to wait twenty-one years before becoming American citizens. The party declines as quickly as it rose, but not before securing nine governorships and winning control of the legislatures in six states, each having a significant immigrant population.

1855   There are now thirty-one states in the Union, with all but five (Maine, Massachusetts, Vermont, New Hampshire, and Rhode Island) limiting the franchise to whites only.

Connecticut requires that its citizens be able to read any provision of the Constitution or any statute in order to qualify to vote.

1856   North Carolina becomes the last state to eliminate a property requirement to vote; it continues to require voters to pay public taxes, however.

1857   In *Dred Scott v. Sandford* the U.S. Supreme Court in a seven to two decision rules that blacks, whether they happen to be slaves or free, are not citizens of the United States.

Twenty-four states now prohibit the franchise to those convicted of a criminal offense. Some states, such as New York, allow for restoration of the vote upon receipt of a pardon by the governor.

Massachusetts requires that its citizens be able to write their name and read the Constitution in English in order to qualify to vote.

Oregon allows declarant aliens the right to vote but also prohibits any individual who is a native of China from voting in its elections. It is also the first state to provide for absentee voting.

1859   Kansas allows declarant aliens the right to vote.

1864   Nevada institutes a poll tax.

1866   Congress passes the Fourteenth Amendment, which declares all citizens born or naturalized in the United States to be its citizens and that no state may abridge the privileges and immunities of U.S. citizens; or deny them life, liberty, or property without due process of law; or deny to them the equal protection of the laws. It further provides that if any state denies to any of its male inhabitants the right to vote other than for rebellion or other crime, that state shall have its representation in Congress reduced by the percentage of people being denied. Finally, Congress is given the power to enforce these provisions.

Congress legislates to abolish racial qualifications for voting in the District of Columbia.

Congress prohibits imposing any racial tests for voting in existing or future U.S. territories.

Georgia institutes a poll tax.

1867   Congress passes the Reconstruction Act, making each southern state's readmission to the Union contingent upon its ratification of the Fourteenth Amendment and its acceptance of a state constitution that grants blacks the same voting rights as whites.

Alabama and Nebraska allow declarant aliens the right to vote.

1868   The Fourteenth Amendment to the Constitution is ratified.

Arkansas, Florida, and Georgia allow declarant aliens the right to vote.

1869   Congress approves the Fifteenth Amendment, prohibiting the United States and any state government from denying or abridging the right to vote on the basis of race, color, or previous condition of servitude. Congress is given the power to enforce this provision.

Elizabeth Cady Stanton and Susan B. Anthony establish the National Woman Suffrage Association, which targets its energies at the federal government, while the American Woman Suffrage Association, founded by Lucy Stone and Henry Blackwell, focuses on advancing the right to vote at the state level.

The Wyoming Territory extends to women the right to vote.

Texas allows declarant aliens the right to vote.

1870   The Enforcement Act becomes law, making it a federal crime to interfere with the right to vote.

Missouri allows declarant aliens the right to vote.

Tennessee institutes a poll tax.

The Utah Territory extends the right to vote to women (Congress will annul it in 1887).

The Fifteenth Amendment is ratified, guaranteeing all men twenty-one years of age or older the right to vote regardless of race, color, or previous condition of servitude.

1871   The Second Enforcement Act places congressional elections under the supervision of the federal government.

The Third Enforcement Act, also known as the Ku Klux Klan Act, becomes law, giving the president the authority to send federal troops to a state in order to protect the electoral process.

1872   Virginia Minor files suit against the registrar of St. Louis, Missouri, for denying her the opportunity to register to vote and thereby interfering with her

1872
(cont.)

freedom of speech and the "privileges and immunities" (Fourteenth Amendment) she enjoys as a U.S. citizen. Three years later, the U.S. Supreme Court will rule against her, arguing that citizenship does not automatically imply the right to vote. Rather, it rests with the states to make that determination.

Susan B. Anthony, one of the leading advocates of women's suffrage, votes illegally in the presidential election, is arrested, and pays a minor fine.

Congress requires that congressional districts contain "as nearly as possible an equal number of inhabitants."

1876

The day following a tightly contested presidential election, Republican Rutherford B. Hayes has 165 electoral votes, while Democrat Samuel J. Tilden is conceded to have 184 and the lead in the popular vote. An additional 19 electoral votes from four states are contested, with both parties accusing each other of fraud, bribery, and intimidation during the voting process. In each of these four states, the Republican and Democratic parties submit their own set of election returns to Congress. With each house of Congress controlled by a different party, there is ample opportunity for mischief, including the possibility that the Democratic House will choose Tilden, and the Republican Senate, Hayes, thereby leaving the nation with two claimants to the office. Cooler heads prevail, however, and Congress instead passes the Electoral Commission Law, signed by President Ulysses S. Grant just three days before the deadline for the opening and counting of ballots. Composed of five senators, five members of the House, and five Supreme Court justices, the commission is authorized to rule in those cases where a state submits double returns. Under the law, the commission's rulings can be overturned only if both houses of Congress agree. By a vote of eight to seven the commission accepts the Hayes electors. Not surprisingly, the Democratic

House votes to reject this ruling, while the Republican Senate votes to accept it. Thus, with the Congress unable to agree, the commission's ruling stands, and Hayes is certified as the winner.

In what was to be the first of several court cases that would erode the significance of the Fourteenth and Fifteenth Amendments, the Supreme Court rules in *U.S. v. Cruikshank* that the vagueness of the Enforcement Acts, as well as their focus upon race, renders them not enforceable under the Fifteenth Amendment. In another case (*United States v. Reese*) the Court rules that the Fifteenth Amendment does not allow Congress and the states to impose penalties for hindering any person from voting for any reason, but rather only because of race, color, or previous condition of servitude.

Colorado joins the Union, permitting women to vote in school elections and providing for a referendum on women's suffrage. It also allows declarant aliens the right to vote.

1877   Georgia requires the payment of all taxes as a condition for voting, and repeals the right of declarant aliens to vote.

1878   An amendment is introduced in the U.S. Senate prohibiting denial of the right to vote on the basis of sex.

1879   California prohibits any individual who is a native of China from voting in its elections.

Louisiana allows declarant aliens the right to vote.

Missouri and North Carolina establish literacy tests for voting.

1882   South Carolina institutes an "eight-ballot" law forcing voters to place their eight ballots in eight separate boxes, each designated for a specific candidate. The

1882 (cont.)	purpose of this procedure is to disqualify illiterate blacks from voting.
1883	Texas institutes a poll tax.

The Territory of Washington extends to women the right to vote, but the Supreme Court of the territory rules it unconstitutional in 1887.

1884 Iowa Territory is the first to repeal its law allowing to vote those aliens who have filed papers to become U.S. citizens. (By 1926, eighteen states will withdraw the franchise, with most doing so in the first two decades of the twentieth century.)

The Supreme Court rules (*Elk v. Wilkins*) that the Fourteenth Amendment does not confer citizenship on American Indians.

1887 Congress, not wanting a repeat of the 1876 election, passes legislation specifying procedures for raising and resolving challenges to presidential ballots. Known as the Electoral Count Act, it specifies that objections be made in writing and signed by at least one member of each house. Each house then separately considers the challenge, which prevails only if both houses concur. In a clear attempt by Congress to shift the burden of resolving disputed ballots to the states, the law further stipulates that in any controversy arising over the appointment of a state's electors, a state's determination of that matter shall be final provided (1) a state has a law for determining such controversies; (2) the law was enacted prior to the date set for appointing electors; and (3) the ruling on such a controversy was made at least six days prior to the date when the electors voted. Should a dispute arise over which state officials are authorized to certify electors, then both houses acting separately will make the determination. If double returns are submitted and the state has made no determination as to which are valid, then both houses, provided they agree, shall decide. If both houses do not agree, the votes certified by a state's executive will be counted.

The General Allotment Act confers citizenship on American Indians who are leading a "civilized life" and agree to accept private allotments of what was formerly tribal land.

An amendment prohibiting denial of the right to vote on the basis of sex is defeated on the floor of the U.S. Senate.

The Territory of Montana extends to women the right to vote.

1888   Democratic president Grover Cleveland, the popular vote winner in the presidential election by a margin of 95,096 votes, nevertheless loses to the Republican challenger, Benjamin Harrison, who receives 233 electoral votes to Cleveland's 168.

Kentucky and Massachusetts become the first states to adopt the Australian ballot—a secret ballot prepared, distributed, and tabulated by public officials at public expense.

1889   Florida institutes a poll tax and adopts the "eight ballot" law (see 1882).

New York becomes the first state to adopt the paper ballot for all statewide elections.

Wyoming establishes a literacy test for voting.

Idaho prohibits from voting in its elections any individual who is a native of China.

Montana, North Dakota, South Dakota, and Washington enter the Union allowing women to vote in school elections. Montana also allows women who pay taxes to vote on tax issues. All four states allow declarant aliens the right to vote.

1890   In order to deter blacks from voting, Mississippi insti-
            tutes a literacy test and poll tax.

            South Carolina is the first state to adopt the "grandfa-
            ther clause," a mechanism to exempt poor whites
            from the poll tax, stiff residency requirements, and/or
            literacy tests, provided they or their ancestors had
            voted prior to 1867.

            Wyoming enters the Union extending to women the
            right to vote.

            The Supreme Court rules (*Davis v. Beason*) that an indi-
            vidual can be denied the right to vote while in prison.

            The National Woman Suffrage Association and the
            American Woman Suffrage Association combine
            forces in a newly created National American Woman
            Suffrage Association.

1891   Federal legislation providing for federal officials to
            supervise congressional elections, thereby giving
            teeth to the Second Enforcement Act (1871), goes
            down to defeat in Congress.

            Forty-one states have now adopted the Australian
            ballot.

1892   The Populist Party calls for the direct election of U.S.
            senators and a "legislative system known as initiative
            and referendum."

1893   Maine establishes a literacy test for voting.

            Arkansas institutes a poll tax.

            Colorado extends to women the right to vote.

1894   Michigan and Montana terminate the right of declar-
            ant aliens to vote.

1895   South Carolina establishes a literacy test for voting
            and institutes a poll tax.

Florida and Wyoming terminate the right of declarant aliens to vote.

Utah decides that only property owners can vote on referenda creating a special tax or public indebtedness.

By now there are twelve states that exclude paupers from voting (Arkansas, Delaware, Louisiana, Maine, Massachusetts, New Hampshire, New Jersey, Rhode Island, South Carolina, Texas, Virginia, and West Virginia).

1896   Idaho and Utah extend to women the right to vote.

Vermont is the first state to pass a statute allowing the absentee vote to civilians and military personnel.

1897   Delaware eliminates a taxpaying requirement for voting.

1898   The Democrats, having regained control of both the executive and legislative branches, repeal the Enforcement Acts passed in the early 1870s.

In *Williams v. Mississippi*, the Supreme Court upholds the constitutionality of both the literacy test and the poll tax.

Louisiana establishes a literacy test for voting, as well as a poll tax. It also terminates the right of declarant aliens to vote.

South Dakota becomes the first state to adopt the initiative and referendum.

1900   Delaware institutes a literacy test for voting.

Utah adopts the initiative and referendum.

Minneapolis, Minnesota, is the first jurisdiction in the country to use the direct primary in nominating officials to public office.

1901   The Florida state legislature becomes the first to pass a law permitting political parties to choose their presidential nominee or delegates by primary.

Alabama institutes a poll tax and terminates the right of declarant aliens to vote.

Congress requires that congressional districts be constructed of "compact territory."

1902   New Hampshire requires that voters be able to read the Constitution in English and write.

Connecticut establishes a literacy test, requiring voters to be able to read the state constitution or its statutes.

Virginia adopts a literacy test requiring the reading of any provision of the state constitution. Exemptions are granted to property owners, veterans, and their descendants.

Oregon adopts the initiative and referendum.

The American Federation of Labor, under the leadership of Samuel Gompers, passes a resolution at its national convention calling for the initiative and referendum at the national level.

The Women's Trade Union League is organized for the purpose of bringing women into the trade union movement.

1903   Alabama institutes a literacy test, requiring that a voter be able to read any provision in the state constitution. Exemptions are granted to owners of forty acres of property or real estate with an assessed value of at least $300.

1904   In *Pope v. Williams*, the Supreme Court rules that as long as there is no evidence of discrimination, residency laws imposed by state and local governments are constitutional.

Nevada adopts the initiative and referendum.

1905   The Wisconsin state legislature passes a law requiring that all delegates to the Democratic and Republican national conventions be chosen by a primary.

1906   Pennsylvania passes legislation allowing candidates for delegate to place the name of their presidential preference on the ballot.

Montana adopts the referendum.

1907   Georgia and Oklahoma establish literacy tests for voting.

Oklahoma adopts the initiative and referendum.

The Oklahoma legislature also decides that only taxpayers can vote to have a town or city incur debt.

A new and more militant women's suffrage group, the Equality League, is established.

1908   Michigan determines that an individual must own taxable property in order to vote on any referendum concerning public money or bonds.

Wisconsin terminates the right of declarant aliens to vote.

Michigan and Missouri adopt the initiative and referendum.

Maine adopts the referendum.

Oregon adopts the recall for all elected officials.

1909   Arkansas adopts the initiative and referendum.

1910   The citizens of Oregon decide to establish the first presidential "preference" primary in which voters are given the opportunity to express their preferences for a presidential candidate and then vote separately (on

1910 *(cont.)*	the same ballot) for the individuals they want as delegates. These delegates are legally bound to vote for the candidate who wins the "preference" vote.

Colorado adopts the initiative and referendum.

Arizona Territory determines that only property holders may vote on a bond issue or special assessment. It also adopts the referendum.

New York limits voting for school board members to taxpayers and parents with children.

Congress votes to limit the size of the U.S. House of Representatives to 435 members.

1911   The governor of South Dakota is recalled.

California establishes a literacy test for voting, and also extends to women the right to vote. The state adopts the initiative, referendum, and recall for all elected officials.

New Mexico adopts the referendum.

1912   Washington and Arizona extend to women the right to vote, and establish a literacy test for voting.

Kansas and Oregon extend to women the right to vote.

Nebraska and Ohio adopt the initiative and referendum.

Washington and Idaho adopt the referendum.

Arizona, Colorado, and Nevada adopt the recall for all elected officials. Washington does as well, except for judges of record.

The Progressive Party comes out in favor of granting women the right to vote.

In a pair of decisions (*Pacific States Telephone and Telegraph v. Oregon* and *Kiernan v. City of Portland*), the U.S. Supreme Court responds to the claim that the initiative is unconstitutional by ruling that the matter is a political question, and not a matter for determination by the courts.

1913   The Seventeenth Amendment to the Constitution is adopted, requiring that United States senators be directly elected by the citizens of their state, and in the event of a vacancy, authorizing the governor to make a temporary appointment until an election is held.

The Illinois state legislature allows women to vote for presidential electors.

New Hampshire institutes a poll tax.

North Dakota terminates the right of declarant aliens to vote.

Michigan adopts the recall for all elected officials except judges of record.

On the day of Woodrow Wilson's inauguration, some five thousand women converge on Washington, D.C., demanding the right to vote. Wilson, however, says this is a matter for the states to decide.

1914   The territory of Alaska and the states of Montana and Nevada extend to women the right to vote.

Kansas adopts recall except for judges of record.

North Dakota adopts the initiative and referendum.

Oregon terminates the right of declarant aliens to vote.

Congress passes a statute requiring that the time set for senatorial elections coincide with election of members to the U.S. House of Representatives.

1914 (cont.)	For the first time, an amendment is proposed to the Constitution requiring that a national referendum be conducted on the decision to go to war. It attracts little support.
1915	The Supreme Court rules (*Guinn v. U.S.*) that the only purpose behind "grandfather laws" is to discriminate against blacks, and therefore, they constitute a violation of the Fifteenth Amendment.
	The Supreme Court also decides (*Myers v. Anderson*) that tax and property requirements for voting are constitutional.
	Under the leadership of Samuel Gompers, the American Federation of Labor vigorously endorses the right of women to vote.
	Maryland adopts the referendum.
1916	The Women's Party is founded and led by Alice Paul, a Quaker and veteran of suffragette protests in England.
	Senator Robert LaFollette proposes a bill allowing one percent of the voters in twenty-five states to petition for a national advisory referendum to be held on whether to declare war. It is defeated.
1917	New York extends to women the right to vote.
	Kentucky adopts the referendum.
	Kansas terminates the right of declarant aliens to vote.
1918	Michigan, Oklahoma, and South Dakota extend to women the right to vote.
	Massachusetts adopts the initiative and referendum.
	Nebraska, South Dakota, and Texas terminate the right of declarant aliens to vote.

Having been picketed outside the White House by the National Women's Party a year earlier, and aware that the cause of women's suffrage has generated unstoppable momentum, President Wilson discards his previously held position that women's suffrage is a state, not a federal, matter. He asks members of the House to support the Sixteenth Amendment as an "act of right and justice." Appearing before the U.S. Senate some eight months later, with his entire cabinet present, he informs that body that the important role of women in the war effort justifies granting them the right to vote.

1919   In contrast to the Democrats, whose party is heavily influenced by the state's rights perspective, the Republican Party platform endorses women's suffrage, albeit in muted tones.

Ratification of the Nineteenth Amendment, which states in part, "The right of citizens of the United States to vote shall not be denied or abridged by the United States or any state on account of sex." Congress is given the power to enforce this provision.

More than half the states are now allowing absentee voting for work-related reasons.

1920   Most states are now prohibiting felons in prison from voting, and upon completing their sentences, condition a restoration of their right to vote on a pardon by the governor.

North Dakota adopts the recall for all elected officials.

Voters of North Carolina eliminate the poll tax and reduce residency requirements.

1921   New York establishes a literacy test for voting.

Indiana terminates the right of declarant aliens to vote.

1923   All states are requiring individuals to establish residency as a requirement for voting. Although six

1923
(cont.)   southern states (Alabama, Louisiana, Mississippi, North Carolina, South Carolina, and Virginia) require a two-year residency for voting at the state level, most states require only one year. For local elections, the required period of residency typically ranges from thirty days to six months.

1924   Oregon establishes a literacy test for voting.

                Missouri terminates the right of declarant aliens to vote.

                The Citizenship Act passed by Congress declares that any Indian born in the United States is a citizen.

1926   California does away with exclusion of native Chinese from voting, as does Oregon the following year.

                Arkansas terminates the right of declarant aliens to vote.

                Wisconsin adopts the recall for all elected officials.

1927   In *Nixon v. Herndon*, the Supreme Court declares in violation of the Fourteenth Amendment a Texas statute that prohibits blacks from voting in Democratic primary elections.

1928   Rhode Island decides to allow men and women who do not own property to vote in municipal elections.

1933   Pennsylvania eliminates its requirement that an individual pay taxes in order to be eligible to vote.

                Idaho adopts the recall for all elected officials except judges.

1934   In *Blue v. State ex rel. Brown*, the Supreme Court rules that states may impose voter registration requirements provided they meet the tests of reasonableness and uniformity.

The Ludlow amendment, named for its author, Democratic congressman Louis Ludlow of Indiana, calls for a constitutional amendment requiring that war be declared only after a majority of voters so approve in a nationwide referendum. Over the next several years the proposal attracts considerable support among members of Congress, opinion leaders, and the general public.

1935   With the Court having ruled (see 1927) that states cannot prohibit blacks from voting in a party's primary, a number of southern states now seek to exclude them by defining parties as private clubs, as such entitled to determine their own membership. In *Grovey v. Townsend*, the U.S. Supreme Court concludes that because political parties had been so defined by state laws, parties can exclude nonmembers from their state political conventions.

1936   Following a strong lobbying effort by the Roosevelt administration, the House votes not to discharge the Ludlow amendment from committee, thereby killing it (see 1934).

1937   In *Breedlove v. Suttles*, the Supreme Court rules that the imposition of a poll tax by the state of Georgia in state and local elections violates neither the Fourteenth nor Fifteenth Amendment.

1939   The Supreme Court rules in *Lane v. Wilson* that penalties imposed by states on individuals for not voting are in violation of the Fifteenth Amendment.

1940   By this time poll taxes have been repealed in all northern states, paupers are still excluded from voting in twelve states, and the insane are excluded from voting in nearly every state.

1942   Congress passes the Soldier Voting Act, which grants to military personnel the right to vote absentee in federal elections and exempts them from having to pay a poll tax.

1942 (cont.)	Senators Arthur Vandenberg and Jennings Randolph sponsor, without success, a constitutional amendment lowering the voting age to eighteen.
	The U.S. House of Representatives passes legislation outlawing the poll tax, but it is filibustered to death in the Senate.
1943	Georgia becomes the first state to lower the voting age to eighteen.
1944	The Supreme Court in *Smith v. Allwright* reverses its earlier ruling (*Grovey v. Townsend*) and now declares that political parties that bar blacks from voting in their primaries are in violation of the Fifteenth Amendment, because the conducting of a primary amounts to engaging in a state function.
	The U.S. House of Representatives again passes legislation outlawing the poll tax, and it is again filibustered to death in the Senate.
1945	Georgia repeals its poll tax.
1946	Under the chairmanship of General Electric president Charles Wilson, President Harry Truman appoints a Committee on Civil Rights, which issues a report (*To Secure These Rights*) that among other things highlights the laws and practices used to disenfranchise blacks and Native Americans and frustrate the efforts of immigrants to gain citizenry.
1948	Idaho, Mississippi, Washington, Maine, Arizona, and New Mexico repeal their laws prohibiting Native Americans from voting.
	President Truman sends a message to Congress calling for a Joint Congressional Committee on Civil Rights, the formation of both a federal Civil Rights Commission and a Civil Rights Division in the Justice Department, and the abolition of the poll tax. None of these proposals receives serious attention by Congress.

1949   The U.S. Supreme Court lets stand (*Schnell v. Davis*) a lower court decision declaring unconstitutional an Alabama law requiring that those registering to vote must be able to "understand and explain" any provision of the state constitution.

1951   In response to the unprecedented number of years (nearly twelve and one-half) served by Franklin Roosevelt in the presidency, the Twenty-second Amendment is ratified. It states that no individual may be elected to more than two terms as president. In addition, if an individual has served more than half of an unexpired term, then he/she may be elected to only one additional term. This restriction does not apply to the president serving (Harry Truman) at the time it is ratified.

1954   President Dwight Eisenhower advocates lowering the legal voting age to eighteen.

1955   The Federal Voting Assistance Act calls for the establishment of a federal Voting Assistance Program housed in the Defense Department and designed to assist members of the armed forces in registering to vote.

        Kentucky decides to lower the voting age to eighteen, becoming the second state to do so.

1956   In view of the various practices used to prevent blacks from voting—including literacy tests, poll taxes, failure to provide receipts for payment of poll taxes, good character tests, purging voter lists, and intimidation—President Eisenhower instructs his attorney general, Herbert Brownell, to prepare a civil rights bill for submission to Congress.

        Alaska is admitted to the Union with a suffrage age requirement of nineteen.

1957   The Civil Rights Act creates a temporary six-person Civil Rights Commission charged with investigating

1957
(cont.)

instances of voting irregularities based upon race, and reporting to Congress in two years; the attorney general is authorized to secure injunctions when necessary in order to prevent interfering with the right to vote; and practices of intimidation in connection with the right to vote are made a federal crime.

1959

In *Lassiter v. Northhampton County Bd. of Electors,* the U.S. Supreme Court upholds the constitutionality of state laws requiring as a condition for voting the ability to read and write English, provided they are not applied in a discriminatory manner.

Alaska adopts the referendum and the recall for all elected officials except judges.

Hawaii is admitted to the Union with a suffrage age requirement of twenty.

1960

The second Civil Rights Act extends the life of the Civil Rights Commission, authorizes the federal courts to appoint voter referees, and requires that voting records be preserved for two years.

The U.S. Senate passes a constitutional amendment outlawing the poll tax, but the House of Representatives defeats it.

In *United States v. Raines,* the U.S. Supreme Court upholds the constitutionality of the 1957 Civil Rights Act empowering the attorney general to seek injunctions in order to prevent interference with the right to vote.

Southern states, in yet another effort to neutralize the black vote, configure voting districts in ways that dilute the black vote by spreading it out, or, alternatively, concentrating it in one area. The U.S. Supreme Court in *Gomillion v. Lightfoot* rules that gerrymandering of this sort, practiced in this instance in Tuskegee, Alabama, is in violation of the Fifteenth Amendment.

1961   The Twenty-third Amendment is ratified, assigning to the District of Columbia electoral votes to be cast for president, which may be no greater in number than those of the least populous state. (The least populous state is Alaska, with three electoral votes.)

1962   At the instigation of several philanthropic organizations, the Kennedy administration announces the Voter Education Project—a program designed to register blacks in the South. During its first twenty-one months, the project reports registering 327,000 new voters, 287,000 of whom are black.

     Breaking with its long-held view that the malapportionment of legislative districts is a political question not suitable for resolution by the courts, the U.S. Supreme Court now rules in *Baker v. Carr* that federal courts have jurisdiction on this issue.

1963   In *Gray v. Sanders* the U.S. Supreme Court, rejecting a Georgia primary system that gave heavier weight to rural votes than to urban votes, requires that in primary elections for U.S. senators and state executive officers, the weight of each person's vote must be equal.

     President John Kennedy's Commission on Registration and Voting Participation reports that millions of Americans are disenfranchised by "restrictive legal and administrative procedures in registration and voting." Among other things it proposes that registration be allowed closer to election day, that absentee registration and voting be made easier, that the voting age be lowered to eighteen, that literacy tests and the poll tax be eliminated, and that new residents be allowed to vote in presidential elections.

1964   The Twenty-fourth Amendment is ratified. It prohibits the imposition of a poll tax in any *federal* election, primary or general. Congress is empowered to enforce this provision. Within the year, black registration in the South increases to 40 percent.

1964   The U.S. Supreme Court rules in *Wesberry v. Sanders*
(cont.)   that congressional districts must be substantially
          equal in population, and in a related ruling (*Reynolds
          v. Sims*), that both houses of a bicameral state legisla-
          ture must be apportioned on the basis of population.

          Fulton and De Kalb counties in Georgia become the
          first jurisdictions to use punchcard and computer
          tally machines.

1965   With a voter registration drive in Selma, Alabama, hav-
          ing led to the arrest of Martin Luther King and the
          murder of two civil rights workers, President Lyndon
          Johnson goes before a joint session of Congress and in
          a stirring address implores the membership to pass a
          voting rights act that will assure blacks the unimpeded
          opportunity to vote. The Voting Rights Act, passed be-
          fore the year is out, provides for the immediate sus-
          pension of literacy tests and other devices in those
          states where fewer than 50 percent of the voters voted
          in 1964. Such suspensions are to be maintained for five
          years. The attorney general is authorized to dispatch
          federal examiners to southern states for the purpose of
          enrolling blacks and observing registration practices.
          Governments in the targeted areas are prohibited from
          changing their election procedures unless given per-
          mission by the Civil Rights Division of the Justice De-
          partment. Finally, the Justice Department is instructed
          to go to court to test the constitutionality of the poll tax.

          In *Carrington v. Rush,* the U.S. Supreme Court declares
          unconstitutional a Texas statute denying military per-
          sonnel the right to establish residency.

          In another ruling (*Drueding v. Devlin*) the U.S.
          Supreme Court upholds the right of states to impose a
          residency requirement of one year for voting in presi-
          dential elections.

          The Supreme Court rules in *Louisiana v. United States*
          that an "interpretation" test for voter registration re-

quiring that a prospective registrant interpret a provision of the federal or state constitution violates the Fourteenth and Fifteenth Amendments.

1966   The U.S. Supreme Court rejects (*South Carolina v. Katzenbach*) the contention that the Voting Rights Act constitutes an unconstitutional interference in the state's power, ruling instead that the act is a valid means of the federal government to enforce provisions of the Fifteenth Amendment.

In *Katzenbach v. Morgan* the U.S. Supreme Court strikes down a New York English-language literacy test, the use of which resulted in the disqualification of Puerto Rican American citizens who had been educated in Spanish-speaking schools.

In *Harper et al. v. Virginia Board of Education et al.* the U.S. Supreme Court rules that the poll tax violates the Equal Protection Clause of the Fourteenth Amendment by creating an invidious distinction on the basis of wealth.

1968   At the tumultuous Democratic National Convention, Vice President Hubert Humphrey defeats Senator Eugene McCarthy (MN) for the presidential nomination. McCarthy, the antiwar (Vietnam) candidate, ran in nearly all the primaries, while Humphrey entered not a single one. Yet at the convention, Humphrey, the candidate of the party bosses, walks off with the nomination, besting McCarthy 1,760 votes to 601. The McCarthy forces, charging that Humphrey supporters have unfairly manipulated the process for selecting delegates to the convention, call for an investigation. The convention adopts a resolution creating the Committee on Party Structure and Delegate Selection. Known as the McGovern-Fraser Commission, after the names of its two co-chairs, it ultimately calls for sweeping reforms in how convention delegates are chosen.

Wyoming adopts the referendum.

1968
(cont.)

The Supreme Court in *Williams v. Rhodes* finds unconstitutional the state of Ohio's requirement that third parties, in order to get on the ballot, must obtain signatures equal to 15 percent of the number of votes cast in the previous gubernatorial election (in 1968 this amounted to 433,000 signatures). Such a requirement, the Court argues, is unduly onerous, depriving individuals of their right to advance their political beliefs through freedom of association, and the right of voters to cast their votes unimpeded, no matter their political persuasion.

1969

The U.S. Supreme Court rules in *Gaston County, NC, v. United States* that the Voting Rights Act can be interpreted to bar even those literacy tests employed without any apparent bias.

In another case (*Kramer v. Union Free School District*) the Court rules unconstitutional election laws that deny the vote to individuals not owning taxable property. Nor, according to the Court (*Cipriano v. Houma*), can voting on bond issues be restricted only to taxpayers.

The U.S. House of Representatives approves an amendment abolishing the Electoral College and replacing it with direct popular election of the president and vice-president. In the event that no candidate receives a majority of the popular vote, a runoff will be held between the first- and second-place finishers. The U.S. Senate declines to consider this proposal.

Maine decides that two of its electoral votes will be awarded to the presidential candidate who wins statewide, while the remaining are to be determined by the vote in each congressional district.

President Richard Nixon sends a message to Congress asking that the office of presidential elector be eliminated, with the electoral votes of a state instead being automatically awarded to the winner of its popular vote. In addition, he calls for abolishing the winner-take-all allocation of electoral votes, and a mandatory runoff election in the event that no candidate receives 40 percent of the electoral vote. These proposals find little support in Congress.

1970   The Voting Rights Act, extended for five more years, lowers the minimum voting age in all federal elections from twenty-one to eighteen, prohibits states from imposing a residency requirement greater than thirty days in presidential elections, and provides uniform national rules for absentee registration and voting in presidential elections.

The U.S. Senate holds hearings on a proposed constitutional amendment that would allow for a national voter initiative. The proposal never makes it out of committee, but it is the subject of considerable discussion over the next several years.

In *Oregon v. Mitchell*, the U.S. Supreme Court declares that the Voting Rights Act empowers Congress to ban literacy tests in state as well as federal elections. The Court also rules that Congress has the authority to allow eighteen-year-olds to vote in federal elections but lacks the authority to extend it to state and local elections.

In *Phoenix v. Kolodziejski* the Supreme Court rules unconstitutional an Arizona law limiting voting on general obligation bonds only to property owners, the Court arguing that all voters have an interest in the outcome of such an election.

In *Evans v. Cornman* the Supreme Court rules that the state of Maryland is in violation of equal protection of the laws by denying residency, and thus the right to vote, to citizens within its boundaries who happen to be living in a federal enclave.

The McGovern-Fraser Commission recommends, and the Democratic Party adopts, extensive reforms in how delegates to its national convention are chosen, the consequence of which is to greatly reduce the

1970
(cont.)
influence of party elites. The reforms include reducing the number of delegates who can be appointed by the party organization; reducing the number of party types who can attend as *ex officio* delegates; democratizing the caucus/convention method of choosing delegates; and eliminating "blind primaries," in which those running for delegate do not have to disclose which presidential candidate they support. The Republican Party ultimately adopts most of these reforms as well.

Illinois adopts the initiative and referendum.

1971
The Twenty-sixth Amendment to the Constitution, lowering the legal voting age to eighteen in all elections, is ratified at breakneck speed in order to allow some eleven million new voters to cast their ballots in the 1972 presidential election.

Congress passes and President Nixon signs the Revenue Act, creating a general campaign fund for presidential and vice presidential candidates to be financed by allowing taxpayers to divert (i.e., "checkoff") a dollar of their tax liability to it. As a condition for signing the bill, the president insists that Congress include in it a provision stating that the bill will not take effect until 1976.

Congress passes and President Nixon signs the Federal Election Campaign Act, which mandates more rigorous reporting of campaign contributions and expenditures by federal candidates at both the nominating and general election stages. The act also places limits on media expenditures by presidential and congressional candidates.

1972
The U.S. Supreme Court rules in *Dunn v. Blumstein* that residency requirements of a year in state elections, and ninety days in local elections, are excessive. It suggests instead a time period of thirty days. In subsequent rulings the Court is willing to accommodate up to fifty days.

In *Bullock v. Carter* the Supreme Court voids a Texas law allowing a party committee to apportion the cost of running a primary among the candidates. With the fee levied on candidates running as high as $8,900, and with candidates not being able to gain access to the ballot any other way, the Court rules that Texas is denying equal protection of the laws to the candidates, and to the voters by depriving them of the right to vote for candidates of their choice.

Montana adopts the initiative.

1973   The District of Columbia Self-government and Government Reorganization Act gives the residents of Washington, D.C., the right to elect a mayor and city council.

Minnesota introduces registration by mail and election-day registration. Kentucky joins in adopting mail registration.

1974   The U.S. Supreme Court rules in *Richardson v. Ramirez* that denying the right to vote to ex-felons does not violate the Equal Protection Clause of the Fourteenth Amendment.

The Southwest Voter Education Project is launched to register Hispanic voters throughout the Southwest and California.

In the aftermath of the Watergate scandals, Congress enacts wide-ranging amendments to the Federal Election Campaign Act (see 1971), including imposing limits on how much money individuals and groups may contribute to federal candidates as well as spend on behalf of them, how much they may contribute to a political action committee and a political party, and an overall limit for all giving categories. The legislation also imposes spending limits on how much money federal candidates can spend on their campaigns as well as how much of their own money they can spend. In addition, the legislation provides for partial public

1974
(cont.)
financing of presidential candidates at the nominating stage and full funding of presidential nominees at the general election stage. Also created by the amendments is a Federal Election Commission, charged with receiving reports on campaign contributions and spending by federal candidates, and with enforcing the laws applicable to campaign financing.

1975
The Voting Rights Act is extended for an additional seven years and moves beyond blacks to include "language minorities" (i.e., Hispanics, Indians, Alaska Natives, and Asian Americans). It also requires that ballots and voter registration materials be bilingual.

Having suspended the use of literacy tests in the 1965 Voting Rights Act, Congress now decides to ban them permanently.

1976
The presidential primary has now become the most common method for choosing delegates to the national conventions in both parties, replacing the caucus-convention.

The National Coalition on Black Voter Participation is organized to stimulate, fund, and coordinate black voter registration efforts among black organizations across the country.

Arguing that they constituted a violation of the First Amendment right to freedom of speech, the Supreme Court in *Buckley v. Valeo* strikes down all spending limits imposed by campaign finance reform legislation (see 1974), whether by a candidate's campaign, the candidate personally, or individuals and groups spending independently on behalf of a candidate. The Court also declares unconstitutional the procedure for appointing members to the Federal Election Commission on the grounds that it violates the separation of powers principle.

Montana adopts the recall for all elected officials except judges.

1977 The state of Michigan allows voters to register when they apply for or renew their driver's license.

President Jimmy Carter sends to Congress legislation titled the National Uniform Registration Act, which mandates allowing voters to register on election day. Congress, fearful that a raft of new voters could lead to unpredictability, declines to pass the bill.

Initiative America is formed in Washington, D.C., for the purpose of advocating a national initiative. It succeeds in winning endorsements from more than two hundred congressional candidates running in the 1978 election.

For the first time a Senate committee holds hearings on the idea of a national initiative and referendum.

1978 At the recommendation of its reform commission (the Winograd Commission) the Democratic Party decides to require that all primaries and caucus/conventions for selecting delegates to its national convention be closed.

Florida adopts the initiative.

California and Oregon allow their citizens unrestricted absentee voting, thereby requiring neither notarization nor a reason (e.g., illness) for requesting an absentee ballot.

Georgia adopts the recall for all elected officials.

1979 The United States Senate votes down an amendment to abolish the Electoral College and replace it with election of the president and vice president by popular vote.

1980 In *City of Rome v. United States,* the U.S. Supreme Court rules unconstitutional changes in voting procedures that have the effect of discriminating against a

1980
(cont.)
group, even though there is no conscious attempt to do so.

Congressman Richard Gephardt (D-MO) calls for the establishment of a national advisory referendum that would allow voters to vote directly on a few proposed laws, but the results would not be binding on members of Congress.

The Election Crimes Branch of the Public Integrity section of the U.S. Department of Justice is created for the purpose of prosecuting criminal violations of federal election laws.

1982
The Voting Rights Act is extended for an additional twenty-five years. In a new provision, it specifies that voting practices may be in violation of the law if their effect is to discriminate, even though their intent is otherwise.

Human Service Employees Registration and Voter Education (Human SERVE) is organized to promote the registration of citizens at day-care centers and public assistance agencies.

The Midwest Voter Education Project is created in Chicago to register Hispanics.

1983
The Supreme Court rules unconstitutional (*Anderson v. Celebrezze*) the early filing deadline imposed on independent candidates—in this case, presidential candidate John Anderson, who did not declare his independent candidacy until April 1980, thereby failing to meet Ohio's March 20 deadline. The Court sees the statute as impeding a diversity of ideas in the electoral process and unduly impeding a candidate's ability to put together a winning coalition of votes.

1984
The Voter Accessibility for the Elderly and Handicapped Act requires that polling places be accessible to the elderly and handicapped in federal elections.

Where none is available, a political subdivision is required to provide an alternative means. It must also offer registration and voting aids.

On Susan B. Anthony's birthday, the Women's Vote Project, representing more than sixty organizations, launches a national voter registration drive.

1985   Although the Supreme Court has generally upheld disenfranchisement for criminal behavior, in *Hunter v. Underwood* it rules that such exclusion cannot be applied in a discriminatory manner, as it was in this case against blacks seeking to cash a worthless check—a crime categorized as a misdemeanor.

1986   The Supreme Court establishes in *Thornburgh v. Gingles* criteria to determine if at-large or multimember districting plans unfairly dilute the votes of African Americans: (1) the minority has to be geographically large and compact enough to constitute a majority of a single district; (2) it must be "politically cohesive"; and (3) there must be evidence that voting by whites in a bloc over an extended period results in blacks usually being defeated.

In *Tashjian v. Republican Party of Connecticut*, the Supreme Court overturns a Connecticut state law prohibiting open primaries. In preventing the Republican Party from having an open primary, the Court argues the state of Connecticut is denying it the right to define its own membership and thereby violating the party's right to freedom of association guaranteed by the First Amendment.

The Democratic Party decides to prohibit winner-take-all presidential primaries, requiring that they be proportional instead. This means that the number of convention delegates a candidate wins in a given state is proportional to the number of votes he or she receives.

The Republican Party continues to allow each state to make this determination.

1986
(cont.)
The Uniformed and Overseas Citizens Absentee Voting Act requires that states and territories permit most U.S. citizens to register for and vote by absentee ballot. Included are members of the Uniformed Services and Marines, along with their families, employees of the federal government living outside the United States, and all other private citizens residing outside the United States. Citizens intending to vote absentee must fill out a federal postcard application, which can be obtained at U.S. embassies, consulates, or military bases. The law, administered by the Pentagon's Voter Assistance Program, also provides for a federal write-in ballot for those living in remote areas.

The Commission on National Elections, chaired by Republican Melvin Laird and Democrat Robert Strauss, calls for the establishment of a National Registration Day to be held in the fall of each election year. It urges as well that states allow election-day registration.

1991
The Supreme Court rules that the Voting Rights Act also applies to voting for state (*Chisom v. Roemer*) and local (*Houston Lawyer's Association v. Attorney General of Texas*) trial judges.

1992
The Supreme Court in *Burdick v. Takushi* upholds Hawaii's prohibition against write-in votes, noting that because the state already provides several easy means for candidates to achieve ballot access, the statute barring write-in votes does not impose an undue burden on the electoral process.

Following the lead of Maine, Nebraska decides that two of its electoral votes will be awarded to the presidential candidate who wins statewide, while the remaining three are to be determined by the vote in each congressional district.

1993
In *Shaw v. Reno*, the Supreme Court rules that if the drawing of districts leads to boundaries that are so "bizarre" as to be inexplicable on any grounds other

than to insure the election of a minority group, then whites would have cause for arguing that gerrymandering is being directed against them.

The National Voter Registration Act (also known as the Motor Voter bill) becomes law. It requires that citizens be allowed to register while applying for or renewing their driver's license, to register in state offices that provide welfare and disabled assistance, or to register by mail with the use of a standardized form. It also permits purging of voting rolls only for change of residence, and not for failure to vote.

1995   In *U.S. Term Limits v. Thornton,* the Supreme Court rules that states lack the authority under the Constitution to impose term limits on representatives elected to Congress.

1996   In an effort to stem the stampede by states to hold their primaries and caucuses at the front end of the nominating process, where all the action is, the Republican National Convention adopts a bonus plan for the year 2000 whereby states holding off their contests until March 15 will have their state delegations expanded by 5 percent. The bonus grows to 7.5 percent for states that defer until April 15, and to 10 percent for those that hold off until May 15. These incentives will ultimately have little effect on lessening the problem of frontloading in the 2000 nomination contest.

In *Shaw v. Hunt* and *Bush v. Vera,* the Supreme Court strikes down the drawing of three congressional districts, concluding that race was the overriding consideration in determining the configuration of each district.

1997   In a blow to minor parties, the U.S. Supreme Court rules in *Timmons v. Twin Cities Area New Party* that states have the right to prohibit candidates from appearing on the ballot under the label of more than one

1997
(*cont.*)   party. In this particular case, a minor party on the left sought to nominate a candidate for the state legislature who had already been nominated by the Democratic Party. The Court rules that states have the right to prevent manipulation of the election ballot and factionalism among the voting population.

1999   The Supreme Court rules in *Hunt v. Cromartie* that the courts cannot intervene to overturn the drawing of district lines unless they are convinced that race was the most important consideration in doing so.

In an effort to reduce the wear and tear on presidential candidates and disperse the influence that certain states and regions may have over the nominating process, the National Association of Secretaries of State proposes a series of regional primaries, each separated by one month, beginning with the eastern region, followed by the South, Midwest, and West. In the next election, the East would be moved to the end of the "line" and the South would go first, and so on. In order to preserve the "retail politics" that Iowa and New Hampshire allow for, they would continue to be allowed to hold their contests before the first regional primary. This proposal is not adopted by either party.

2000   In *California Democratic Party v. Jones,* the U.S. Supreme Court rules the California "blanket primary" unconstitutional. An extreme form of open primary, the blanket primary allows a voter to vote for candidates in both parties, although not for the same office. This form of primary, the Court argues, denies to a party (in this case the Democrats) the ability to define its own membership, and thus its right to freedom of association guaranteed under the First Amendment.

The Brock Commission, appointed by the Republican National Committee to address the problem of primaries bunching up at the front end of the presidential nominating process, proposes that for 2004 the primaries and caucuses occur in four waves, beginning with the smallest states and ending with the largest. Each wave is to be separated by one month. This plan, it is argued, will reduce the likelihood of some candidates being eliminated from the race prematurely. Very much wanting a harmonious convention in 2000, and fearful that this plan could lead to a floor fight, forces for candidate George W. Bush prevent it from being brought before the convention for a vote.

The Reform Party advocates a constitutional amendment to establish a national voter initiative.

With the Florida State Supreme Court having ordered a recount of Florida undervotes as presidential candidate Al Gore requested, candidate Bush appeals to the U.S. Supreme Court to overturn the order. The Court does indeed halt the recount pending a review of the case. In its historic decision (*Bush v. Gore*), the Court overturns the Florida Supreme Court, with seven justices arguing that by ordering a recount without specified standards for what constitutes a valid ballot, Florida voters are being denied equal protection of the law (Fourteenth Amendment), in this instance the right of each vote to be counted equally. (This decision is rendered just two hours before the deadline for counting all votes, thereby making it impossible to have a recount with specified standards for what qualifies as a valid vote.) Three justices also argue that when the Florida Supreme Court extended the deadline for certifying the election results—a deadline established by the Florida legislature—it was violating Article II of the U.S. Constitution, which gives to state legislatures the *sole* authority to determine the manner of choosing presidential electors.

For only the third time in U.S. history (excluding the election of 1824, decided in the U.S. House of Representatives), the presidential candidate with the most popular votes loses the presidential election. Vice President Al Gore outpolls his Republican opponent,

2000
(cont.)

George W. Bush, by more than 500,000 votes, but Bush inches past Gore in electoral votes, garnering 271 to the vice president's 267, thereby making this one of the closest popular and electoral vote elections in American history.

Democratic voters in Arizona become the first in the nation to vote online in a binding election, in this case, its state's primary.

2001

A joint study by the Massachusetts Institute of Technology and the California Institute of Technology finds that four to six million votes went uncounted in the 2000 presidential election due to faulty voting equipment, confusing ballots, voter error, and polling places with long lines, short hours, and inconvenient locations.

The state of Florida eliminates punch card voting machines, mandates a handcount of overvotes as well as undervotes in any election in which the margin of votes is within one-fourth of 1 percent, and directs the secretary of state to establish uniform statewide standards for dealing with disputed ballots.

The National Commission on Election Reform, chaired by former presidents Gerald Ford and Jimmy Carter, releases its recommendations, calling for every state to adopt a system of statewide voter registration, provisional voting, restoration of voting rights to convicted felons after serving their sentences, and the creation of statewide standards for what constitutes a valid vote. The commission also calls upon Congress to make election day a national holiday, ease requirements for overseas absentee voter registration, develop a comprehensive set of voter equipment standards, provide federal assistance to the states for election administration, and the creation of an Election Administration Commission to assist in these matters.

2002   The U.S. Justice Department announces that it is filing lawsuits against several jurisdictions in Florida, Missouri, and Tennessee, charging them with violations of voting rights in the 2000 presidential election. The violations include treating minority voters differently from whites, not providing disabled voters with appropriate access to the polls, and not giving adequate assistance to voters with limited English proficiency.

In response to the misfirings that occurred in the process during the 2000 presidential election, particularly in the state of Florida, President Bush signs into law the Help America Vote Act, authorizing $3.9 billion to assist the states in meeting new national standards with respect to voting. To qualify for these funds, states must take steps to give voters an opportunity to check their ballots for errors, provide at least one voting machine per precinct for disabled voters, define what constitutes a legal vote for each type of voting machine used in a state, limit the error rate of their voting system to that established by the Federal Election Commission Office of Administration, create a centralized and computerized statewide voter registration database, and continue to provide ballots in other languages, as mandated by the 1965 Voting Rights Act. The bill also directs states to establish procedures whereby first-time voters must present valid photo identification when registering. Voters lacking a driver's license may instead provide the last four digits of their Social Security number. Voters lacking either of these are to be assigned a unique identifier. If a citizen's eligibility to vote is in question, then he or she must be provided a provisional ballot to be cast but not counted until eligibility is determined. States will also be eligible to receive $4,000 per voting precinct for the purpose of replacing punchcard and lever voting machines. Finally, the bill mandates the establishment of a four-member Election Assistance Commission, appointed by the president and charged with providing funds through the grant programs overseeing the creation of voluntary election standards.

2002
(cont.)

The Bipartisan Campaign Reform Act (known as Mc-Cain-Feingold) becomes law. It increases from $1,000 to $2,000 the amount an individual can contribute to a candidate per election (primaries and general elections count as separate elections) and indexes it to the rate of inflation. In addition, it raises from $25,000 to $37,000 the total amount an individual can contribute each year to all federal candidates, political parties, and political action committees. It also prohibits the national parties from accepting any "soft money" contributions, but allows state and local parties to accept up to $10,000 in soft money each year per individual for the purpose of get-out-the-vote and voter registration efforts in federal elections. Finally, unions, corporations, and nonprofit groups are prohibited from paying for broadcast advertisements if the ads refer to a specific candidate and run within thirty days of a primary election and sixty days of a general election.

2003

In *Georgia v. Ashcroft,* the Supreme Court gives its approval to a new approach to racial redistricting that permits consideration of the overall minority influence in the political process, above and beyond the number of minority voters in a given district.

The Supreme Court upholds (*Federal Election Commission v. Beaumont*) the long-standing bans on corporate contributions to federal candidates even when, as in this case, those corporations are organized for the purpose of ideological advocacy.

For the first time in California's history, and only the second time in the history of the United States, Californians by a vote of 55 percent to 45 percent recall their second-term governor, Gray Davis (D), replacing him with Arnold Schwarzenegger, who in a separate vote wins with 49 percent of the vote.

The Michigan Democratic Party allows Internet voting in its presidential caucus.

In *McConnell v. Federal Election Commission,* the Supreme Court upholds the major provisions of the

Bipartisan Campaign Reform Act (McCain-Feingold), including raising the individual contribution limit from $1,000 to $2,000 and banning national political parties and their committees from accepting "soft money" contributions, but allowing state and local parties to accept up to $10,000 in individual soft money contributions provided the money is raised locally and used for party-building activities. The Court also upholds prohibiting candidates from soliciting soft money contributions and bars labor unions and corporations from using money in their general treasuries to pay for political advertisements that refer to a specific candidate and are broadcast within 30 days of a primary or within 60 days of a general election. The Court declines, however, to uphold the ban on contributions by individuals under the age of 18, arguing that such a provision "sweeps too broadly."

4

Biographical Sketches

The individuals described in this chapter have made a significant contribution to voting and elections in America. Some
were instrumental in securing the right to vote; others fought
to protect that right, once granted; still others played a lead role
in expanding the opportunities for Americans to exercise the
franchise, or rendering its use more accessible. There are also
those who have helped us to better understand how the electoral
process is functioning, directing our attention to potential trouble
spots that could diminish the value of the voting act, and offering
remedies to make the process work better.

Susan Brownell Anthony (1820–1906)

It is not altogether surprising that Susan B. Anthony would become an activist. She was born into a Quaker family, her parents
were active in the fight to abolish slavery—Frederick Douglass
was a frequent guest in their home—and they were strong supporters of the temperance and women's rights movements. Her
father, Daniel Anthony, took pains to foster in his daughters personal discipline, self-reliance, self-confidence, and the importance
of standing for something—all of which would, later in life, carry
her through long periods of abuse and ridicule, and an impossi-
bly demanding travel and lecture schedule.

Daniel Anthony was a teacher by training but became
owner of a cotton mill, and some years later manager of another,
but lost his position during the financial crisis of 1837. Susan was
called upon to help support the family, which she did by teaching
in the New York State school system. The unequal treatment of
females was driven home to her when she learned she was being

paid one-fifth of what male teachers were receiving. She vigorously protested this inequity, which, along with her visits to the homes of African Americans, led to her dismissal. Not long thereafter, she was hired as principal of the girl's department of Canajoharie Academy, where she remained for ten years.

Her attention then turned to the temperance movement, seen by women as the only way to stop the abusive treatment they received in the home at the hands of husbands and other male family members. In 1851 she became head of her community's Daughters of Temperance and in this capacity attended a temperance convention in Seneca Falls, New York, where she would meet for the first time Elizabeth Cady Stanton, the woman destined to become her lifetime comrade in arms. The following year Anthony decided to attend a meeting of the Sons of Temperance in Albany, New York—an event that proved to be a defining moment in her life. Up to this point, she had given little thought to woman's suffrage, but after being told that she could not speak at the meeting but must instead remain silent, listen, and learn, Susan Anthony came to the realization that women would not achieve social reform until they had first become full participating members in the political process.

She joined with Elizabeth Cady Stanton to form the New York State Temperance Society, which throughout the 1850s was a vanguard organization in the state for women's rights, presenting the legislature with a host of demands related to achieving equality for women in the areas of voting, property and custody rights, divorce laws, and certain specified jobs performed by women. Her political tactics, which she would ultimately replicate at the national level, were to educate the public through a grueling lecture schedule, pamphlets, and newspaper subscriptions, in conjunction with appeals to sign petitions that would then be presented to public officials. Her efforts produced results on property rights and child custody but met stiff resistance on the suffrage.

With the start of the Civil War, she turned her attention to the abolition movement, and the target of her efforts shifted from the state to the national level, as she devoted more than a year to organizing a nationwide petition to pressure Congress into eliminating slavery through a constitutional amendment. As corresponding secretary for the American Equal Rights Association, formed in 1866, she pushed for universal suffrage and oversaw petition campaigns to get states to amend their constitutions accordingly. Between 1868 and 1870 she edited a feminist weekly named *Revolution*, a turn in her life that proved to be the low point in an otherwise admirable career. In need of funds to support the paper, she became allied with a wealthy racist (George Francis Train), which helped to explain why she and Stanton withdrew their support of the Fifteenth Amendment and now claimed that the enfranchisement of blacks would pose a threat to the safety of white women.

Believing that the cause of woman's suffrage would be advanced by the creation of an organization separate from the equal rights movement, in 1869 she and Cady Stanton formed the National Woman Suffrage Association—an organization that would ultimately merge with the American Woman Suffrage Association in 1890 to become the National American Woman Suffrage Association (NAWSA). Under her leadership the organization took a new tack on woman's suffrage, claiming that the Fourteenth and Fifteenth Amendments, when correctly read together, already guaranteed women the right to vote. Anthony undertook yet another punishing lecture tour to defend this proposition, and ultimately decided to put it to the test, insisting that she be allowed to register in an upcoming election in her home town of Rochester, New York, on the grounds that nothing in the Fourteenth and Fifteenth Amendments stated that the privilege of voting was limited to men. Her insistent demeanor proved persuasive, and she was allowed to register, as were fifty other women the following day. On election day Anthony and sixteen other women cast their ballots, only to be arrested three days later. In a poor excuse for a trial, the judge refused to let Anthony testify and instructed the jury to find her guilty, but then declared the trial over before they had a chance to declare their verdict! Motion for a new trial was denied, and Anthony was fined $100, which she refused to pay.

With a U.S. Supreme Court decision in 1874 ruling that states had the authority to determine the political rights of women, Anthony now concluded that a constitutional amendment was the only way to secure the suffrage. Accordingly, over the course of the next decade she worked tirelessly to this end, traveling the country, more than willing to speak in the smallest of towns as well as the biggest of cities. She also followed her compatriot Elizabeth Cady Stanton as president of the NAWSA, a position she held until her eightieth birthday. She had ready access to all women's organizations throughout the country, was routinely sought after for interviews, and in the autumn of her years continued to travel the nation as well as abroad in the cause of women's rights.

Although she never lived to see her goal achieved—dying thirteen years before the Nineteenth Amendment was ratified—it is a measure of her importance to the movement that those in it referred to the Nineteenth Amendment as the "Susan B. Anthony Amendment."

Joseph Little Bristow (1861–1944)

Like others of a strong reformist bent, Joseph Bristow would sink his teeth into a problem and not let go until it was corrected. Such tenaciousness was instrumental in achieving for Americans one of the most significant expansions in the opportunities to vote in our history.

Born in Kentucky to a circuit-riding Methodist minister, he moved to Kansas after his marriage at the age of eighteen. There he enrolled at Baker University, intending to become a minister like his father, but his work at a newspaper while attending college redirected his career interests to journalism. He graduated with honors in 1896, while also managing to get himself elected district clerk of Douglass County. Four years later he purchased a Republican newspaper in Salina, Kansas, and then turned his attention more directly to Republican politics, serving as chair of the Republican state committee and private secretary to the governor for two years. In his role as head of the Kansas Republican Party he crossed paths with William McKinley in the presidential election campaign of 1896, and upon the latter's ascendancy to the presidency McKinley appointed Bristow as fourth assistant postmaster general, a post he held until 1905.

McKinley sent him to investigate the postal frauds in Cuba—a task that Bristow pursued with relentless determination and efficiency. Quickly earning a reputation for unimpeachable integrity and administrative skill, he was assigned by President Theodore Roosevelt to investigate more postal scandals, to which Bristow brought his customary determination and thoroughness—so much so, in fact, that some Republican politicians grew uneasy about what he was unearthing. Accordingly, they prevailed upon Roosevelt to find other employment for him. In 1905, the president appointed him special Panama railroad commissioner.

The following year Bristow went home to Kansas and made an unsuccessful bid for the U.S. Senate. In 1908, however, he managed to capture the Republican senatorial nomination in the first statewide primary ever held in that state, promising Kansans that among other things, he would support direct election of U.S. senators.

As more and more information came to light on the role of state legislatures in picking senators, public support for abolishing legislative selection increased. It was not unusual for state legislatures to deadlock on choosing a senator, leading to last-minute selections of often unqualified individuals who did not represent the views of a state's voters. In some instances, the office was simply left unfilled for extended periods of time, to say nothing of the bribery scandals that had been uncovered as monied interests sought to place their retainees in the position.

Five times between 1892 and 1902 the U.S. House of Representatives passed resolutions calling for direct election of U.S. senators, and each time they met a quick death in the Senate.

Not long after his entry into the U.S. Senate in 1909, Joseph Bristow joined up with other Progressives, who became known as the "Insurgents." Believing that farmers were being severely hurt by the railroads and eastern corporate/financial interests, Bristow and his supporters were determined to do something about it in the Senate. One important way of doing so would be to take the selection of U.S. senators out of the hands of state legislatures, whom Bristow and others saw as in the grips of big business, and turn it over to the people. For a man of Bristow's rectitude, the urgency to do so was all the more compelling given repeated revelations of corruption surrounding the choosing of senators in various state legislatures throughout the country.

Wasting no time, in July 1909 Bristow proposed direct election of senators as an amendment to a joint resolution calling for a constitutional amendment to give the federal government the power to impose an income tax. He argued that direct election was warranted now that the population had much more information at its disposal. Bristow's amendment was quickly ruled out of order at the urging of powerful eastern senator Nelson Aldrich. When the Senate reconvened that December, Bristow proposed a freestanding resolution calling for direct election of senators and, upon the advice of Idaho senator William Borah, requested that it be referred to the Judiciary Committee rather than the usual Committee on Privileges and Elections, which had served as a graveyard for all previous such resolutions coming from the House.

The Judiciary Committee delayed moving on the resolution, but Bristow, who would earn the reputation as "six feet of protest; one hundred and sixty pounds of defiance," kept badgering the committee chair, who finally agreed to appoint a special subcommittee to consider it. At Bristow's suggestion, Senator Borah was made a member and proved to be instrumental in achieving a favorable report of the resolution out of the Judiciary Committee in January 1911. Unfortunately, southern Democrats in the committee had succeeded in attaching an amendment to it providing that the "times, places, and manner of holding elections for Senators shall be prescribed in each state by the legislature thereof." This provision was to replace the constitutional requirement (Article I, Sec. 4) giving the states such authority *subject to regulation by Congress.* The purpose behind the change was to insure that southern states would be able to continue the many practices then being used to disenfranchise blacks. On the Senate floor, Senator George Sutherland of Utah offered an amendment striking this paragraph, thereby returning the resolution to the original Bristow version.

Senate debate quickly became bogged down over the Sutherland amendment. Many southern senators actually supported direct election but only if states were guaranteed the right to determine the "times, places, and manner" of doing so. Opponents of direct election, meanwhile, recognizing that inclusion of such a provision, with its clear racial implications, would be a sure way to kill the proposal, wanted to defeat the Sutherland amendment. Bristow was so set on direct election that at one point he was willing to defeat the Sutherland amendment too, believing that his proposal would otherwise not be able to attract enough votes from southern senators. In this less-than-admirable bit of political expediency, he was joined by the likes of Senators William Borah and Robert LaFollette.

The Sutherland amendment ultimately passed, and, as Bristow had feared, his proposal for direct election went down to defeat by a vote of 54 to 33. Bristow vowed to keep fighting, however, and when the next Congress convened, he reintroduced his resolution. This time the political terrain was more hospitable to his proposal, for ten of the senators who had voted against it during the previous session were no longer in the Senate. The House, meanwhile, had passed the direct election resolution, but with the controversial provision that states would have the right to determine the "times, places, and manner of elections." When the resolution was sent to the Senate for consideration, the Senate Judiciary Committee reported it to the floor with a favorable recommendation. Bristow, now convinced that the "times, places, and manner" provision would kill it yet again, immediately proposed an amendment from the floor removing it. Following days of often contentious debate on the Bristow amendment, the vote was called on June 12, 1911. The result was a 44-to-44 tie, with the vice president (James S. Sherman) as president of the Senate having to cast the deciding vote, which he did in Bristow's favor. The Senate president then called for an immediate vote on the main resolution for direct election, which secured the necessary two-thirds support, with 64 voting in favor and 24 against.

Joseph Bristow's quest for direct election of U.S. senators achieved fulfillment on April 8, 1913, when the thirty-sixth state ratified the Seventeenth Amendment to the Constitution.

Carrie Chapman Catt (1859–1947)

The daughter of farmers, Carrie Chapman Catt was born in Ripon, Wisconsin, later moving to Charles City, Iowa. She enrolled at Iowa State Agricultural College (now Iowa State), graduating in 1880. The fact that her mother was not allowed to vote so offended her that she organized a debate on woman's suffrage while in college, and incidentally broke the tradition of an all-male debating team by joining up.

After graduation, she studied law for a year, followed by a stint of high school teaching in Mason City, Iowa. She would ultimately rise to the position of superintendent of schools, a reflection of the fact that others saw early on her considerable gifts for organization and administration.

In 1885, she married Leo Chapman, owner of a newspaper Carrie would help edit, and in which she initiated a regular column on issues related to women's rights. Her husband later died in San Francisco, and Carrie remained there for some time after his death, working for a newspaper. During that time she became a member of the Woman's Christian Temperance Union, which in addition to its fight for Prohibition took some interest in the franchise for women.

During her attendance at a conference of the Iowa Woman Suffrage Association in 1889, Chapman was chosen as state lecturer and organizer. As a reflection of her organizational gifts, she quickly brought on line ten new Political Equality Clubs. The following year she became a member of the newly formed National American Woman Suffrage Association (NAWSA) and also found a new husband, George Catt, a wealthy engineer who generously directed his money in support of Carrie's movement activities.

In 1892 the Catts moved to New York, where Carrie's organizational and administrative talents flourished as she bolstered local suffrage groups, created new ones, and through her formidable public speaking skills roused women around the state to action. At Susan B. Anthony's initiative, Catt's appointment to a newly created business committee of the NAWSA represented part of an effort to bring new blood into that organization. Her responsibility was to recruit new women to the movement, which she did by lining up speakers and organizing lecture tours for them, and to create new woman's clubs and reinvigorate existing ones. Her efforts attracted attention, and in 1890 she was elected president of the NAWSA—a position she would hold until 1904, resigning due to her husband's poor health.

In 1893 she attended a Congress of Representative Women of All Lands, where she met women from twenty-seven countries. It proved to be a defining experience, inspiring her to create the International Woman's Suffrage Alliance (IWSA) in 1902 during a meeting in Washington, D.C., despite Susan B. Anthony's strong opposition. It was arguably Catt's most important achievement, for the organization became a rallying point for women in Western countries.

Despite failing health, in 1911 she took a trip around the world—returning at the end of 1912—during which she introduced women in many parts of the world to the concept of women's rights. The esteem with which she was held was evidenced by the decision of her peers to again place her at the head of the NAWSA, where she would remain until passage of the Nineteenth Amendment. Although the suffrage movement was now divided between those who thought its efforts should be directed at the national level, pressuring Congress for a constitutional amendment, and those espousing a state-by-state approach, Catt pushed the NAWSA toward both approaches. She had the wisdom to recognize on the one hand that an exclusively national focus ignored the reality that states would ultimately have to ratify any amendment proposed by Congress and, on the other, that an exclusively state-centered strategy overlooked the reality that some states, if left to their own devices, simply would not adopt woman's suffrage.

When war broke out in Europe in 1917, Catt committed the NAWSA to assisting in the war effort and was subject to considerable criticism for doing so, particularly since she had long been opposed to war and had helped found the Woman's Peace Party in 1915. NAWSA's support of the war, however, through such activities as knitting clothes and selling war bonds and thrift stamps, served to neutralize the argument that if you don't fight, you shouldn't vote.

In this same year Catt led a suffrage campaign in New York that included the last great suffrage parade, snaking its way as it did through the streets of New York City. The New York state legislature responded to the call, adopting a suffrage amendment in 1917, and six other states did likewise that same year. Responding to these ever-mounting pressures, a woman's suffrage committee was established in the House, which would approve the Nineteenth Amendment in January 1918, to be followed by Senate adoption in June 1919. With ratification of the amendment by the state of Tennessee on August 18, 1920, Carrie Chapman Catt's lifelong dream became a reality.

Believing that the NAWSA needed new blood, Catt bowed out; the organization subsequently morphed into the League of Women Voters, which had—and continues to have—as its goals the development of an informed and participating electorate. She devoted the rest of her life to peace issues, in 1925 organizing the first annual Conference on the Cause and Cure of War, which, among other things, worked in support of creating a World Court and the League of Nations.

While women such as Susan B. Anthony and Elizabeth Cady Stanton had been instrumental in elevating the issue of woman's suffrage into the national conscientious, it was the organizational skills and political savvy of Carrie Chapman Catt that played a major role in making that demand a reality.

Richard Henry Dana III (1851–1931)

The man who helped start the process for the most profound ballot reform in U.S. history was born in Cambridge, Massachusetts, to a patrician family that instilled in him the responsibility for service to the community that comes with a high station in life.

He received an impeccable education, graduating from Harvard in 1874 and its law school in 1877.

His interest in elections had been kindled by a friend of his father's, William Vernon Harcourt, a member of the British Parliament whom young Richard had visited, and who wrote to Richard from time to time. One of these occasions was in 1886 when he asked Dana, now thirty-five and a Boston lawyer, why the American political process seemed to attract so many mediocre individuals. Dana would later recall that this searching question directed his attention to the way elections were run in his country. He joined up with the Mugwump Party in Massachusetts—a group of citizens who were put off by patronage politics and the corruption that attended it.

With political parties handing out ballots and monitoring the voting process in which ballots were cast publicly, there was ample opportunity for bribery, intimidation of voters, and stuffing of ballot boxes. This latter problem was largely eliminated in the 1880s by the use of ballot boxes with counting devices, but the parties continued to distribute the ballots, thereby precluding the opportunity to cast a vote in secret.

Dana had already made a reputation as a reformer of the civil service system in Massachusetts, drafting its sweeping Civil Service Reform Act of 1884. He now turned his attention to ballot reform, raising the issue of a secret ballot one evening at the Dutch Treat—a dining club of distinguished Bostonians united by a passion for reform. One of its members, Henry Sprague, chaired the committee on election laws in the Massachusetts legislature, and when the body convened in 1888, he asked Dana to draft legislation on ballot reform. With careful shepherding by Henry Sprague, Dana's proposal for a ballot of uniform shape and size, printed by the state and cast in secret (known as the Australian ballot), was presented to the Massachusetts Senate and House and was quickly passed.

The Australian ballot was first used in the state's 1889 election. Dana, as treasurer of the Ballot Act League, an organization created in that year to educate citizens to the new ballot, traveled the state explaining and defending it, and gave testimony before legislative committees in and outside the state. Indeed, the Massachusetts Ballot Act would serve as a model for other states, thirty-eight of which adopted some version of it by 1892.

Curtis B. Gans (1937–)

Curtis Gans's life has been a blend of political activist, writer, sage political observer, and director. He graduated from the University of North Carolina in 1959 with a degree in philosophy and English. Eight years later he was leading the movement to deny President Lyndon Johnson reelection, and in 1968 he became the staff director for the presidential campaign of Minnesota senator Eugene McCarthy. He subsequently did stints as a reporter for the *Miami News* and United Press International.

In 1977 his career took another turn as he, along with Maurice Rosenblatt, founded the Committee for the Study of the American Electorate—a nonpartisan, nonprofit, tax-exempt research institution, the primary purpose of which is to focus on issues relating to citizen engagement in politics. In operation for nearly thirty years now, it has become the authoritative source of information and analysis regarding registration and voter turnout in American elections. The committee has also issued reports on voter registration laws, campaign advertising, campaign finance, the impact of media on politics, and citizen education. Whether appearing on National Public Radio, public television, morning network news programs, or writing for a host of prominent news magazines (e.g., *Atlantic Monthly, New Republic, The Nation, Washington Monthly*), Curtis Gans has provided the public with reliable data on participation in elections, on where the problem areas are in the functioning of our electoral process, and on what consequences are likely to follow from proposals to address them. He and the Committee for the Study of the American Electorate have, in short, made a valuable contribution to the ongoing dialogue regarding the democratic character of the electoral process in the United States. Not surprisingly, his counsel has been sought by a number of institutions and organizations, including the Democratic Policy Council, the Woodrow Wilson Center for International Scholars, and the National Committee for an Effective Congress.

Lyndon Baines Johnson (1908–1973)

Although one would scarcely have predicted it, Lyndon Johnson did more to advance the civil rights of African Americans than any president since Abraham Lincoln.

Born in Stonehill, Texas, on August 27, 1908, to a not particularly successful father and a nurturing but demanding mother,
Johnson went through a difficult adolescence, at one point running away from home and ending up in California. He eventually returned to the fold, upon which his mother, who had always
hoped for great things from him, prevailed upon him to go to college. Following graduation from Southwest State Teacher's College in San Marcos, he taught school in Houston and Pearsall,
Texas. The poverty of the students he taught—many of them
Mexican American—left a lasting impression and helped to kin-
dle in him an empathy for and commitment to improving the
lives of the less fortunate.

In 1931 Johnson had the opportunity to go to Washington as
a secretary for Congressman Richard M. Kleberg, and he immediately became the star among congressional secretaries. There followed a two-year stint as the Texas director of the National Youth
Administration, interrupted in 1937 when Johnson decided to
run for a vacancy created by the untimely death of a congressman in Texas's tenth district. At the age of twenty-eight he was
elected to Congress and taken under the wing of President
Franklin Roosevelt, who, along with other Democratic Party stal-
warts, was duly impressed by the robust campaign that had been
waged by the young Texan.

As fate would have it, in 1941 Johnson was presented with
the opportunity to fill another vacancy in the state—this one following the death of one of its U.S. senators. Once again, he
waged a tireless campaign but ultimately came up short, losing to
the then governor by 1,311 votes. That December he joined the
navy; he was honored with the Silver Star in 1942 and returned to
Washington when he and other congressmen were ordered back
by the president.

In 1948 Johnson finally won election to the United States
Senate, challenging a former governor in what proved to be a
highly contentious and closely fought battle—to say nothing of
the controversy surrounding it. The ambitious young Texan
emerged victorious by a mere eighty-seven votes—earning him
the nickname "landslide Lyndon," as well as charges never fully
put to rest that he had stolen the election.

It did not take long for Lyndon's fellow senators to recognize
his quick mind, political acumen, and boundless energy, and they
elected him Democratic "whip" just three years into his term. In
1953 they would elevate him yet again, this time to the position of
minority leader. Following the 1954 election in which Democrats

managed to gain control of both houses of Congress, Johnson became the majority leader of the U.S. Senate—the youngest senator
ever to hold that office, and also the most masterful.

Johnson entered the presidential sweepstakes in 1960 but
proved no match for the dashing young senator from Massachusetts, John F. Kennedy. Although the motivations behind, and circumstances surrounding, Johnson's selection as Kennedy's vice-
presidential running mate remain in dispute, there is no doubt
that his elevation to the second-highest office in the land proved
to be one of the most frustrating periods in his life, just as it had
for previous occupants of this office, such as John Nance Garner
who characterized the vice presidency as not even worth "a
pitcher of warm spit." A man of very considerable talent, with an
ego to match, Johnson now found himself totally eclipsed, dependent on the captivating young president for whatever substan-
tive responsibilities he was given, which were few.

Once again, however, fate would intervene, when an assas-
sin's bullet thrust him into the office he had long craved. Five
days after taking the oath of office on *Air Force One* at Love Field
in Dallas, Texas, following Kennedy's assassination on November 22, 1963, President Johnson appeared before a joint session of
Congress and pledged to complete the unfinished agenda of the
slain president.

Both the crisis of the moment and Johnson's unequalled
grasp of the legislative process combined to achieve many of the
legislative goals that had eluded his predecessor, including the
historic 1964 Civil Rights Act outlawing racial discrimination in
employment, voting, public accommodations, and education.
With his reelection, Johnson moved beyond the Kennedy agenda,
ultimately achieving a legislative record second only to that of
Franklin Roosevelt.

Lyndon Johnson had not been a longtime champion of civil
rights for blacks. A product of his upbringing, his views on race
were not radically different from others of his generation living in
the South. In 1937 he had voted against an antilynching bill, and
during the 1940s and 1950s he would vote against civil rights legislation. He did, to be sure, shepherd the first civil rights bill in
eighty-two years through the Senate in 1958, but he did not resist
efforts to water it down in significant ways. But as Johnson later
noted, the presidency can be transforming: "Nothing makes a man
come to grips more directly with his conscience than the Presidency," he wrote. "Sitting in that chair involves making decisions
that draw out a man's fundamental commitments. The burden of

his responsibility literally opens up his soul. No longer can he accept matters as given. No longer can he write off hopes and needs as impossible. So it was for me. When I sat in the Oval office after President Kennedy died and reflected on civil rights, there was no question in my mind as to what I would do" (Johnson 1971, 157).

Despite passage of the 1964 Civil Rights Act, the number of blacks on the registration rolls in southern states was still pitifully low—only 6 percent in Mississippi. In his State of the Union Address delivered in January 1965, President Johnson called for the elimination of "every remaining obstacle to the right and the opportunity to vote" and privately instructed his attorney general to draft voting rights legislation. In his view, voting rights legislation would be even more important than the 1964 act, for it would provide blacks with political leverage over the political process—leverage they created themselves.

Despite growing pleas for more forceful action on the protection of voting rights, Johnson moved cautiously, convinced that having digested the 1964 Civil Rights Act, the congressional appetite for yet another piece of civil rights legislation had not yet developed. He bided his time, waiting for the press of events to create the propitious moment for action—and they did. During a nonviolent protest march in Selma, Alabama, in March 1965, local authorities unleashed bullwhips, nightsticks, and billy clubs against the marchers, seriously injuring more than fifty men and women. This unprovoked assault, replayed time and again on the three television networks, created a national public outrage, fueled further by the clubbing death of a Boston Unitarian minister in Selma a few days later. Johnson dispatched federal troops to Selma to protect the marchers and, sensing that the time was ripe, went before a joint session of Congress to demand that it pass voting rights legislation. The address, which concluded with "And . . . we . . . shall . . . overcome," brought the Congress to its feet and was the most memorable speech of the Johnson presidency. It also led to the most significant and effective legislation ever passed to protect the right of African Americans to vote—the 1965 Voting Rights Act. Within three years of its passage more than a million blacks were registered to vote.

Robert Marion LaFollette (1855–1925)

One of the leading members of the Progressive movement, Robert LaFollette led the way in expanding the vote beyond the choosing of candidates in the general election to affording voters a role in deciding who those choices would be. The direct primary has been and continues to be an institution unique to the American political process.

Born into a farming family in Primrose, Wisconsin, LaFollette attended the University of Wisconsin, where he came under the influence of its president, John Bascom, who stressed the importance of engaging in public service. Bascom's importunings apparently took, for shortly after being admitted to the bar, LaFollette was elected district attorney in 1880 and congressman in 1884. Like many other Republicans, however, he was swept out of office in 1890 following a Democratic landslide.

Returning to his home state, LaFollette opened a law practice, during which time he also began to see the corrupting influence that business interests such as the railroads, timber companies, and electrical power monopolies were having on the state's politics and government. He was keenly aware as well of farmers' profound resentment at eastern banking interests, which controlled their access to money and credit. Convinced that the people were being taken advantage of, he sought to reform Wisconsin politics by forging an alliance of farmers, laborers, small businessmen, and professionals. A man with considerable personal charisma and formidable speaking skills, he traveled about the state inveighing against machine politics, speaking with such conviction that he soon became known throughout Wisconsin as "Fighting Bob LaFollette." He sought the Republican nomination for governor in 1896 and 1898 but lost both times, his message proving too strident and threatening to some within the party establishment. In response, he toned down his reform message just enough to win the governorship in 1900. The Wisconsin legislature, however, was still not ready to take on the trusts and political machine, so he took his case to the voters, asking them to elect legislators who would ally themselves with its progressive reform agenda. The voters responded, reelecting him to office in 1902 and giving him a legislature that was ready to act. Not only did it legislate into law his proposals on corporate taxes and extensive civil service reform, but it also enacted the first statewide direct primary law in 1903, removing from the party machines the power to nominate candidates for office, and placing it instead directly in the hands of the voters. By 1917, this landmark change was adopted for most nominations in all but a few states.

After the 1904 Republican National Convention declined to recognize LaFollette's Progressive Republican delegate slate, opting instead to seat the Stalwart Republican wing of the party, LaFollette and his supporters in the legislature decided that the only fair way to choose national convention delegates was to let the people do it. Accordingly, in 1905 the state legislature passed a law allowing rank-and-file voters to directly elect delegates to the party's national nominating convention—another first in U.S. national politics.

By then the dominating presence in Wisconsin politics, LaFollette was elected to the U.S. Senate in 1906, where he continued to ruffle the feathers of the establishment, violating some of the Senate traditions and espousing both foreign and domestic policies out of line with his party. Continuing to advocate policies that would prove to be ahead of their time, he organized other party insurgents in the Senate, put out a Progressive weekly magazine carrying his name, and ultimately ran for presidential nomination in 1924 on an independent Progressive ticket. He managed to tally 17 percent of the popular vote but was labeled a "Bolshevik" by his opponents for his "radical views," including public ownership of railroads, child labor laws, collective bargaining, and the recalling of federal judges. LaFollette's decision to run for president as an independent also brought severe reprisals from his party, namely his expulsion from the Senate's Republican Conference and the loss of all his committee assignments. Exhausted and depressed, he died a year later.

The long view of history, however, has been much kinder to him than were his immediate Senate colleagues. In 1957, the Senate honored him as one of the five most significant senators to serve in that body—the others being Henry Clay, Daniel Webster, John C. Calhoun, and Robert Taft.

Robert Parris Moses (1935–)

The son of a janitor, Robert Moses was born in Harlem, New York. He received degrees in English and philosophy from Hamilton College in 1956 and the following fall enrolled at Harvard to study for a doctorate in philosophy. His father's illness forced him to interrupt his studies to return to New York and care for him. In 1960 Moses crossed paths with the noted black civil rights leader and intellectual Bayard Rustin, who prevailed upon him to work with the newly created Student Nonviolent Coordinating Committee (SNCC) on a voter registration campaign based in Atlanta, Georgia. This approach had strong appeal for Moses, who believed that improving the conditions of his race lay not in sit-ins, freedom rides, and direct action but ultimately in the acquisition of political power through the exercise of the ballot.

While traveling through Mississippi in 1960, seeking recruits for the upcoming SNCC conference, he was encouraged by a local NAACP leader there to come back to the state with more volunteers. The following summer Moses, now the field secretary for SNCC, did precisely that, organizing a voter registration drive in this hotbed of racism. In the 1960s, Mississippi was the poorest state in the Union, with 86 percent of its nonwhite population living in poverty, and only 5 percent of the black citizenry registered to vote, even though African Americans made up fully 45 percent of the state's population.

During the next two years, a civil rights worker who helped SNCC in Mississippi was murdered, as was Medgar Evers, and Moses himself was at various times beaten and jailed. In 1963 Moses was named director of the Council of Federated Organizations—a collection of civil rights groups. Under his leadership it launched a program called "Mississippi Freedom Summer" that brought nearly a thousand, mostly well-to-do, college students from around the country to help register black voters; organized a "Freedom Democratic Party" that would compete with the all-white Mississippi Democratic Party; and opened "freedom schools" where black children could learn math and reading.

Under the leadership of Bob Moses, the Mississippi Freedom Democratic Party (MFDP) fielded four candidates in the 1964 primary to be delegates to the Democratic National Convention that year. All lost, but the regular Mississippi Democratic Party refused to support the civil rights plank adopted by the national party, thereby violating an oath of loyalty to the party required by the Democratic National Committee. The MFDP then held its own convention and selected sixty-eight individuals as an alternative slate of delegates to represent Mississippi at the Democratic National Convention. Many of its members testified before the Credentials Committee (charged with determining who can be seated as delegates) at the convention, setting forth all the obstacles placed in their paths when trying to register to vote. The plight of the MFDP was now attracting considerable national attention, but President Johnson feared that if they were seated, other southern states would walk out of the convention. Ultimately, the decision was made to seat two of them as at-large delegates—a compromise that did not sit well with Moses. Accordingly, on two evenings during the convention he instructed the MFDP delegation, which received help clandestinely from other state delegations in gaining access to the floor, to occupy the seats allocated to the state of Mississippi. Although there were some initial attempts to remove them, the powers that be decided to let them remain, believing that the spectacle of ejecting the delegation before millions of viewers on national television would not serve the party well.

The Democratic Party's failure to recognize the Freedom Party delegates as the official delegation of Mississippi left Moses feeling bitter and reluctant to continue participating in politics. In addition, threats on his life grew, forcing him to change his name (to Robert Parris). To make matters worse, he saw SNCC being taken over by Black Power enthusiasts who advocated far more aggressive tactics than he was prepared to accept. So he left the organization in 1965.

When the Vietnam War intensified, he spoke out against it, applied for conscientious objector status and was rejected, and so fled first to Canada and then to Tanzania, where he became head of the mathematics department at one of the country's prominent schools. Taking advantage of President Jimmy Carter's Amnesty Program, established in 1977, he returned to the United States and resumed his doctoral study at Harvard. In 1982 he was awarded the highly prized MacArthur Fellowship, which he used to start the Algebra Project—a program designed to engage more than 40,000 rural and inner-city students in the study of mathematics. In recent years he has been further honored with the Heinz Award for the Human Condition (2000), the Margaret Chase Smith American Democracy Award (2001), and the James B. Conant Award of the Education Commission of States.

A self-effacing individual who is not a flashy personality, Bob Moses has not attracted as much attention as other members of the civil rights movement, but his contributions to advancing the political rights of blacks are significant. His courageous program to register blacks in one of the most racially hostile states in the nation, and to create a parallel political party (MFDP) there as well, drove home to whites that the 1964 Civil Rights Act was not enough to secure voting rights for blacks, and demonstrated to blacks the importance of organizing for political power.

Alice Paul (1885–1977)

Highly intelligent, tenacious, and uncompromising, Alice Paul represented the hard edge of the fight for women's suffrage. She was born in Moorestown, New Jersey, to well-off Quaker parents who, in typical Quaker fashion, raised her to take seriously matters of equality, social justice, and public service. She graduated from Swarthmore College in 1905, worked briefly at a settlement house in New York City, and then traveled to London in 1906 to pursue further graduate study. There Paul joined up with the militant end of the suffrage movement, going to jail three times and taking part in hunger strikes that on one occasion required her to be force fed for one month. She also managed to find time for study; indeed, the University of Pennsylvania agreed to count her coursework from two British universities, which proved sufficient to earn her an M.A. (1907) and Ph.D. (1912) .

Upon her return to the United States, Paul was asked to head the Congressional Committee of the National American Woman Suffrage Association (NAWSA). The militant tactics to which she had become accustomed in London, and transported back to the U.S., did not sit well with most members of NAWSA, however, and so Paul left the organization, taking with her some other women who signed on to her more aggressive approach. Together they formed the Congressional Union for Woman Suffrage, with Alice Paul serving as the first national chair. The group organized a march on Washington timed for the day of Woodrow Wilson's first inauguration; and march they did, some five thousand strong, which evoked a sufficiently violent response from inaugural bystanders that the army, police, and militia had to come to their rescue. It is generally agreed, however, that the demonstration gave the movement a needed shot in the arm.

The Congressional Union abjured the state-by-state approach to securing the right to vote advocated by NAWSA, instead focusing its efforts on a constitutional amendment. The organization also resolved to hold the party in power (Democrats) responsible for lack of progress on this front. Accordingly, in 1914 it went after Democrats running in the nine states where women could vote, and a year later it had an organization in every state. Not coincidentally, that same year both houses of Congress created committees on woman's suffrage and draft suffrage bills as well, with the Senate bill escaping passage by just one vote.

Paul and her compatriots kept up the pressure. There were protests outside the White House as well as hunger strikes, with Paul putting up such a fight against being force fed that she was committed to a mental institution and placed in solitary confinement, until friends won her release a week later.

The Congressional Union merged with the Woman's Party to become the National Woman's Party in 1917, with Alice Paul serving as chair of its national executive committee and the committee on international relations. Once the Nineteenth Amendment was passed, she immediately turned her considerable energies and talents to lobbying for an equal rights amendment, drafting the very first such amendment and having it placed before Congress in 1923.

Recognizing that a knowledge of the law would aid her in fighting to overturn the many legal barriers erected against women, she proceeded to earn bachelor's and doctoral degrees in law and D.C.L. In the 1930s she would expand her focus to the international plight of women, heading the Nationality Committee of the Inter-American Commission of Women. Elected president of the National Woman's Party in 1942, she used this perch to continue her quest for equal rights for all women, achieving a very considerable victory in 1946 when she persuaded the General Assembly of the United Nations to adopt a Woman's Suffrage Resolution.

Alice Paul continued to lobby Congress for an equal rights amendment well into the autumn of her years, sidelined only by a stroke, the consequences of which took her life at the age of ninety-two.

Frances Fox Piven (1931–) and Richard A. Cloward (1931–2001)

It has been said that those who can't do it, teach it, and those who can't teach it, teach about teaching. True or not, this statement certainly does not apply to Frances Piven and Richard Cloward, both of whom have not only taught it but also done it by helping to achieve change in the very political process they have taught and written about.

Piven, the recipient of a Ph.D. from the University of Chicago in 1962, is now Distinguished Professor of Political Science and Sociology at the Graduate School and University Center of the City University of New York. Cloward received a master's degree in social work and a Ph.D. in sociology from Columbia University, where he taught in the School of Social Work until his death. The two of them collaborated to produce several books, including *Regulating the Poor: The Functions of Public Welfare; The New Class War; Poor People's Movements: Why They Succeed, How They Fail; The Politics of Turmoil: Essays on Poverty, Race, and the Urban Crisis;* and *Why Americans Still Don't Vote.* This latter publication achieved considerable visibility, with the authors arguing that the decline in voting turnout is not traceable to social and psychological factors but rather is the result of procedural requirements instituted for voting at the turn of the twentieth century, and the party response to them.

As their joint scholarship clearly shows, Piven and Cloward have long had a concern for the poorer segments of our society and how they are adversely affected by public policy. That concern extended to the electoral process as well, where the poor show very low rates of participation—a fact that the authors believe is significantly related to the kinds of decisions government makes. Believing that cumbersome registration procedures deter the poor from voting, they set about trying to streamline them.

Out of a meeting they had with a former antipoverty legal services attorney in 1982, Piven and Cloward came up with the idea of registering voters on a massive scale by using public workers to register citizens in welfare and assistance agencies, Medicaid offices, and unemployment agencies, as well as workers employed in a host of private social agencies such as settlement houses, senior and day care centers, family planning agencies, community health centers, and other community-centered organizations. To this end, in 1983 they cofounded Human Service Employees Registration and Voter Education (Human SERVE).

Although Human SERVE had registered more than 400,000 people by 1984, this was far short of the organization's goal of four to five million. Private agencies, as Piven and Cloward soon realized, were not wholly enthusiastic about undertaking such a task. The reasons were varied. Some feared their clients would think the services provided were conditional upon registering to vote; others saw the whole undertaking as unsuited to their training and mission; still others feared losing their tax-exempt status, or ruffling the feathers of politicians who determined their grant-funding; finally, in the case of some social agencies (e.g., Head Start, Legal Services) the legislation creating them prohibited such activity.

Human SERVE decided to try a different tack, namely, persuading public officials to make voter registration available on a regular basis in state, county, and municipal agencies. The state of Michigan, for example, had done so back in 1975, allowing individuals to register when licensing their automobiles—a procedure that came to be known as "motor-voter registration." Four other states had done so by 1983, and by 1984 Human SERVE had persuaded governors in four more states to issue executive orders allowing voter registration in social agencies and the Department of Motor Vehicles.

As a consequence of Human SERVE's dogged efforts, with Piven and Cloward leading the charge, more and more states adopted some kind of public agency registration over the next several years, but there was still resistance to national legislation mandating such procedures. This resistance, too, was ultimately overcome, however, once evidence from the states demonstrated that agency registration could be handled administratively, was cheap to do, and was not burdened by fraud, and, most important, once it had become clear that making registration easier would not advantage either political party. Accordingly, in 1993 the National Voter Registration Act was signed into law, mandating that voters be allowed to register while licensing their car, at welfare offices, or by mail, and that voter registration rolls not be purged except for change of residency. Although this legislation has had a significant effect on increasing the number of registered voters, it has yet to demonstrate a similar impact on the number who turn out at the polls.

The contributions made by Piven and Cloward both to the understanding of voting participation and to efforts to increase it have been widely recognized: In 1986 they were both honored with the Bryant Spann Memorial Prize from the Eugene V. Debs Foundation for their scholarship on voter registration; in 1994 the National Association of Secretaries of State awarded them the Jim Waltermire Award in recognition of their efforts to make voter registration easier; and the Tides Foundation did likewise in 1996, presenting them with the James Bagley Lehman Award for Excellence in Public Advocacy.

Elizabeth Cady Stanton (1815–1902)

In her roles as writer, editor, and activist for women's rights, Elizabeth Cady Stanton never left her listeners and readers in doubt about where she stood, nor did she shy away from the controversy spawned by those views.

Elizabeth Cady was one of eleven children born to a well-to-do family in Johnstown, New York; her father was a prominent lawyer and later a congressman. The talk among women in her father's law office made her aware early on of the distinctions the law made between men and women, and a comment made to Elizabeth by her father upon the death of the Cadys' oldest son made it clear that he too made distinctions between the two sexes: "Oh my daughter, I wish you were a boy."

The family's religious and social conservatism was tempered by Elizabeth's visits to her free-spirited cousin, Gerrit Smith, a philanthropist and committed abolitionist, with equally strong views on the pitfalls of religion. During a lengthy stay with her cousin in 1839, she was introduced to another abolitionist of some prominence, Henry Brewster Stanton, whom she married in 1840—a marriage greeted with restrained enthusiasm by her family.

At Henry's initiative, he and Elizabeth journeyed to England for the World Anti-Slavery Convention, which proved to be a fateful event in Elizabeth's life. It was there that she met Lucretia Mott, destined to become a close comrade in the fight for women's rights. Both she and Mott were denied seats as delegates because of their gender. It was this indignity that caused them to resolve, upon their return to the United States, to convene a conference on women's rights. The conference did indeed take place, albeit some eight years later, and it issued a "Declaration of Sentiments," which in structure is very similar to the Declaration of Independence, and set forth the long train of abuses by males against females, calling for women to be treated equally with men in the political process and before the law.

This conference spawned a number of others across the country during the following decade, yielding petitions demanding that women be granted property and voting rights. Cady Stanton, a forceful and incisive writer, conveyed her views through the antislavery and women's press, insisting that men were unable to represent the interests of women and that women had an inalienable right to wages and property and to separate themselves from physically and psychologically damaging marriages. Nor, as her writings made clear, was she at all receptive to religious claims that the Bible contemplated gender inequality, pleading with members of her sex to speak out against those churches that preached such beliefs.

In 1851 Cady Stanton met Susan B. Anthony, with whom she would develop a lifelong friendship. Both were now living in New York and together launched a campaign in 1854 to pressure the state legislature into changing some of its laws regarding women. Anthony provided the organizational skills behind the movement while Cady Stanton marshaled the case for reform. Although the legislature would not budge on the suffrage question, in 1860 it did make changes in economic and custody rights of married women and widows.

With the outbreak of the Civil War, and anticipating its outcome, she began to advocate and lecture on the subject of universal suffrage, convening the Equal Rights Association in 1866 to promote this cause. To her great surprise, however, Republicans and abolitionists opposed states granting women the right to vote—a stance that infuriated Cady Stanton. She (and Anthony) reversed field and now argued against adoption of the Fifteenth Amendment, directing rather harsh attacks against black men. These sentiments were probably engendered by the fact that the weekly magazine (*Revolution*) of which she was now senior editor and the major writer was being kept afloat with an injection of funds from a notorious racist (George Francis Train).

Convinced that seeking the right to suffrage through the states would not yield results, Cady Stanton in 1869 undertook what would prove to be the most far-reaching campaign of her career—the "National Protection of National Citizens." Arguing that the right to vote was much too precious to be left to the states to safeguard, she called for a constitutional amendment to provide such a guarantee to all citizens; and to advance this proposal she founded the National Woman Suffrage Association. Under her leadership, it asserted the cause of women more aggressively than the more gradualist and state-oriented approach taken by the American Woman Suffrage Association.

For eight years Cady Stanton worked to petition Congress for a constitutional amendment. Supporters in Congress annually introduced an amendment, and in 1880 both houses appointed select committees on women's suffrage, each of which recommended its approval. Not until 1887, however, was such an amendment brought to the floors of Congress for a vote, only to be defeated by a wide margin.

After 1880, Cady Stanton became less active on the front lines of the suffrage movement, living abroad with her children for several years. She did, however, continue to give voice to her views through writing—five books and several hundred articles—as well as a few major speeches each year. She had remained nominally head of the National Woman Suffrage Association only at the urging of Susan B. Anthony, but she stepped down in 1892, upset that the organization was attracting evangelical church types and southern women lukewarm to the idea of a federal guarantee of the vote.

Once the New York constitutional convention turned down the suffrage amendment, a profoundly disappointed Cady Stanton cast aside the notion of universal suffrage and began arguing instead for an "educated suffrage," believing that skeptics might find it more acceptable. Placing the emphasis on education, she believed, could possibly open the door to woman's suffrage since level of education was something women could change; gender was not. In her final years, Cady Stanton also became even more critical of religion—and more controversial as well—as she twice published *The Woman's Bible* (1895, 1898), which contained a collection of essays by various movement members critical of the demeaning way in which religion portrayed women.

Even in her last days, Cady Stanton continued to fight with the pen, an unmailed letter having been found on her desk addressed to Theodore Roosevelt, pleading with him to support women's right to vote.

William Simon U'Ren (1859–1949)

William U'Ren was born in Lancaster, Wisconsin. His father was a blacksmith and homesteader who also had a keen interest in ideas beyond the conventional, having become a strong socialist in the latter part of his life. Son William would evince the same inclination to imagine alternative realities.

During William's youth, the family lived in four different states, one of which was Colorado, where he worked for a while in the coal mines and then blacksmithed in Denver. He enrolled in evening studies at Denver Business College, studied law with the firm of France and Rogers, and was admitted to the bar in 1881. He also found time to do some campaigning for Republican candidates, which, to his dismay, exposed him to some of the corruption in the state's politics.

U'Ren had an inquisitive mind that was quite comfortable with, and excited by, ideas. He read *Progress and Poverty*, by Henry George, a leading social reformer and economist of the period, and was much taken by his proposal for the more equitable raising of public monies by use of a single tax. During his journey to Oregon in 1889, U'Ren also happened to read a pamphlet advocating use of the initiative—a mechanism he immediately saw as a vehicle for securing adoption of the single-tax proposal.

Once in Oregon, he quickly gravitated to reformer E. W. Bingham, secretary of the Australian Ballot League, and together they fashioned a proposal for a secret ballot, which gained adoption by the legislature in 1891.

U'Ren's flowering interest in spiritualism brought him into contact with the similarly inclined Lewelling family, who also happened to be prominently involved in reform politics in Milwaukee, Oregon. During a meeting at their house, U'Ren's life was once again to be changed by something he read, as he was told of J. W. Sullivan's book *Direct Legislation by the Citizen through the Initiative and Referendum*. Indeed, so enamored was he of the idea set forth by Sullivan that his reformist zeal was diverted from the single tax and toward the initiative and referendum, firmly convinced that these two reforms would make it possible to achieve any reform.

Under the auspices of the Milwaukee Alliance, U'Ren, now a Populist, became secretary of a newly created joint committee in 1893 tasked with seeking passage of the initiative and referendum. He also became secretary of the Oregon Populists and, for the only time in his life, won election to the Oregon House in 1896, where he continued to push for the adoption of direct legislation. Though he made a number of converts to the cause among his peers, certain of his tactics did not sit well with some legislators. U'Ren decided to depart after completing his term.

He continued his efforts on the outside, founding the Non-Partisan Direct Legislation League of Oregon in 1898, a year which also saw him return to the Republican Party and fall out with the Lewelling family. Persistent campaigning by the league proved instrumental in gaining adoption of the initiative and referendum in 1902.

U'Ren was not done, however, for he now turned his attention to pushing for a direct primary. To that end, he founded the Direct Primary League in 1903. It was he who drafted the direct primary legislation that would be enacted into law in 1904. On the heels of this achievement, he organized the People's Power League, which he used for initiative campaigns that led to laws on corrupt practices, the establishment of the recall, and requiring legislators to select U.S. senators favored by the voters.

Despite his many achievements, he was unable to persuade Oregonians either to adopt the single tax or to elect him to office. In 1914 he ran for governor and lost; he suffered the same fate in runs for the legislature in 1934 and 1935. The remainder of his years were devoted to a modest law practice and a newfound interest—advocating the creation of voluntary worker colonies. Three years prior to his death in 1949, the University of Oregon recognized his public spiritedness by awarding him an honorary master's degree in public service.

Over the course of a rich and varied career, U'Ren had played a key role in achieving for the Oregon political process several key reforms—the secret ballot, initiative and referendum, recall, and direct primary. It is small wonder that at the height of his career the *Portland Oregonian* was moved to comment that "in Oregon the state government is divided into four departments— the executive, judicial, legislative and U'Ren" (July 17, 1906). No less of a tribute came from noted journalist and reformer Lincoln Steffens, who referred to U'Ren as the "lawgiver."

Earl Warren (1891–1974)

Arguably the most influential chief justice of the United States since John Marshall, Earl Warren was born in Los Angeles, where as a youth he worked for the railroad as a "call boy"—an experience that left him with a disdainful view of corporate power as he witnessed workers laid off without notice and callous treatment of minorities and injured employees. As a law student at the University of Berkeley, he worked on the unsuccessful gubernatorial campaign of Republican Hiram Johnson, one of the state's leading Progressives and a critic of corporate influence over the political process.

Following service in World War I, Warren returned to California, where he filled a one-year vacancy for district attorney and then won election to that same post in 1926. His record on fighting crime and corruption was so impressive that it attracted national attention and propelled him into the race for California attorney general, which he won by a landslide in 1938. His campaign against corruption continued in this role, but Warren also became caught up in the anticommunist campaigns of the period and the hysteria over the considerable numbers of Japanese citizens and aliens within California, adding his voice to the calls for their internment during World War II. He would later profoundly regret this action and argue for denying to the government any such power in future national emergencies.

In 1942 he challenged the incumbent governor, winning an impressive victory. He would win again in 1946 and 1950—no mean feat in a Democratic state. He was very much an activist and progressive governor, achieving reforms in civil service, pensions, and parole regulations, as well as upgrading conditions in prisons and mental institutions. The fact that he was a Republican who headed a big Democratic state made Warren an appealing prospect for the national Republican ticket. In 1948 he was chosen as Thomas E. Dewey's vice-presidential running mate in the Republican's unsuccessful bid to unseat incumbent President Harry S. Truman. Warren would enter national election politics again in 1952, this time as a presidential candidate, running in the few primaries but failing to make any headway against the widely popular Dwight Eisenhower.

Impressed with Warren's political career and ability, President Eisenhower decided to appoint him interim chief justice of the U.S. Supreme Court in 1953, filling the vacancy created by the death of Chief Justice Carl Vinson. He was confirmed for permanent appointment to that position by the Senate in the following year. It was an appointment that Eisenhower would later come to regret, however, for Warren turned out to be far too activist for the more conservative president. Under his apt leadership, the Supreme Court broke new ground in the areas of criminal procedure, freedom of religion, and civil rights. With respect to this last area, the Warren Court asserted the authority of the national government to protect the right to vote in the face of various nefarious state practices. It was Chief Justice Warren himself who wrote the opinion of the Court (in *South Carolina v. Katzenbach*) upholding the constitutionality of the crucially important Voting Rights Act of 1965, giving African Americans at long last the federal protections they needed against the assorted roadblocks erected by southern states to discourage them from voting. Where Warren did not himself author the opinions upholding protection of voting, he could nevertheless be found, without exception, joining those opinions—opinions sustaining the right of eighteen-year-olds to vote in federal elections, and declaring unconstitutional a number of state practices including poll taxes, literacy tests, and excessive residency requirements.

The Warren Court also made landmark rulings in protecting the value of the vote. Overturning the Supreme Court's long-held view that it must stay out of redistricting disputes because they involved "political questions," the Warren Court in 1962 abandoned that position (in *Baker v. Carr*), asserting instead that the vast differences in the populations of legislative districts violated the Equal Protection Clause of the Fourteenth Amendment. Two years later, in a massive opinion authored by Chief Justice Warren, the Court invoked the same amendment (in *Reynolds v. Sims*), declaring that both houses of state legislatures must be apportioned on the basis of population and that districts must be as nearly equal in population as possible, noting that "legislators represent people, not trees or acres." Warren would later state that reapportionment was the most significant issue decided by the Court during his stewardship, believing that had legislative districts originally been created on the basis of "one man, one vote," African Americans would have been able to gain remedies for their grievances through the political process rather than the courts.

On his last day as chief justice of the United States Supreme Court, Earl Warren was asked how he would like the court to be remembered, to which he replied, "I would like the Court to be remembered as the people's Court." That hope, it is fair to say, has been realized.

Fred Wertheimer (1939–)

Although Fred Wertheimer has devoted his career to addressing a variety of public issues, including government ethics, budget and tax reform, and nuclear arms control, on none has he been more thoughtful, relentless, and influential than the role of money in politics. Indeed, the *New York Times* described him as the "country's leading proponent of campaign finance reform," and the *Wall Street Journal* allowed as how he was "perhaps the capital's longest-toiling advocate of reducing the role of money in politics."

He had been well prepared for such a task. Educated at the University of Michigan and Harvard Law School, he was taken on as an attorney with the Securities and Exchange Commission, counsel to the House Small Business Committee, and legislative counsel to the late Massachusetts congressman Silvio Conte. In 1976, he served as legal counsel to the nonpartisan citizens' lobby Common Cause in the landmark Supreme Court case (*Buckley v. Valeo*) on the Federal Election Campaign Act, arguing that the Court should uphold the constitutionality of contribution and spending limits.

In 1981 he became the president and chief executive officer of Common Cause, succeeding its founder, John Gardner. During his stewardship the organization carefully monitored the role of money in elections, drew public and congressional attention to efforts by candidates to circumvent the rules, and recommended changes in the law to stop such abuses. In 1995 he left Common Cause, and after brief visiting positions at Harvard's Shorenstein Center for the Press, Politics, and Public Policy (1996) and the Yale Law School (1997), he established and continues to serve as president of Democracy 21, another nonpartisan, nonprofit organization dedicated to eliminating the influence of money in American politics, ensuring the integrity of elections and government decisions, and increasing the involvement of citizens in their government.

His thinking on the role of money in politics and how to address it is systematically set forth in "Campaign Finance Reform: The Unfinished Agenda," published in the *Annals of the American Academy of Political and Social Science;* "Campaign Finance Reform: A Key to Restoring the Health of Our Democracy," in the *Columbia Law Review;* and "TV Ad Wars: How to Cut Advertising Costs in Political Campaigns," which can be found in the *Harvard International Journal of Press/Politics.*

References

Cloward, Richard A., and Frances Fox Piven, eds. 1974. *The Politics of Turmoil: Essays on Poverty, Race, and the Urban Crisis.* New York: Pantheon Books.

Johnson, Lyndon Baines. 1971. *The Vantage Point: Perspectives of the Presidency, 1963–1969.* New York: Holt, Rinehart, and Winston.

Piven, Frances Fox, and Richard A. Cloward. 1971. *Regulating the Poor: The Function of Public Welfare.* New York: Vintage Books.

———. 1985. *The New Class War.* Revised and expanded ed. New York: Vintage Books.

———. 2000. *Why Americans Still Don't Vote.* Boston: Beacon Press.

Stanton, Elizabeth Cady. 1895. *The Woman's Bible*. New York: Arno Press.

Wertheimer, Fred. 1986. "Campaign Finance Reform: The Unfinished Agenda." *Annals of the American Academy of Political and Social Science* 486 (July): 86–102.

———. 1997. "TV Ad Wars: How to Cut Advertising Costs in Political Campaigns." *The Harvard International Journal of Press/Politics* 2 (Summer): 93–101.

Wertheimer, Fred, and Susan Weiss Manes. 1994. "Campaign Finance Reform: A Key to Restoring the Health of Our Democracy." *Columbia Law Review* 94 (May): 1126–1159.

Cases Cited

Baker v. Carr 369 U.S. 186 (1982)
Buckley v. Valeo 424 U.S. 1 (1976)
Reynolds v. Sims 377 U.S. 533 (1964)
South Carolina v. Katzenbach 383 U.S. 301 (1966)

5

Data and Quotations

This chapter is divided into two parts, the first of which contains data on a number of subjects, including milestone events in the quest for an inclusive suffrage, information on state practices in connection with the selection of their delegates to national party conventions, direct democracy (i.e., initiative, referendum, and recall), voter registration procedures, the casting and counting of votes, and term limits. Also included are data on the participation of Americans in presidential primaries and general elections, as well as the reasons they give for not participating, and presidential election outcomes since 1789, with emphasis on how they were affected by the Founding Fathers' curious creation known as the Electoral College.

The second half of this chapter contains more than sixty quotes related to the importance of the vote in democratic government, the quest for the right to vote in America, and assessments of how well various facets of the electoral process are functioning. The authors of these quotations are wide-ranging in background, consisting of important figures from history, philosophers, scholars, poets, officeholders, a comedian, members of commissions, political commentators, interest group advocates, and corporate officers. Their observations are included because they offer an eloquent plea, a compelling argument, a wise caution, a telling fact, or an incisive question.

Survey Data

The Right to Vote

The federal principle is one of the defining characteristics of the American political process, creating as it does two distinct levels of government ruling the same people, with certain powers allocated to the national government, others reserved to the states, and still others that can be exercised by both levels. The federal arrangement, it is fair to say, proved to be both a hindrance and an asset in the march toward a more inclusive electorate.

Certainly it frustrated attempts by blacks to gain the franchise, even after that right had been guaranteed with passage of the Fifteenth Amendment. Southern states, exercising their powers to decide the qualifications for voting, conduct elections, and redistrict, erected all kinds of subtle and not so subtle roadblocks to the black franchise, including the poll tax, literacy tests, grandfather clauses, placing polling places away from black neighborhoods, white primaries, the "eight ballot" law, and racial gerrymandering. Most of these devious practices had to await more robust interpretations of the Fourteenth and Fifteenth Amendments by the Supreme Court in the 1950s and 1960s, and the Voting Rights Act of 1965, before they were brought to an end.

But if the federal arrangement provided some states with an opportunity to stymie black voting rights, it must also be said that in other ways states provided an arena to push for political changes that the federal government, seeing no national consensus for them, was not yet prepared to accept. Thus, it was the state of Wyoming that first chose to fully enfranchise women, to be followed a few years later by Utah and Idaho (Keyssar 2000, table A20). As they campaigned across the country for universal women's suffrage, one of the compelling arguments made by suffragettes was that none of the untoward consequences predicted by opponents of the vote had in fact materialized in states where the franchise had already been granted. This same argument, among others, would also be made by the champions of younger citizens after Georgia led the way in 1943 as the first state to lower the voting age to eighteen, with Kentucky, Alaska, and Hawaii doing likewise in the next two decades (see Table 5.1).

It was also at the state level that one of the most significant efforts to expand voters' control over government occurred as many of them were given the tools to preempt (*initiative*) or overrule (*referendum*) the actions of elected officials, and even revoke (*recall*) their election to office (see Table 5.2). South Dakota was the first state to adopt the initiative and referendum, in 1898, and an additional twenty-three states would ultimately follow its lead, while Oregon pioneered the use of the recall in 1908, with seventeen states deciding to follow suit, including California,

TABLE 5.1
Milestones in the Expansion and Protection of the Suffrage

Date	Event
1791	Vermont is the first state to impose no property qualifications on white males and free African American males as a condition of voting.
1850	The Seneca Falls Convention of women, organized by Lucretia Mott and Elizabeth Cady Stanton, marks the beginning of women's struggle for the right to vote.
1868	Ratification of the Fourteenth Amendment, which defined citizenship, prohibited states from denial of the suffrage under penalty of having their representation in Congress reduced, guaranteed equal protection of the laws, and prohibited denial of life, liberty, and property without due process.
1870	Ratification of Fifteenth Amendment, which prohibits states from denying citizens the right to vote on the basis of race, color, or previous condition of servitude.
1889	Wyoming becomes the first state to fully enfranchise women.
1898	South Dakota becomes the first state to adopt the initiative and referendum.
1905	Wisconsin passes a law requiring that all delegates to both parties' national conventions be chosen by primary.
1908	Oregon becomes the first state to adopt the recall.
1910	Oregon establishes a binding presidential preference primary, requiring convention delegates to vote for the candidate winning the primary.
1913	Seventeenth Amendment is ratified, requiring the direct election of U.S. senators.
1919	Nineteenth Amendment is ratified, extending the right to vote to women.
1924	Citizenship Act is enacted into law, declaring that any American Indian born in the United States is a citizen.
1926	California does away with the exclusion of native Chinese citizens from voting, as does Oregon the following year.
1943	Georgia becomes the first state to lower the voting age to eighteen.
1944	Supreme Court rules in *Smith v. Allright* that political parties cannot prohibit blacks from voting in their primaries.
1946	Committee on Civil Rights appointed by President Truman issues a report highlighting the laws and practices used to disenfranchise blacks and Native Americans.
1957	Civil Rights Act is enacted into law, creating a commission to investigate voting irregularities, making intimidation in connection with the right to vote a federal crime, and authorizing the attorney general to seek injunctions to prevent interference with the right to vote.
1960	Civil Rights Act is enacted, extending the life of the Civil Rights Commission, authorizing courts to appoint voter referees, and requiring states to preserve voting records for two years.
1961	Twenty-third Amendment is ratified, allowing residents of the District of Columbia the right to vote for president.
1961	The Supreme Court rules in *Gomillion v. Lightfoot* that racial gerrymandering is a violation of the Fifteenth Amendment.
1964	The Twenty-fourth Amendment is ratified, prohibiting the imposition of a poll tax in any federal election, primary or general.
1965	Voting Rights Act is enacted into law, suspending literacy tests for five years, dispatching federal examiners to southern states for the purpose of registering blacks and observing registration practices, requiring jurisdictions with a history of discrimination against blacks to clear any changes in voting procedures with the U.S. Justice Department, and instructing the department to test the constitutionality of the poll tax in court.

(continues)

TABLE 5.1

Milestones in the Expansion and Protection of the Suffrage (continued)

Date	Event
1966	The Supreme Court rules in *Harper et al. v. Virginia Board of Elections et al.* that the poll tax is unconstitutional.
1969	The Supreme Court rules in *Kramer v. Free School District* that election laws denying the vote to those not owning taxable property are unconstitutional.
1970	Voting Rights Act, extended for five more years, lowers voting age to eighteen in federal elections, prohibits a residency requirement any greater than thirty days in federal elections, and provides uniform rules for absentee registration and voting in federal elections.
1970	The Supreme Court rules that the Voting Rights Act empowers Congress to ban literacy tests in state as well as federal elections.
1970	The Democratic Party adopts the recommendations of the Committee on Party Structure and Delegate Selection (known as the McGovern-Fraser Commission)—changes that serve to greatly expand the opportunities for party rank-and-file members to participate in the presidential nominating process.
1971	The ratification of the Twenty-sixth Amendment, lowering the legal voting age to eighteen in all elections.
1975	Congress permanently bans the use of literacy tests and renews the Voting Rights Act for an additional seven years and makes its provisions applicable to "language minorities" (i.e., Hispanics, Indians, Alaska Natives, and Asian Americans).
1982	Voting Rights Act is extended for an additional twenty-five years, and a new provision specifies that voting practices may be in violation of the law if their effect is to discriminate, even though their intent was not.
1984	Enactment of the Voter Accessibility for the Elderly and Handicapped Act, requiring that polling places in federal elections be accessible to both groups.
1986	Uniformed and Overseas Citizens Absentee Voting Act requires that states and territories permit U.S. citizens living abroad to register and vote by absentee ballot.
1993	The National Voter Registration Act is enacted, requiring citizens to be allowed to register to vote when licensing their car, or at welfare offices, to register by mail, and to have their names purged from the voting rolls only for change of residence.
2002	In response to balloting irregularities in the Florida presidential vote of 2000, the Voter Help Act is enacted, providing states with federal money to meet new national voting standards. States are required to afford voters the opportunity to check their ballots, define what constitutes a legal ballot, create a centralized voter registration database, and allow provisional voting.

which for the first time in its history launched a successful campaign to recall its recently reelected governor, Gray Davis.

Although the recall has never caught on at the national level, calls for a constitutional amendment establishing a national referendum procedure did gain some traction in the 1930s with the introduction of the Ludlow Amendment, which called for a national referendum on a decision to go to war; and in 1980, when then Democratic Party majority leader Richard Gephardt (MO) came out for the establishment of a nonbinding national advisory referendum enabling voters to express their preferences on a few proposed laws. If his public comments since then are

TABLE 5.2
Initiatives, Referendums, and Recall Procedures in the States

State	Initiative	Referendum	Recall
Alabama	yes	no	no
Alaska	yes	yes	yes
Arizona	yes	yes	yes
Arkansas	yes	yes	no
California	yes	yes	yes
Colorado	yes	yes	yes
Connecticut	no	no	no
Delaware	no	no	no
Florida	yes	no	no
Georgia	no	no	yes
Hawaii	no	no	no
Idaho	yes	yes	yes
Illinois	yes	no	no
Indiana	no	no	no
Iowa	no	no	no
Kansas	no	no	yes
Kentucky	no	yes	no
Louisiana	no	no	yes
Maine	yes	yes	no
Maryland	no	yes	no
Massachusetts	yes	yes	no
Michigan	yes	yes	yes
Minnesota	no	no	yes
Mississippi	yes	no	no
Missouri	yes	yes	no
Montana	yes	yes	yes
Nebraska	yes	yes	no
Nevada	yes	yes	yes
New Hampshire	no	no	no
New Jersey	no	no	yes
New Mexico	no	yes	no
New York	no	no	no
North Carolina	no	no	no
North Dakota	yes	yes	yes
Ohio	yes	yes	no
Oklahoma	yes	yes	no
Oregon	yes	yes	yes
Pennsylvania	no	no	no
Rhode Island	no	no	yes
South Carolina	no	no	no
South Dakota	yes	yes	no
Tennessee	no	no	no
Texas	no	no	no

(continues)

TABLE 5.2
TABLE 5.2
Initiatives, Referendums, and Recall Procedures in the States *(continued)*

State	Initiative	Referendum	Recall
Utah	yes	yes	no
Vermont	no	no	no
Virginia	no	no	no
Washington	yes	yes	yes
West Virginia	no	no	no
Wisconsin	no	no	yes
Wyoming	yes	yes	no

Sources: Initiative and Referendum Institute, "Information on the Statewide Initiative Process in the United States," http://www.iandrinstitute.or/statewide_1&r.htm; American Society of Legislative Clerks and Secretaries, "Initiative, Referendum, and Recall: The Process," by Jennifer Drage, *Journal of the American Society of Legislative Clerks and Secretaries* 5, 2 (Winter 2000), available online at http://www.ncsl.org/prorams/legman/aslcs/drag00.htm. Accessed March 11, 2003.

any guide, it would have to be said that his proposal has not been an all-consuming passion. Mild interest was shown in the initiative during the 1970s when Congress held hearings on a proposal for a national initiative, but it was never reported out of committee. An organization known as the National Initiative for Democracy (see Chapter 6) continues to carry the torch for supporters of this reform.

Presidential Nominating Process

The presidential nominees in each of our two major political parties are chosen by national party conventions consisting of delegates from each of the fifty states and territories. State political parties have traditionally used one of three ways to pick their delegates—*caucus/convention, primary,* or *state party committee.* The caucus/convention method, of which Iowa is perhaps the most noteworthy example, involves rank-and-file party members assembling at the precinct level to select delegates to a county caucus; the county caucus then chooses delegates to attend a congressional district caucus, whose members then select delegates to the party's state convention, which in turn chooses the delegates to attend the national convention. It is important for candidates to turn out as many of their supporters as possible at the precinct level since the number of delegates chosen to go on to subsequent stages will reflect the number of supporters they have at this first stage.

The primary is the most widely used method for selecting national convention delegates. Democratic Party rules require that all primaries be proportional, meaning that the number of delegates presidential candidates receive from their state's party is proportional to the number of votes they won in the primary. The Republican Party, in contrast, leaves to each state the decision of how it will run its primary; thus, some Republican primaries are proportional, but a number are also run on a winner-take-all basis.

The third method for choosing delegates, the state party committee, allows for the least participation by rank-and-file members of the party, for the delegates are simply picked by the members of the party's state committee.

As can be seen in Table 5.3, some state parties use more than one method to pick their delegates. The New York and Washington Republican parties, for example, choose part of their state delegations by closed primary and part by state party committee. The Democratic Party in Texas does likewise.

These three methods of delegate selection underwent considerable change following the contentious 1968 Democratic National Convention, which pitted Vice President Hubert Humphrey against anti–Vietnam War candidate Eugene McCarthy (D-MN). The former did not enter a single primary whereas the latter entered nearly all of them, and yet Humphrey walked off with the nomination, receiving nearly three times as many delegate votes as McCarthy. The reason this could happen is because *most of the delegates to the convention at that time were chosen by either caucus/ convention or state party committee, both of which selection methods were controlled by the party bosses,* very few of whom supported McCarthy. Although primaries were not usually totally ignored by presidential candidates—though some did—they typically entered just a few and only to demonstrate their vote-getting ability to the party elites.

McCarthy supporters cried foul, arguing that their candidate had taken his case to the people in the primaries whereas Humphrey did not, and further, that the party bosses had in many instances rigged the caucus-convention selection process so as to prevent McCarthy supporters from being able to compete fairly. These charges led to the creation of the McGovern-Fraser Commission, which was charged with looking into delegate selection methods in all the states and, where appropriate, proposing changes. Although their proposals were many and varied,

TABLE 5.3
National Convention Delegate Selection Methods in the Fifty States

State	Methods of Selection	
	Republican	Democrat
Alabama	open primary	open primary
Alaska	caucus/convention	caucus/convention
Arizona	closed primary	closed primary
Arkansas	open primary	open primary
California	closed primary	closed primary
Colorado	open primary	open primary
Connecticut	open primary	closed primary
Delaware	caucus/convention	caucus/convention
Florida	closed primary	closed primary
Georgia	open primary	open primary
Hawaii	caucus/convention	caucus/convention
Idaho	open primary/state party committee	caucus/convention
Illinois	state party committee with nonbinding presidential preference poll	open primary
Indiana	open primary; state party committee	open primary
Iowa	caucus/convention	caucus/convention
Kansas	closed primary with Independents allowed	closed primary with Independents allowed
Kentucky	closed primary	closed primary
Louisiana	closed primary	closed primary
Maine	closed primary with Independents allowed	closed primary with Independents allowed
Maryland	closed primary with Independents allowed	closed primary
Massachusetts	closed primary with Independents alowed	closed primary with Independents allowed
Michigan	open primary	caucus/convention
Minnesota	caucus/convention	caucus/convention
Mississippi	open primary	open primary
Missouri	open primary	open primary
Montana	caucus/convention with nonbinding primary	open primary
Nebraska	caucus/convention with nonbinding primary	closed primary
Nevada	caucus/convention	caucus/convention
New Hampshire	closed primary with Independents allowed	closed primary with Independents allowed
New Jersey	open primary	closed primary with Independents allowed
New Mexico	closed primary	closed primary
New York	closed primary; state committee	closed primary
North Carolina	closed primary with Independents allowed	closed primary with Independents allowed
North Dakota	chosen by state committee	chosen by state party committee
Ohio	open primary	open primary
Oklahoma	closed primary	closed primary
Oregon	closed primary	closed primary
Pennsylvania	closed primary; state party committee	closed primary
Rhode Island	closed primary with Independents allowed	closed primary with Independents allowed
South Carolina	open primary	open primary

(continues)

TABLE 5.3
National Convention Delegate Selection Methods in the Fifty States *(continued)*

	Methods of Selection	
State	Republican	Democrat
South Dakota	closed primary	closed primary
Tennessee	open primary	open primary
Texas	open primary	open primary; state party committee
Utah	closed primary with Independents allowed	closed primary with Independents allowed
Vermont	open primary	open primary
Virginia	open primary	caucus/convention
Washington	closed primary	caucus/convention caucus/convention
West Virginia	open primary	closed primary
Wisconsin	open primary	open primary
Wyoming	caucus/	convention caucus/convention

Source: The Green Papers. "State-by-State Summary: 2004 Presidential Primaries, Caucuses, and Conventions."
Available online at http://www.thegreenpapers.com/P04/tally.phtml. Accessed March 30, 2004.

suffice it to say that their recommendations led to a significant reduction in the number of delegates who could be appointed by
state party committee—the reason being that this method provided no opportunity for voters to participate. Other significant
changes served to open up the caucus/convention method of delegate selection so that it could not be manipulated by the party
bosses within a state. The McGovern-Fraser Commission also required that state parties make every possible effort to insure that
groups that had for many years been grossly underrepresented
(women, blacks, and young people) in the pool of national convention delegates were now included in a state's delegation in
reasonable proportion to their numbers in that state.

Although some of these recommendations would be fine-
tuned over the next twenty-five years, the fact remains that they
served to revolutionize the presidential nominating process by
greatly reducing the influence of the party elites and opening it
up to more rank-and-file participation. The Republican Party incorporated a number of these changes into its party rules as well.

The McGovern-Fraser Commission never required that any
state select its delegates by primary, but after 1968 more and more
states began doing so, abandoning the caucus/convention selection method (see Table 5.4). The reasons for doing so varied. Some
states felt the complex McGovern-Fraser Commission reforms

could be implemented more easily in a primary than in a caucus/convention system. Others, no doubt perceiving the broad-based sentiment for greater participation in the nominating process, saw the primary as best able to meet that goal. Still others could not ignore the fact that primaries attract more media coverage than caucuses and thus provide a much bigger boost to a state's economy, since candidates must spend considerably more on a primary than on a caucus (DiClerico and Davis 2000, 22).

Regardless of the reasons for switching, the fact remains that what now amounts to a president-by-primary process has opened up the presidential nominating process to far greater numbers of participants than ever occurred prior to 1972. As Table 5.4 suggests, turnout in presidential primaries is typically not very high, but it far outdistances the number participating in the caucus/convention—the most common method of selecting delegates prior to 1972. It is instructive to compare turnout in eight states (Arizona, Kentucky, Michigan, Minnesota, Mississippi, Missouri, Oklahoma, and Texas) that switched from the caucus/convention to the primary method between 1984 and 1988. The total number of people participating in those states' caucuses in 1984 was 550,973, in contrast to the total turnout in their primaries in the following presidential election: 4,178,180—nearly 7.5 times greater (DiClerico and Davis 2000, 53).

TABLE 5.4
Number of Primaries and Number of Voters by Party, 1972–2000

Year	Democratic Party Number of Primaries	Republican Party Number of Primaries
1972	21	20
1976	27	26
1980	35	35
1984	30	25
1988	37	37
1992	40	39
1996	36	43
2000	39	42

Note: Only those primaries in which delegates are selected and bound by the primary results are included in the above counts.
Source: Adapted from Harold W. Stanley and Richard G. Niemi, *Vital Statistics on American Politics, 2001–2002* (Washington, DC: Congressional Quarterly Press, 2001), p. 64.

Voter Registration

Our democracy imposes three general tests as a condition for voting—*interest, competence,* and *social compliance* (Hyneman 1968, 66–71). The first is used to make certain that prospective voters have a stake in what it is they will be deciding. Thus, U.S. citizenry and residency are employed to insure that only those with a stake in an election will be voting in it. European citizens, for example, cannot vote for president or any elected office in the United States, residents of Ohio cannot vote for the governor of Michigan or vice versa, and those residing in Monongalia County, West Virginia, cannot vote for members of the county commission in Kanawha County, West Virginia, or vice versa; nor are the dead entitled to have a ballot cast on their behalf! A few states also deny the vote to paupers—those supported at the public expense—on the ground that they do not have a sufficient stake in the community.

A general test of competence is also imposed by the government to insure that the voting pool will possess a certain minimum level of knowledge regarding the electoral process. Thus, those under the age of eighteen are ineligible to vote as are, in most states, those in mental institutions.

Finally, most states, believing that voting is a privilege that comes with good citizenship, deny that privilege to those institutionalized for having failed to comply with the laws of the society—a denial that, following release from confinement, may continue for a specified period of time, or even permanently in some states (see Table 5.5).

Voter registration, established by all but one state (see Table 5.6) is intended to insure that the potential voting pool meets the tests of voter eligibility. The cutoff period to register ranges from a high of thirty days in some states to a low of election day itself, on which those going to the polls may register right before voting. On the ground that election interest is likely to increase as one moves closer and closer to election day, some have argued that allowing citizens to register up until a week before election day, and even better, on election day, would have a salutary effect upon voter turnout (Wolfinger and Rosenstone 1980, 77, 78; Patterson 2002, 178). This view receives further reinforcement from the state turnout figures in the 2000 presidential election. More specifically, the two states (Minnesota and Wisconsin) with the highest turnout allowed election-day registration (see Table 5.6).

TABLE 5.5
Felony Disenfranchisement Laws by State

State	Law
Alabama	Must not have been convicted of a felony punishable by imprisonment in the penitentiary (or must have had civil and political rights restored)
Alaska	Must not be a convicted felon (unless unconditionally discharged)
Arizona	Must not have been convicted of treason or a felony (or must have had civil rights restored)
Arkansas	Must not be a convicted felon (or must have completely discharged sentence or been pardoned)
California	Must not be imprisoned or on parole for the conviction of a felony
Colorado	Must not be confined as a prisoner or serving any part of a sentence under mandate
Connecticut	Must have completed confinement and parole if previously convicted of a felony, and have had voting rights restored by registrars of voters
Delaware	Felons are eligible if fines and sentences are completed at least five years prior to application date and felony convictions were not one of the disqualifying felonies (murder, sexual offenses, or crimes against public administration involving bribery or improper influence or abuse of office)
Florida	Must not have been convicted of a felony without civil rights having been restored pursuant to law
Georgia	Must not be serving a sentence for having been convicted of a felony
Hawaii	Must not be incarcerated for a felony conviction
Idaho	Must not have been convicted of a felony, and without having been restored to the rights of citizenship, or confined in prison on conviction of a criminal offense
Illinois	Must not currently be in jail for a criminal conviction
Indiana	Must not currently be in jail for a criminal conviction
Iowa	Must not have been convicted of a felony (or must have had rights restored)
Kansas	Must have completed the terms of sentence if convicted of a felony; a person serving a sentence for a felony conviction is ineligible to vote
Kentucky	Must not be convicted of a felony, or if convicted of a felony, civil rights must have been restored by executive pardon
Louisiana	Must not currently be under an order of imprisonment for conviction of a felony
Maine	No requirement regarding felony disenfranchisement
Maryland	Must not be under sentence or on probation following conviction for an infamous crime (this includes a felony, treason, perjury, or any other crime involving an element of deceit, fraud, or corruption) and must not have been convicted more than once of an infamous crime without a pardon
Massachusetts	Must not currently be incarcerated for a felony conviction
Michigan	Must not be confined in a jail after being convicted and sentenced
Minnesota	Must not be convicted of treason or a felony (or must have had civil rights restored)
Mississippi	Must not have been convicted of murder, rape, bribery, theft, arson, obtaining money or goods under false pretense, perjury, forgery, embezzlement, or bigamy; or must have had rights restored as required by law
Missouri	Must not be on probation or parole after conviction of a felony, until finally discharged from such probation or parole, and must not have been convicted of a felony or misdemeanor connected with the right of suffrage
Montana	Must not be in a penal institution for a felony conviction
Nebraska	Must not have been convicted of a felony (or must have had civil rights restored)

(continues)

TABLE 5.5
Felony Disenfranchisement Laws by State *(continued)*

State	Law
Nevada	Must not currently be laboring under any felony conviction
New Hampshire	Must not have been denied the right to vote by reason of a felony conviction
New Jersey	Must not be serving a sentence or on parole or probation as the result of a conviction of any indictable offense under the laws of this or another state or of the United States
New Mexico	If convicted of a felony, must have completed all condition of probation or parole, served the entirety of the sentence, or have been granted a pardon by the governor
New York	Must not be in jail or on parole for a felony conviction
North Carolina	Must have rights of citizenship restored if convicted of a felony
North Dakota	No voter registration
Ohio	Must not be convicted of a felony and currently incarcerated
Oklahoma	Must not have been convicted of a felony, for which a period of time equal to the original sentence has not expired, or for which the voter has not been pardoned
Oregon	No requirement regarding felony disenfranchisement
Pennsylvania	No requirement regarding felony disenfranchisement
Rhode Island	Must not be serving a sentence, including probation or parole, for which the voter was imprisoned, upon final conviction of a felony imposed on any date; and must not be serving a sentence, whether incarcerated or suspended, on probation or parole, upon final conviction of a felony committed after November 5, 1986
South Carolina	Must not have been convicted of a felony or offense against election laws, or if previously convicted, must have served entire sentence, including probation or parole, or have received a pardon for conviction
South Dakota	Must not be under sentence of imprisonment for a felony conviction
Tennessee	Must not have been convicted of a felony, or if convicted, have had full rights of citizenship restored or received a pardon
Texas	Must not be finally convicted of a felony (felons regain the right to register when pardoned, after receiving a certificate of discharge from the appropriate correction institution, or after completing a period of probation)
Utah	Must not be a convicted felon currently incarcerated for commission of a felony
Vermont	No requirement regarding felony disenfranchisement
Virginia	Must not have been convicted of a felony (or must have had civil rights restored)
Washington	Must not be convicted of infamous crime, unless restored to civil rights
West Virginia	Must not be under conviction, probation, or parole for a felony, treason, or election bribery
Wisconsin	Must not have been convicted of treason, felony, or bribery (or must have had civil rights restored)
Wyoming	Must not be convicted of a felony (or must have had rights restored by a competent authority)

Source: Federal Election Commission, State Voter Registration Requirements, http://www.fec.gov.votregis/state reg requirements02.htm. Accessed March 11, 2003.

As noted earlier, all but a few states deny the vote to individuals serving in prison; a majority extend that denial to include the period during which an individual is on probation or parole; and over ten states make the denial permanent, unless an individual is pardoned or has his or her civil rights restored by the

TABLE 5.6
Deadlines for Voter Registration in the Fifty States

State	Closing Date for Registration before General Election (in days)
Alabama	10
Alaska	30
Arizona	29
Arkansas	30
California	15
Colorado	29
Connecticut	14
Delaware	20
Florida	29
Georgia	5th Monday before general election
Hawaii	30
Idaho	Election Day
Illinois	28
Indiana	29
Iowa	10
Kansas	15
Kentucky	29
Louisiana	30
Maine	Election Day
Maryland	21
Massachusetts	20
Michigan	30
Minnesota	Election Day
Mississippi	30
Missouri	28
Montana	30
Nebraska	Received 2nd Friday before election or postmarked by 3rd Friday before election
Nevada	By 9:00 p.m. on 5th Saturday preceding any election
New Hampshire	Election Day
New Jersey	29
New Mexico	28
New York	25
North Carolina	25
North Dakota	No voter registration
Ohio	30
Oklahoma	24
Oregon	21
Pennsylvania	30
Rhode Island	30
South Carolina	30
South Dakota	15
Tennessee	30
Texas	30

(continues)

TABLE 5.6
Deadlines for Voter Registration in the Fifty States (continued)

State	Closing Date for Registration before General Election (in days)
Utah	8
Vermont	By noon on 2nd Saturday before election
Virginia	28
Washington	15
West Virginia	30
Wisconsin	Election Day
Wyoming	Election Day

Source: The Book of the States: 2002 Edition, vol. 34 (Lexington, KY: Council of State Governments, 2002), pp. 261–262.

governor or some other authority—a process that is typically lengthy and difficult (see Table 5.5).

The number of convicted felons has been growing steadily in this country. Indeed, the United States now has a greater percentage of its population incarcerated than any other country in the world—a number that, according to one recent study, has been a key factor in helping to explain the declines in voting turnout since 1972 (McDonald and Popkin 2001, 963–971). These prohibitions against voting have fallen particularly hard on the black population, as reported by the Sentencing Project, which found that of the 10.6 million black males living in the United States in 1997, 1.46 million had lost the right to vote. Of these, 950,000 were ineligible because they were in prison, and 510,000 were permanently barred after having returned to society and become in all other respects fully functioning citizens (Butterfield 1997). In the 1998 midterm elections more than 20 percent of the black male population was barred from voting (Suro 1998). The number of blacks in prison, moreover, has been rising steadily, reaching its highest rate in 2003 with an estimated 12 percent of the African American male population between the ages of twenty and thirty-four behind bars (Butterfield 2003).

Although a good case can be made for denial of the right to vote during incarceration and even during the period of parole or probation, one can certainly question the fairness of barring from the ballot box those who have paid their penalty and have been returned to society, where they are required to bear all the burdens and responsibilities of citizenship, while continuing to be denied one of its greatest privileges. One convicted felon who had been imprisoned in New York, was released, and while living in Florida, made the point well: "I've been in this community for five years. I'm a taxpayer. I help mold this community through my work. The sheriff is a friend of mine. But voting is the power by which you truly shape and mold, and I'm being denied that. I watch my sons see me stay home when my wife goes off to vote. I'm appalled by it" (Twohey 2001, 46).

Voting, Not Voting

As noted in Chapter 2, a great many political observers bemoan the overall downward trend in voting turnout since 1960 (see Tables 5.7–5.9), arguing that the millions upon millions who stay away from the polls is an indicator of their sense of disconnectedness from the political process. Others, meanwhile, contend (1) that the situation is not as bleak as it appears, for the way voting turnout is calculated by the government artificially deflates the turnout figures; (2) that while a sense of alienation from the political system may be regrettable, it is not a significant factor in determining whether people decide to vote; and (3) that election outcomes would not, in any event, have turned out differently had the nonvoters voted.

In perusing the reasons people give for why they did not vote (see Table 5.10) three stand out from the others. Nearly 15

TABLE 5.7
Voting Turnout in Presidential Elections, 1924–2000

Year	Turnout (%)	Year	Turnout (%)
1924	48.9	1964	61.9
1928	51.8	1968	60.9
1932	52.6	1972	55.2
1936	56.8	1976	53.5
1940	58.8	1980	52.6
1944	56.1	1984	53.1
1948	51.1	1988	50.1
1952	61.6	1992	55.2
1956	59.4	1996	49.0
1960	62.8	2000	51.0

Source: Center for Voting and Democracy, http://www.fairvote.org/turnout/preturn.htm. Accessed March 11, 2003.

TABLE 5.8
Comparison of Voters and Nonvoters by Election Years, 1924–2000

Year	Voters	Nonvoters*	Year	Voters	Nonvoters*
1924	29,091,417	37,322,583	1964	70,645,000	43,445,000
1928	36,879,424	34,305,586	1968	73,212,000	47,073,000
1932	39,732,000	36,036,000	1972	77,625,000	62,443,000
1936	45,643,000	34,531,000	1976	81,603,000	68,524,000
1940	49,900,000	34,828,000	1980	86,515,221	76,245,779
1944	47,977,000	37,677,000	1984	92,652,793	81,283,207
1948	48,794,000	46,779,000	1988	91,595,000	91,033,000
1952	61,551,000	38,378,000	1992	105,867,768	83,176,232
1956	62,027,000	42,488,000	1996	92,712,803	103,798,197
1960	68,838,000	40,834,000	2000	105,404,546	108,549,477

*Based upon estimated voting-age population.
Sources: International Institute for Democracy and Electoral Assistance, *United States Voter Turnout from 1945 to Date*, http://www.idea.int/vtcountry_view.cfm; *Presidential Elections since 1789* (Washington, DC: Congressional Quarterly Inc., 1991), p. 97; Committee for the Study of the American Electorate, Press Release on Voter Turnout, June 18, 2000, http://www.gspm.org/csae.html. Accessed on March 11, 2003.

percent note that it was due to illness, disability, or a family emergency. There is probably no quick-fix solution for those in this category. Assuming absentee voting was not an option, being able to vote at home via the Internet might have helped some individuals, but such a system, free from the potential for corruption, is presently not available. Anywhere from 12 to 16 percent of the nonvoters decided to stay home because they did not think their vote would make a difference. Whether some of these people thought the 1996 and 2000 elections in particular were already decided, and thus their vote would not matter, or whether they have simply concluded that voting in any election does not matter very much, these individuals would also appear to be beyond the reach of any immediate change that might turn them around.

The biggest reason given for not voting—fully 20 percent— was that people were simply too busy, had schedule conflicts, or were unable to get time off from work. These reasons, to be sure, have the flavor of "boilerplate" excuses many of us have given at one time or another for not doing something we should have done, but if we assume that they were in fact legitimate deterrents to voting, these obstacles would seem to be a problem that could be addressed. It has been proposed, for example, that the

TABLE 5.9
Turnout as a Percentage of Voting-Age Population in Each State, 1960–2000

State	'60	'64	'68	'72	'76	'80	'84	'88	'92	'96	'00	Average
AL	30.8	36.0	52.7	43.3	46.3	48.7	49.9	45.8	52.2	47.7	50.0	46.0
AK	43.7	44.0	50.0	46.9	48.1	57.2	59.3	55.7	63.8	56.9	66.4	53.8
AZ	52.4	54.8	49.9	47.4	46.1	44.4	46.1	46.1	52.9	44.7	42.3	47.9
AR	40.9	50.6	54.2	48.1	51.1	51.5	51.8	47.3	53.6	47.2	47.8	49.5
CA	65.8	65.4	61.6	59.5	50.0	48.9	49.6	47.1	49.4	43.9	44.1	53.2
CO	69.7	68.0	64.8	59.5	58.8	55.8	55.1	67.6	60.8	52.8	56.8	60.9
CT	76.1	70.7	68.8	66.2	62.8	61.0	61.0	58.3	64.5	56.2	58.4	64.0
DE	72.3	68.9	68.3	62.1	57.2	54.6	55.5	50.2	55.6	49.4	56.3	59.1
FL	48.6	51.2	53.1	48.6	49.2	48.7	48.3	44.7	51.0	48.0	50.6	49.3
GA	29.3	43.3	43.9	37.3	42.0	41.3	42.1	39.4	46.2	42.4	43.8	41.0
HI	49.8	51.3	53.8	49.4	46.7	43.5	44.3	43.0	41.9	40.5	40.5	45.9
ID	79.7	77.2	73.3	63.3	60.7	67.7	59.9	58.3	65.2	57.1	54.5	65.2
IL	75.5	73.2	69.3	62.3	59.4	57.7	57.1	53.3	58.9	49.3	52.8	60.8
IN	76.3	73.5	69.8	60.0	60.1	57.6	55.9	53.3	55.2	48.8	49.0	60.0
IA	76.5	72.9	69.8	64.0	63.1	62.8	62.3	59.3	65.3	57.7	60.7	64.9
KS	69.6	65.1	64.8	48.0	58.8	56.6	56.8	54.3	63.0	56.1	54.1	58.8
KY	57.7	53.3	51.2	48.0	48.0	49.9	50.8	48.2	53.7	47.4	51.6	50.9
LA	44.6	47.3	54.8	44.0	48.7	53.1	54.6	51.3	59.8	57.0	54.2	51.8
ME	71.7	65.1	66.4	60.3	63.7	64.5	64.8	62.2	72.0	71.9	67.3	66.4
MD	56.5	54.1	54.4	49.8	49.3	50.0	51.4	49.0	53.6	46.6	51.6	51.5
MA	75.6	70.0	67.4	62.0	61.7	59.0	57.6	58.1	60.2	55.0	57.6	62.2
MI	72.2	67.9	65.7	59.4	58.8	60.0	57.9	54.0	61.7	54.4	57.5	60.9
MN	76.4	75.8	73.8	68.7	71.5	70.0	68.2	66.3	71.6	64.1	68.8	70.5
MS	25.3	33.9	53.3	44.2	48.0	51.8	52.2	49.9	52.8	45.4	48.6	45.9
MO	71.5	67.1	64.3	57.3	57.3	58.7	57.3	54.8	62.0	54.0	57.5	60.2
MT	70.3	69.3	68.1	67.6	63.3	65.0	65.0	62.4	70.1	62.1	61.5	65.9
NE	70.6	66.5	60.9	56.4	56.2	56.6	55.6	56.7	63.2	55.9	56.5	59.6
NV	58.3	52.1	54.3	49.5	44.2	41.2	41.5	44.9	50.0	38.3	43.8	47.1
NH	78.7	72.4	69.6	63.6	57.3	57.1	53.0	54.8	63.1	57.3	62.5	62.7
NJ	70.8	68.8	66.0	50.8	57.8	54.9	56.6	52.2	56.3	51.0	51.0	58.7
NM	61.7	62.0	60.7	57.7	53.4	50.8	51.3	47.4	51.6	45.4	47.4	53.6
NY	66.5	63.3	59.3	56.4	50.7	48.0	51.2	48.1	50.9	47.5	50.4	53.8
NC	52.9	52.3	54.4	42.8	43.0	43.4	47.4	43.4	50.1	45.6	50.3	47.8
ND	78.0	72.0	70.0	68.3	67.2	64.6	62.7	61.5	67.3	56.0	60.0	66.2
OH	70.7	66.6	63.3	57.3	55.1	55.3	58.0	55.1	60.6	54.3	55.8	59.3
OK	63.1	63.4	61.2	56.7	54.9	52.1	52.2	48.7	59.7	49.7	48.8	55.5
OR	72.0	68.9	66.6	62.1	61.3	61.3	61.8	58.6	65.7	57.1	60.6	63.3
PA	70.3	67.9	65.3	56.0	54.2	51.9	54.0	50.1	54.2	49.0	53.7	57.0
RI	75.1	71.6	67.2	61.0	59.7	58.6	55.9	53.0	58.4	52.0	54.3	60.6
SC	30.4	39.4	46.8	38.3	40.3	40.4	40.7	38.9	45.0	41.6	46.6	40.8
SD	77.6	74.2	73.2	69.4	64.1	67.2	62.6	61.5	67.0	60.5	58.2	66.9
TN	49.9	51.7	53.7	43.5	48.7	48.7	49.1	44.7	52.4	46.9	49.2	49.0
TX	41.2	44.6	48.7	45.0	46.3	44.8	47.2	44.2	49.1	41.3	43.1	45.0

(continues)

TABLE 5.9
Turnout as a Percentage of Voting-Age Population in Each State, 1960–2000 *(continued)*

State	'60	'64	'68	'72	'76	'80	'84	'88	'92	'96	'00	Average
UT	78.2	78.4	76.7	69.4	68.4	64.6	61.6	60.0	65.2	49.9	52.6	65.9
VT	72.4	70.3	64.1	60.7	55.7	57.7	59.8	59.1	67.5	58.1	64.0	62.7
VA	32.8	41.1	50.1	44.7	47.0	47.5	50.0	48.2	52.8	47.5	53.0	46.9
WA	71.9	71.8	66.0	63.1	59.8	57.3	58.4	54.6	59.9	54.8	56.9	61.3
WV	77.9	75.5	71.1	62.5	57.2	52.7	51.7	46.7	50.7	44.9	45.8	57.9
WI	72.9	69.5	66.5	62.5	66.5	67.4	63.5	62.0	69.0	57.4	66.1	65.8
WY	73.3	74.3	67.0	64.4	58.6	53.2	53.4	50.3	62.3	59.4	59.7	61.4

Source: Federal Election Commission, "Voter Registration and Turnout Statistics," www.fec.gov/elections.html. Accessed April 2, 2003.

TABLE 5.10
Reasons for Not Voting, 1996 and 2000

Reasons	1996 (percent of registered nonvoters)	2000 (percent of registered nonvoters)
Illness, disability, or emergency (own or family's)	14.9	14.8
Out of town or away from home	11.1	10.2
Forgot to vote (or send in absentee ballot)	4.4	4.0
Not interested (felt vote would not make a difference)	16.6	12.2
Too busy/conflicting schedule/no time off	21.5	20.9
Transportation problems/no transportation	4.3	2.4
Did not like candidates or campaign issues	13.0	7.7
Registration problems	0.0	6.9
Bad weather conditions	0.0	0.6
Inconvenient polling place or hours or lines too long	1.2	2.6
Other reasons, not specified	10.3	10.2
Refused or don't know	2.7	7.5

References: United States Census Bureau, Current Population Survey, *Voting and Registration in the Election of November 1996* (P20-504), p. 3, http://www.census.gov/prod/3/98pubs/p.20-504.pdf. Accessed on March 10, 2003; United States Census Bureau, Current Population Survey, *Voting and Registration in the Election of November 2000* (P20-542), p. 10, http://www/census.gov/prod/2002pubs/p20-542.pdf. Accessed on March 10, 2003.

United States, like a number of Western democracies, make election day a national holiday, or else allow voting to occur over a twenty-four-hour period, or on a Sunday. These proposals, to be sure, also have their detractors, who claim that all of them would be expensive, and a national holiday might actually serve to depress turnout further by encouraging people to travel or take a brief vacation (Teixeira 1992, 143).

Voting innovations in two states provide perhaps more viable ways of accommodating the polling place to people's busy schedules (see Table 5.11). Since 1991, voters in Texas have not only been able to cast their ballots at polling locations on election day, but also any time between seventeen and four days prior to the day of the election. In the 1992 presidential election, 25 percent of the Texas ballots were cast before election day, and, significantly, turnout was higher in those counties with a higher proportion of these early voters (Maisel 2002, 109).

The state of Oregon has experimented for a number of years with mail ballots and for the first time in the 2000 presidential election dispensed with polling places and used only mail ballots. It achieved a hefty 75.45 percent turnout (*Washington Post* 2002, A35).

Some political observers, however, are not so sanguine about the desirability of early voting—be it mail ballot or absentee voting—believing that it denies voters the opportunity to factor into their decision important information and events that may become known just before election day. Also lost, it is argued, is the sense of voting as a communal act, where voters travel to a designated place and converse with polling place personnel and probably other voters as well (Nagourney 2002). Nor, according to Curtis Gans, one of the leading authorities on voter participation, does early voting do much to increase turnout: "People who vote earlier and get no-excuse absentee ballots are essentially people who already vote. All my research says this hurts turnout efforts. You are defusing mobilization efforts. You have to spread them out over a 35-day period" (quoted in the *New York Times* 2002, A14). Most important, perhaps, there is no guarantee that a ballot cast by mail is being filled out by the individual for whom it is intended, and without coercion—problems that do not arise in the privacy of the voting booth on election day (Teixeira 1992, 144; Ceaser and Busch 2001, 246, 247; Ornstein 2001, A25).

One of the advantages of our federal system is that states have the opportunity to experiment in a whole range of areas, including the conduct of elections. Over time, the benefits and liabilities of various forms of early voting will no doubt become apparent, leaving other states to decide whether to take them on board or search for other alternatives.

TABLE 5.11
Polling Hours in the Fifty States

State	Polls Open	Polls Close
Alabama	No later than 8:00 a.m.	Between 6 and 8 p.m.
Alaska	7 a.m.	8 p.m.
Arizona	6 a.m.	7 p.m.
Arkansas	7:30 a.m.	7:30 p.m.
California	7 a.m.	8 p.m.
Colorado	7 a.m.	7 p.m.
Connecticut	6 a.m.	8 p.m.
Delaware	7 a.m.	8 p.m.
Florida	7 a.m.	7 p.m.
Georgia	7 a.m.	7 p.m./8 p.m.
Hawaii	7 a.m.	6 p.m.
Idaho	Between 7 and 8 a.m.	8 p.m.
Illinois	6 a.m.	7 p.m.
Indiana	6 a.m.	6 p.m.
Iowa	7 a.m./12 p.m.	9 p.m.
Kansas	Between 6 and 7 a.m.	Between 7 and 8 p.m.
Kentucky	6 a.m.	6 p.m.
Louisiana	6 a.m.	8 p.m.
Maine	Between 6 and 9 a.m./10 a.m.	8 p.m.
Maryland	7 a.m.	8 p.m.
Massachusetts	No later than 7 a.m.	8 p.m.
Michigan	7 a.m.	8 p.m.
Minnesota	7 a.m./10 a.m.	8 p.m.
Mississippi	7 a.m.	7 p.m.
Missouri	6 a.m.	7 p.m.
Montana	7 a.m./12 p.m.	8 p.m.
Nebraska	7 a.m. MST/8 a.m. CST	7 p.m. MST/8 p.m. CST
Nevada	7 a.m.	7 p.m.
New Hampshire	No later than 11 a.m.	No earlier than 7 p.m.
New Jersey	7 a.m.	8 p.m.
New Mexico	7 a.m.	7 p.m.
New York	6 a.m.	9 p.m.
North Carolina	6:30 a.m.	7:30 p.m.
North Dakota	Between 7 and 9 a.m./12 p.m.	Between 7 and 9 p.m.
Ohio	6:30 a.m.	7:30 p.m.
Oklahoma	7 a.m.	7 p.m.
Oregon	7 a.m.	8 p.m.
Pennsylvania	7 a.m.	8 p.m.
Rhode Island	Between 6 and 9 a.m.	9 p.m.
South Carolina	7 a.m.	7 p.m.
South Dakota	7 a.m.	7 p.m.
Tennessee	No later than 9 a.m. CST/10 a.m. EST	7 p.m. CST/8 p.m. EST
Texas	7 a.m.	7 p.m.

(continues)

TABLE 5.11
Polling Hours in the Fifty States *(continued)*

State	Polls Open	Polls Close
Utah	7 a.m.	8 p.m.
Virginia	6 a.m.	7 p.m.
Vermont	Between 6 and 10 a.m.	7 p.m.
Washington	7 a.m.	8 p.m.
West Virginia	6:30 a.m.	7:30 p.m.
Wisconsin	7 a.m./9 a.m.	8 p.m.
Wyoming	7 a.m.	7 p.m.

Source: The Book of the States: 2002 Edition, vol. 34 (Lexington, KY: Council of State Governments, 2002), p. 260.

Casting and Counting the Votes

The 2000 election controversy in Florida served to highlight the flawed voting equipment in some of its counties, as reports came in of unmarked ballots, uncounted ballots, spoiled ballots, and the famous "hanging chads." Although the balloting problems in this state captured nearly all of the national attention—not surprising since the outcome there was to determine the winner of the election—a number of other states (e.g., Georgia, Idaho, Illinois, South Carolina, and Wyoming) and cities (Chicago, New York) had ballot problems that were even more severe than those uncovered in Florida (Caltech/MIT 2001, 17).

According to a joint study of equipment employed nationwide to cast and count votes, "two of every one hundred ballots cast in the last four presidential elections registered no presidential vote. That rate is double in Senate and gubernatorial elections. Analysis of exit polls suggests that seventy percent of these uncounted votes are unintentional. In other words, approximately 1.5 million votes for president were 'cast' but not recorded or counted in 2000. Approximately 2.5 million votes for Senate and governor were 'cast' but not recorded over the last cycle" (Caltech/MIT 2001, 17).

The major offenders in producing uncounted votes (presidential, Senate, and gubernatorial) are the punch card (responsible for the notorious "hanging chads" in Florida 2000) and mechanical lever machines, both used by roughly 25 percent of all the counties in the United States as of November 2002 (see Table 5.12). In contrast, the same study found the paper ballot, and particularly the optical scan equipment, to be the most reliable, with the electronic (touch screen) voting machines finishing in the middle of the pack (Caltech/MIT 2001, 21). Another study, using data from over 2,200 counties in the 2000 election, likewise concluded that punchcard systems are the most error-prone, and optical scan the least so, but it also gave a much higher rating to electronic voting devices than did the earlier study (Brady 2002).

Defenders of electronic voting machines and mechanical levers argue, moreover, that they free election personnel from the time and expense of having to manage all the paper associated with paper ballot and optical scan systems. But those less enthused about electronic and mechanical lever machines make an even more telling point, noting that they "do not provide a separate record of the voter's intent apart from that captured by the machines. Election officials can only record what the machines record, so it is impossible to conduct a thorough audit of the election" (Brady 2002, 19).

That the voting equipment of the world's most advanced democracy falls well short of what one would expect is not wholly surprising, for nearly all states have delegated to local governments the responsibility for administering and paying for elections. For local officials with limited budgets, updating voting equipment is decidedly less sexy than responding to the more palpable complaints about trash collection, road repair, and police protection. The electoral misfirings in Florida 2000, however, served to concentrate the minds of elected officials on the need to take corrective action. Accordingly, in 2002 President George W.

TABLE 5.12
Voting Methods Used in the Fifty States, by County

Type of Voting Equipment Used	Number of Counties	Percent of Counties
Punch Card	460	14.73
Datavote	24	0.77
Lever Machine	330	10.57
Paper Ballots	328	10.50
Optical Scan	1,343	43.00
Electronic	510	16.33
Mixed (more than one system)	128	4.10

Source: Election Data Services Inc., "Voting Equipment Report: November 2002," http://www.electiondataservices.com/content/votingequipment.htm. Accessed on April 2, 2003.

Bush signed into law the Help America Vote Act, authorizing $3.9 billion to assist states in meeting new national standards with respect to voting, including the updating of voting equipment.

Although that effort is proceeding apace, it has not been without problems. Some jurisdictions have complained the new high-tech electronic terminals have lost votes, and a petition signed by more than three hundred computer scientists claims that many of these new machines are susceptible to tampering (voters can vote more than once; poll workers can alter ballots) and computer malfunctions (Keating 2003; Schwartz 2003).

Election Outcomes and the Electoral College

One of the most striking features of the 2000 presidential election was that it was so close in both the popular and electoral votes. Only two twentieth-century elections (1960, 1968) were closer in the popular vote, and none was as close in the electoral vote (see Table 5.13). Indeed, one has to go all the way back to the election of 1876 to find a closer Electoral College contest, one in which the presidential contenders were separated by only one electoral vote.

What will always remain most striking about the 2000 election, however, is that the candidate with fewer popular votes than his opponent was elected president. What decided the election was the 537-vote margin Bush had over Gore in the state of Florida—thereby giving him all of that state's twenty-five electoral votes and a narrow win in the Electoral College—rather than Gore's 539,898-vote margin over Bush in the national popular vote. As Table 5.14 indicates, however, this is not the first time that the Electoral College has visited such an outcome upon the nation. In 1824, no presidential candidate achieved a majority of the electoral vote, and thus the election was forced into the House of Representatives, which proceeded to select John Quincy Adams. It did so, mind you, even though his Democratic-Republican opponent (Andrew Jackson) had received 37,000 more popular votes and fifteen more electoral votes than Adams. In the election of 1876, Republican Rutherford B. Hayes defeated Democrat William Tilden by one vote in the Electoral College, though the latter had bested Hayes in the popular vote by a 254,235-vote margin. Twelve years later, Republican Benjamin Harrison won a comfortable Electoral College victory over the Democrat, Grover Cleveland, but he trailed him in the popular vote by a margin of 90,596 votes.

TABLE 5.13
Electoral and Popular Votes Received by Major Presidential Candidates, 1789–2000

Year	Party	Electoral Votes	Popular Votes	Party	Electoral Votes	Popular Votes
1789	Federalist	69				
1792	Federalist	132				
1796	Federalist	71		Democratic-Republican	68	
1800	Federalist	65		Democratic-Republican	73	
1804	Federalist	14		Democratic-Republican	162	
1808	Federalist	47		Democratic-Republican	122	
1812	Federalist	89		Democratic-Republican	128	
1816	Federalist	34		Democratic-Republican	183	
1820	Independent Democratic-Republican	1		Democratic-Republican	231	
1824	Independent Democratic-Republican	84		Democratic-Republican	99	
1828	National Republican	83	500,897	Democratic-Republican	178	642,553
1832	National Republican	49	484,205	Democratic-Republican	219	701,780
1836	Whig	73	550,816	Democratic	170	764,176
1840	Whig	234	1,275,390	Democratic	60	1,128,854
1844	Whig	105	1,300,004	Democratic	170	1,339,494
1848	Whig	163	1,361,393	Democratic	127	1,223,460
1852	Whig	42	1,386,942	Democratic	254	1,607,510
1856	Republican	114	1,342,345	Democratic	174	1,836,072
1860	Republican	180	1,865,908	Democratic	12	1,380,202
1864	Republican	212	2,218,388	Democratic	21	1,812,807
1868	Republican	214	3,013,650	Democratic	80	2,708,744
1872	Republican	286	3,598,235	Democratic	63	2,834,761
1876	Republican	185	4,034,311	Democratic	184	4,288,546
1880	Republican	214	4,446,158	Democratic	155	4,444,260
1884	Republican	182	4,848,936	Democratic	219	4,874,621
1888	Republican	233	5,443,892	Democratic	168	5,534,488
1892	Republican	145	5,179,244	Democratic	277	5,551,883
1896	Republican	271	7,108,480	Democratic	176	6,511,495
1900	Republican	292	7,218,039	Democratic	155	6,358,345
1904	Republican	336	7,626,593	Democratic	140	5,028,898
1908	Republican	321	7,676,258	Democratic	162	6,406,801
1912	Republican	8	3,486,333	Democratic	435	6,293,152
1916	Republican	254	8,546,789	Democratic	277	9,126,300
1920	Republican	404	16,133,314	Democratic	127	9,140,884
1924	Republican	382	15,717,553	Democratic	136	8,386,169
1928	Republican	444	21,411,991	Democratic	87	15,000,185
1932	Republican	59	15,758,397	Democratic	472	22,825,016
1936	Republican	8	16,679,543	Democratic	523	27,747,636
1940	Republican	82	22,336,260	Democratic	449	27,263,448
1944	Republican	99	22,013,372	Democratic	432	25,611,936

(continues)

TABLE 5.13

Electoral and Popular Votes Received by Major Presidential Candidates, 1789–2000 *(continued)*

Year	Party	Electoral Votes	Popular Votes	Party	Electoral Votes	Popular Votes
1948	Republican	189	21,970,017	Democratic	303	24,105,587
1952	Republican	442	33,936,137	Democratic	89	27,314,649
1956	Republican	457	35,585,245	Democratic	73	26,030,172
1960	Republican	219	34,106,671	Democratic	303	34,221,344
1964	Republican	52	27,177,838	Democratic	486	43,126,584
1968	Republican	301	31,785,148	Democratic	191	31,274,503
1972	Republican	520	47,170,179	Democratic	17	29,171,791
1976	Republican	240	39,147,793	Democratic	297	40,830,763
1980	Republican	489	43,904,153	Democratic	49	35,483,883
1984	Republican	525	54,455,075	Democratic	13	37,577,185
1988	Republican	426	48,886,097	Democratic	111	41,809,074
1992	Republican	168	39,103,882	Democratic	370	44,909,326
1996	Republican	159	39,197,350	Democratic	379	47,401,054
2000	Republican	271	50,456,141	Democratic	266	50,996,039

Source: Internet Public Library. "POTUS, Presidents of the United States." Available online at http://www.ipl.org/div/potus. Accessed March 30, 2004.

Defenders of the current system argue with some justification that these four election misfirings overstate the case against the Electoral College. They insist that only the elections of 1888 and 2000 constitute clear instances of a president being elected with a minority of the popular vote. The election of 1824 does not qualify because at the time only six of the twenty-four states were choosing their electors by popular vote, and thus there is no way of knowing what the national sentiment was for either candidate. Nor does the Tilden/Hayes contest of 1876 fit the bill, because there was so much vote fraud on both sides that a true vote count is impossible to determine.

That there have been only two clear misfirings in fifty-two contested presidential elections suggests to some that such a possibility is worth putting up with when judged against the other strengths of the Electoral College. One of the most important of these, according to supporters, is that the winner-take-all system of awarding electoral votes (used in all but two states) serves to convert narrow popular vote victories into decisive Electoral College victories (see Table 5.15), thereby providing victors with a mandate to govern that would otherwise have eluded them (Ornstein 2001, 12–16; Best 1971, ch. 6). As one po-

TABLE 5.14
Electoral College Anomalies, 1789–2000

Election Anomaly Year	
1800	The House chose Democratic-Republican Thomas Jefferson as the new president after there was a tie in the Electoral College between Jefferson and vice-presidential candidate Democratic-Republican Aaron Burr. This decision led to the creation and ratification of the Twelfth Amendment to the Constitution, which requires separate votes in the Electoral College for president and vice president.
1824	The House chose Democratic-Republican John Quincy Adams as the new president after no candidate had received a majority in the Electoral College, and despite the fact that his opponent (Andrew Jackson) had received 37,000 more popular votes and fifteen more electoral votes than Adams.
1836	The Whigs ran different presidential candidates in different parts of the country. Each candidate would capture electoral votes for the Whigs in the region where he was strongest. The Whig electors would then combine on one candidate or throw the election into the House, whichever seemed to their advantage. The scheme did not work because Martin Van Buren, the Democratic nominee, captured a majority of the electoral vote.
1836	The Senate chose Democrat Richard M. Johnson as vice president after no vice presidential candidate had achieved a majority in the Electoral College.
1872	The Democratic presidential nominee, Horace Greeley, died between the time of the popular vote and the meeting of the presidential electors. The Democratic electors had no party nominee to vote for, and each was left to his own judgment. Forty-two of the sixty-six Democratic electors chose to vote for the Democratic governor-elect of Indiana, Thomas Hendricks. The rest of the electors split their votes among three other politicians: eighteen for B. Gratz Brown of Missouri, the Democratic vice presidential nominee; two for Charles J. Jenkins of Georgia; and one for David Davis of Illinois. Three Georgia electors insisted on casting their votes for Greeley, but Congress refused to count them. (Republican Ulysses S. Grant was reelected president that year.)
1876	The Electoral College chose Republican Rutherford B. Hayes over Democrat Samuel Tilden after Tilden led Hayes in the popular vote.
1888	The Electoral College chose Republican Benjamin Harrison over Democrat Grover Cleveland after Cleveland led Harrison in the popular vote.
2000	The Electoral College chose Republican George W. Bush over Democrat Albert Gore Jr. after Gore led Bush in the popular vote.

litical scientist has noted, the Electoral College "tends to produce larger and more decisive margins for wins when the popular vote is very close, leading to a more definitive judgment of victory, and giving presidents some greater sense of legitimacy and mandate—a necessity in a system of checks and balances where a president relies heavily on intangibles like credibility" (Ornstein 2002, 157). In 1980, for example, Ronald Reagan managed barely over 50 percent of the popular vote but fully 90 percent of the electoral vote, and in 1992 Bill Clinton received an even smaller percentage of the popular vote—43 percent—but it converted into nearly 70 percent of the electoral vote. Although not shown in Table 5.15, one of the most dramatic examples of this multiplier effect was the 1960 election—the closest popular vote election of the twentieth century—where John F. Kennedy finished a slim 114,673 votes ahead of Richard M. Nixon and yet pulled in 303 electoral votes to Nixon's 219.

This presumed strength of the Electoral College did not, of course, materialize in the election of 2000, as George Bush finished just five electoral votes ahead of Al Gore. Skeptics, moreover, can be forgiven for believing that whatever mandate attaches to an election victory results from support expressed to him or her through the *actual* casting of votes by *citizens*. It is rather doubtful that it can be significantly enhanced or diminished through the mechanical conversion of those popular votes into electoral votes.

TABLE 5.15
Popular versus Electoral Vote, 1980–2000

Year	Candidates	Percent of Popular Vote	Percent of Electoral Vote
1980	Reagan	50.8	90.9
	Carter	41.0	9.1
	Anderson	6.6	0.0
1984	Reagan	58.8	97.6
	Mondale	41.0	2.4
1988	Bush	53.4	79.2
	Dukakis	45.7	20.6
1992	Clinton	43.0	68.8
	Bush	37.7	31.2
	Perot	18.9	0.0
1996	Clinton	49.2	70.4
	Dole	40.7	29.6
	Perot	8.4	0.0
	Nader	0.7	0.0
2000	Bush	47.9	50.4
	Gore	48.4	49.4
	Nader	2.7	0.0
	Buchanan	0.4	0.0

Source: http://www.uselectionatlas.org/. Accessed April 2, 2003.

As noted in Chapter 2, the more compelling arguments for retaining the Electoral College are that it serves to marginalize more extreme candidates and discourage third parties, thereby making the task of governing easier through two stable political parties. In addition—and by no means least important—the alternatives to the Electoral College are themselves fraught with no small number of difficulties.

Term Limits

Although the movement to limit the service of elected public officials has been around for many years, it received a significant boost in the early 1990s when Republicans in Congress took the idea on board, making it a plank in their 1994 platform known as the "Contract with America." After gaining control of the House in 1995, however, their enthusiasm for term limits diminished considerably. No such bill passed Congress, and a Supreme Court decision (*U.S. Term Limits v. Thornton*) handed down the same year declared that states could not impose term limits on their congressional delegation.

If the air was let out of the movement to limit service in our national legislature, the same cannot be said for the state level. On the contrary, during the 1990s a number of states imposed limits on their elected officials. Currently, governors are subject to term limits in thirty-six states, and state legislators are likewise limited in seventeen—with most setting the time of service from eight to twelve years (see Table 5.16). In seven of these states (Arkansas, California, Michigan, Missouri, Nevada, Oklahoma, and Oregon) the term limit for service in their legislature is a lifetime restriction, which is to say that they may never again be elected to that body. Seven states (Arizona, Florida, Louisiana, Maine, Ohio, South Dakota, and Utah), in comparison, limit individuals to eight to ten years of *consecutive* service, thereby affording them the option of running again after sitting out a term. Others define the sitting-out period as four years or longer (Dudley and Gitelson 2002, 52, 53). As Table 5.16 indicates, the enthusiasm for limiting service in legislative assemblies grows as one moves from east to west. On the eastern seaboard only the state of Maine has seen fit to impose such a limit; in the Midwest, just Ohio and Michigan; and in the South, Arkansas and Louisiana.

Whether states were showing prudent judgment by legislating such limits is a matter of some debate. Clearly, term limits pre-

TABLE 5.16
Term Limits in States

State	Gubernatorial Term Limits	Legislative Term Limits
Alabama	yes	no
Alaska	yes	no
Arizona	yes	yes
Arkansas	yes	yes
California	yes	yes
Colorado	yes	yes
Connecticut	no	no
Delaware	yes	no
Florida	yes	yes
Georgia	yes	no
Hawaii	yes	no
Idaho	no	no
Illinois	no	no
Indiana	yes	no
Iowa	no	no
Kansas	yes	no
Kentucky	yes	no
Louisiana	yes	yes
Maine	yes	yes
Maryland	yes	no
Massachusetts	no	no
Michigan	yes	yes
Minnesota	no	no
Mississippi	yes	no
Missouri	yes	yes
Montana	yes	yes
Nebraska	yes	yes
Nevada	yes	yes
New Hampshire	no	no
New Jersey	yes	no
New Mexico	yes	no
New York	no	no
North Carolina	yes	no
North Dakota	no	no
Ohio	yes	yes
Oklahoma	yes	yes
Oregon	no	no
Pennsylvania	yes	no
Rhode Island	yes	no
South Carolina	yes	no
South Dakota	yes	yes
Tennessee	yes	no
Texas	no	no

(continues)

TABLE 5.16
Term Limits in States (continued)

State	Gubernatorial Term Limits	Legislative Term Limits
Utah	yes	yes
Vermont	no	no
Virginia	yes	no
Washington	no	no
West Virginia	yes	no
Wisconsin	no	no
Wyoming	yes	yes

References: U. S. Term Limits, "State Gubernatorial Term Limits," http://www.termlimits.org/Current_Info/State_TL/gubernatorial.html. Accessed April 2, 2003; U.S. Term Limits, "State Legislative Term Limits," http://www.termlimits/org./Current_Info/State_TL/index.html. Accessed April 2, 2003.

determine a legislator's service rather than leaving it to the voters, thereby artificially limiting voter choice. Supporters of this restriction also attach less importance to experience in office than to the presumed need to discourage "cozy" relationships with special interests and provide fresh perspectives on issues of the day. Skeptics, however, claim that the constant turnover renders greenhorn legislators even more dependent upon special interests, not only because legislators are likely to have limited information and expertise but also because, in full-time legislatures, at least, they may be looking to those special interests as potential sources of employment after leaving the legislature.

In contrast, the power of incumbency—with all the advantages that come with it—can serve as a powerful discouragement to potential challengers. With that advantage removed through term limits, many individuals are now finding public office a more attractive prospect. In 1998, for example, 67 of the 110 members of the state of Michigan's lower house were forced out by term limits. As a consequence, some 497 individuals filed to enter the primaries—the greatest number of people to do so in thirty-five years (Dudley and Gitelson 2002, 51).

Quotations

Importance of the Vote

It is essential to liberty that the government . . . should have a common interest with the people; so it is particularly essential that the [representatives] should have an immediate dependence on and an intimate sympathy with the people. Frequent elections are unquestionably the only policy by which this dependence and sympathy can be effectually secured.

James Madison
The Federalist, No. 52 (1788)

Voting in the United States is the fundamental act of self-government. It provides the citizen in our free society the right to make a judgment, to state a choice, to participate in the running of his government—in the community, the State, and the Nation. The ballot box is the medium for the expression of the consent of the governed. . . .

It is a tribute to the vitality of our Republic that since the founding of our Nation, we have never cancelled or postponed an election scheduled by the Federal or State constitutions or by statute. No civil war, world war, epidemic, or depression has halted our electoral machinery.

It is also significant that throughout our history of unhindered elections, we have maintained a system of voluntary voting. Nothing in this country makes voting mandatory—unless it is the conscience of the voter himself.

President's Commission on Registration and Voting Participation
Report on Registration and Voting Participation (1963)

There's a paradox at the core of democratic politics. We use elections to tally up our preferences and to determine the future direction and structure of our government, but the existing arrangements powerfully influence our preferences and dramatically limit the choices available to us. The kind of democracy we have, and can imagine, is thus quite path-dependent, like the famous Escher print of a hand drawing itself drawing a hand.

Pamela Karlan, professor of law
"A Bigger Picture," in Robert Richie and Steven Hill, eds.,
Whose Vote Counts? (1999)

The Right to Vote

The same reasoning that will induce you to admit all men who have no property, to vote, with those who have, will prove that you ought to admit women and children; for generally speaking, women and children have as good judgments, and as independent minds as those men who are wholly destitute of property. . . . Depend upon it, Sir, it is dangerous to open as fruitful a source of controversy and altercation as would be opened by attempting to alter the qualifications for voters; there will be no end of it. New claims will arise; women will demand the vote; lads from twelve to twenty-one will think their rights not enough attended to; and every man who has not a farthing will demand an equal voice with any other, in all acts of state.

John Adams (1776)

Experience has but too clearly evinced what, indeed, reason had always foretold, by how frail a tenure they hold every other right, who are denied this (the suffrage) the highest prerogative of freemen. . . .

A regulation which, instead of the equality nature ordains, creates an odious distinction between members of the same community; robs of all share, in the enactment of laws, a large portion of the citizens bound by them, and whose blood and treasure are pledged to maintain them. . . .

Surely it were much to be desired that every citizen should be qualified for the proper exercise of all his rights, and the due performance of all his duties. But the same qualifications that entitle him to assume management of his private affairs, and claim the other privileges of citizenship, equally entitled him, in the judgment of your memorialists, to be entrusted with this, the dearest of all his privileges, the most important of all his concerns. . . .

The enjoyment of all other rights, whether of person or property, they will not deny, may be as perfect among those deprived of the privilege of voting, as among those possessing it. It may be as great under a despotism, as under any other form of government. But they alone deserve to be called free, or have a guarantee for their rights, who participate in the formation of their political institutions, and in the control of those who make and administer the laws. To such as may be disposed to surrender this, or any other immunity, to the keeping of others, no practical mischief may ensue from its abandonment; or if any, none that will not be justly merited. Not so with him who feels as a freeman should; who would think for himself and speak what he thinks; who would not commit his conscience or his liberty to the uncontrolled direction of others. To him the privation of right, of that especially, which is the only safeguard of freedom, is practically wrong. So thought the fathers of the republic. It was not the oppressive weight of the taxes imposed by England on America: it was the assertion of a right to impose any burdens whatever upon those who were not represented; to bind by laws those who had no share, personal or delegated, in their enactment, that roused this continent to arms. . . .

A memorial presented by nonfreeholders of Richmond, Virginia, to the Virginia Constitutional Convention protesting their exclusion from the suffrage (1829)

Today a man owns a jackass worth fifty dollars and he is entitled to vote; but before the next election the jackass dies. The man in the meantime has become more experienced, his knowledge of the principles of government, and his acquaintance with mankind, are more extensive, and he is therefore better qualified to make a proper selection of rulers—but the jackass is dead and the man cannot vote. Now gentlemen, pray inform me, in whom is the right of suffrage? In the man or in the jackass?

Benjamin Franklin
The Casket, Or Flowers of Literature, Wit and Sentiment (1828)

It is far more dangerous to have a large underclass of ignorant and disfranchised men who are neither stimulated, educated, nor enobled by the exercise of the vote . . . to have an ignorant class voting is dangerous, whether white or black; but to have an ignorant class and not have them voting, is a great deal more dangerous . . . the remedy for the unquestionable dangers of having ignorant voters lies in educating them by all the means in our power, and not in excluding them from their rights. . . . Nothing so much prepares men for intelligent suffrage as the exercise of the right of suffrage.

Harold Ward Beecher
"Universal Suffrage: An Argument" (1865)

A New England village of the olden time—that is to say, of some forty years ago—would have been safely and well governed by the votes of every man in it; but, now that the village has grown into a populous city, with its factories and workshops, its acres of tenement-houses, and thousands and ten thousands of restless workmen, foreigners for the most part, to whom liberty means license and politics means plunder, to whom the public good is nothing and their own most trivial interests everything, who love the country for what they can get out of it, and whose ears are open to the promptings of every rascally agitator, the case is completely changed, and universal suffrage becomes a questionable blessing.

Francis Parkman (1878)

The history of mankind is a history of repeated injuries and usurpations on the part of man toward woman, having in direct object the establishment of an absolute tyranny over her. To prove this, let facts be submitted to a candid world.

He has never permitted her to exercise her inalienable right to the elective franchise.

He has compelled her to submit to laws, in the formation of which she had no voice.

He has withheld from her rights which are given to the most ignorant and degraded men—both natives and foreigners.

Having deprived her of this first right of a citizen, the elective franchise, thereby leaving her without representation in the halls of legislation, he has oppressed her on all sides. . . .

From the "Declaration of Sentiments," Seneca Falls Convention (1848)

I think it was Wendell Phillips who said something like this, "if women are like men, then they certainly possess the same brain and that should entitle them to the ballot; if they are not like men, then they certainly need the ballot, for no man can understand what they want." And we ask you upon those lines to give the ballot to women.

Carrie Chapman Catt
Delaware Constitutional Convention (1897)

Mr. Halfhill: Now, gentlemen, this question of franchise is not, as has been sometimes debated and urged, an inalienable right; it is a conferred right, and it must be conferred under our theory of government and under our organization of society.

Mr. Fackler: If suffrage is a conferred right and not a natural one, who conferred that right on us?

Ohio Constitutional Convention (1912)

Discrimination! Why, that is precisely what we propose. That, exactly, is what this Convention was elected for—to discriminate to the very extremity of permissible action under the limitations of the Federal Constitution, with a view to the elimination of every Negro voter who can be gotten rid of, legally, without materially impairing the numerical strength of the white electorate.

Carter Glass, senator
Virginia Constitutional Convention (1901–1902)

I had supposed that this Commission would be unanimous on the fundamental principle that all men are equal in their political rights, but it is not; one member has written, a dissent to the recommendation of the Commission that literacy tests should be abolished. As a result, I think it important to make a more extensive statement in support of the Commission recommendation and the principles upon which it is based.

A democratic system rests ultimately on the belief that each man is the best judge of his own interests and that he should have, through the ballot box, a voice in choosing those who govern him. On what grounds should we deny to the person who has not learned to read the rights we accord to others? That he cannot read the ballot? Then shall we also disfranchise the blind? That he cannot read newspapers? Then shall we disfranchise the deaf because they cannot hear radio and television? That he will not be an "informed" voter? Then shall we require that each voter pass a test in current events?

Evron M. Kirkpatrick
Member, President's Commission on
Registration and Voting Participation Registration
Report on Registration and Voting Participation (1963)

Our fathers believed that if this noble view of the rights of man was to flourish, it must be rooted in democracy. The most basic right of all was to choose your own leaders. The history of this country, in large measure, is the history of the expansion of that right to all of our people.

Many of the issues of civil rights are very complex and most difficult. But about this there can and should be no argument. Every American citizen must have an equal right to vote. There is no reason which can excuse the denial of that right. There is no duty which weighs more heavily on us than the duty we have to ensure that right.

Yet the harsh fact is that in many places in this country men and women are kept from voting simply because they are Negroes.

Every device of which human ingenuity is capable has been used to deny this right. . . .

Experience has clearly shown that the existing process of law cannot overcome systematic and ingenious discrimination. No law that we now have on the books—and I have helped to put three of them there—can ensure the right to vote when local officials are determined to deny it.

In such a case our duty must be clear to all of us. The Constitution says that no person shall be kept from voting because of his race or his color. We have all sworn an oath before god to support and defend that Constitution. We must now act in obedience to that oath.

Wednesday I will send to Congress a law designed to eliminate illegal barriers to the right to vote.

Lyndon B. Johnson, president
Addressing a joint session of Congress on his
proposal for a Voting Rights Act (1965)

Voting Systems

The pure idea of democracy, according to its definition, is the government of the whole people, equally represented. Democracy, as commonly perceived and hitherto practiced, is the government of the whole people by a mere majority of the people, exclusively represented. The former is synonymous with the equality of all citizens; the latter, strangely confounded with it, is a government of privilege, in favor of the numerical majority, who alone possess practically any voice in the State. This is the inevitable consequence of the manner in which the votes are now taken; the complete disenfranchisement of minorities.

John Stuart Mill
Considerations on Representative Government (1861)

Too often the majorities created by winner take all are "artificial" or "exaggerated" majorities plagued by phantom representation; and the successful party and their candidates have used vicious mudslinging in a two-choice field to win by appealing to ill-informed and confused swing voters in swing districts. It is a majority by default in a two-party system where one party *must* win a majority. But that's not necessarily a "representative" majority. And the policies they enact may not at all represent the true will of the majority, making politics feel to the average person like a bit of a crapshoot.

Steven Hill, associate director and cofounder
of the Center for Voting and Democracy
Fixing Elections: The Failure of America's Winner Take All Politics (2002)

If a voting system is to be really fair, more than two alternatives must be allowed to enter the decision process; a decision method must be able to operate on three or more alternatives, but no one method satisfies all the conditions of fairness that have been proposed as reasonable or just. Every method satisfies some and violates others. Unfortunately, there are, so far as I know, no deeper ethical systems or any deeper axioms for decision that would allow us to judge and choose among these conditions of fairness. Hence there is no generally convincing way to show that one decision method is truly better than another.

William H. Riker, political scientist
*Liberalism against Populism: A Confrontation between the
Theory of Democracy and the Theory of the Social Contract* (1982)

Presidential Nominating Process

There ought never to be another nominating convention. . . . The nominations should be made directly by the people at the polls.

Woodrow Wilson, president
First Annual Message to Congress (1913)

The key reform that's needed in both parties is to break up the influence of New Hampshire–Iowa. We've delegated to them the role of picking our presidents.

Morris Udall, congressman
"Roundtable Discussion on Specific Changes in
the Nominating Process," *Common Sense* (1981)

To suggest a diminished role for primaries is a skittish undertaking. Yet the bald reality is that the primary exercise is now madness. We have reformed ourselves into a primary maze that is chaotic and confusing, so costly as to dissuade most good possible candidates from even trying, and subject to massive media misinterpretation.

Terry Sandford
A Danger of Democracy: The Presidential Nominating Process (1981)

When the state primaries became the mode rather than the exception after 1968, a basic safeguard in the presidential election process was lost. Previously an elite of party leaders performed a screening function.

They administered a kind of competence test; they did not always exercise the duty creditably. But they could—and did—ensure that no one was nominated who was not acceptable to the preponderance of the party elite as its leader. Even if the candidate swept the limited number of primaries, he could still be rejected, as Senator Estes Kefauver was in 1952. Usually, then, the nominee was a politician or an administrator or both, of national stature and of demonstrated competence. The party leaders who approved the nomination were prepared to follow the nominee, and to mobilize the party on his behalf.

James L. Sundquist, political scientist
"The Crisis of Competence in Government," in Joseph Pechman, ed., *Setting National Priorities: Agenda for the Eighties* (1980)

In the present nominating system, the determinants of success are the size of the candidate's ambitions, the extent of his leisure time, and the tolerance of his family, his budget, and his job for almost unlimited travel. These characteristics have almost nothing to do with the qualities that make an effective president—as the results show. It is a recklessly haphazard way to choose the candidates for that demanding job.

David Broder, columnist
Washington Post (1980)

Presidential primaries were designed to take the nomination away from the party bosses in the back room and give the decisions to the voters, but they haven't worked out that way. Instead, the current version of primaries turns the decisions over to a new kind of boss. Today, a small, unrepresentative handful of party activists, often only concerned with one issue or with narrow, special interests, dominate the primaries. Because the broad center of moderate and independent voters seldom vote in the primaries, the decisions are abdicated to small groups of motivated extremists of the left or right.

Newton Minnow
Wall Street Journal (1979)

Expensive and demanding though it may be, the president-by-primary process subjects candidates to more protracted and intense scrutiny by the public, media, and even party elites, than ever occurred under the old system. To be sure, this scrutiny does not guarantee that the most qualified candidate will be chosen. No system can. Yet it probably does a better job than the old system of ensuring that we do not select a very bad candidate. Certainly the president-by-primary process has not yet nominated a candidate whose views were so at variance with a majority of Americans as were those of Barry Goldwater (1964). Nor has it produced a nominee whose overall level of competence was as lacking as

Warren Harding's (1920). Nor, finally, has it given us a president whose insensitivity to constitutional requirements approached that of Richard Nixon (1960, 1968, 1972).

Robert E. DiClerico, political scientist
Choosing Our Choices (2000)

Money in Elections

An honest politician is one who, when he is bought, will stay bought.

Simon Cameron (1799–1889), U.S. senator, Pennsylvania
quoted in Daniel M. Friedenberg, *Sold to the Highest Bidder* (2002)

Politicians spend half their time making laws and the other half helping contributors evade them.

American maxim
quoted in Daniel M. Friedenberg, *Sold to the Highest Bidder* (2002)

Funding for elections in a democracy should not depend on an economic elite. When the rich pay for electoral campaigns, the substance of politics is confined to the issues and policies that the wealthy funders approve of. To be sure, the electorate gets to vote. But the choices presented to voters are, at best, those that are acceptable to the wealthy. At worst, of course, such a system is simply corrupt.

Jay Mandle, professor of economics
"Follow the Money," *Commonwealth* (2001)

It [the influence of a campaign contribution] may not come in a vote. It may come in a speech not delivered. The PAC payoff may come in a colleague not influenced. It may come in a calling off of a meeting that otherwise would result in advancing legislation. It may come in a minor change in one paragraph in a 240-page bill. It may come in a witness not invited to testify before a committee. It may come in hiring a key staff member for a committee who is sympathetic to the PAC. Or it may come in laying off or transferring a staff member who is unsympathetic to a PAC.

William Proxmire, former U.S. senator, Wisconsin
quoted in Philip M. Stern, *Still the Best Congress Money Can Buy* (1992)

Restricting private money campaign contributions does not empower the "average constituent," however defined. Rather, it increases the relative influence of an even smaller elite: media people and others whose skills are directly valuable to a candidate or legislator. The best way to assure that a representative does not shirk the public interest for that of narrow interests is to provide as many points of influence as possible. Efforts to ensure equality of inputs to the campaign process are less likely to guarantee popular control than is the presence of multiple sources of political power.

Bradley A. Smith, professor of law
Unfree Speech: The Folly of Campaign Finance Reform (2001)

Contributions to candidates and parties today do not line anybody's pockets, as they did in the heyday of machines like Tammany Hall. Vigilant media and law enforcement now nip improper personal enrichment in the bud. . . .

Political money today instead goes directly into political advertising, a quintessential form of political speech. Our large electoral districts and weak political parties force candidates to communicate directly with large groups of voters. This depends on the use of privately owned mass media. Thus, getting the candidate's message out is expensive. . . .

Nor is there any doubt that restrictions on political money amount to restrictions on political speech. Reformers sometimes say they merely seek to limit money, not speech. But a law, say, barring newspapers from accepting paid political advertisements or limiting the prices of political books would also only limit the exchange of money. Yet none would question that it would inhibit political speech—as do restrictions on campaign finance.

Kathleen M. Sullivan, dean, Stanford Law School
"Paying Up Is Speaking Up," *Washington Post* (1999)

The Supreme Court says they [candidates] may spend their own money on their own campaigns as a way of giving expression to their views of public policy. Restricting all other money—including money that comes from political action committees and political parties—merely gives advantages to the rich and famous, advantages they scarcely need.

So, oddly enough, restricting money in the political system appears to be a good way to assure that more political leaders will be recruited from among the rich. And rich politicians may feel most comfortable giving access to other rich people.

Nelson W. Polsby, political scientist
"Money Gains Access: So What?" *Washington Post* (1997)

Term Limits

In free governments, the rulers are the servants and the people their superiors and sovereigns. For the former, therefore, to return among the latter is not to degrade but to promote them.

Benjamin Franklin (1787)

In order, particularly, that his appointment may as far as possible be placed beyond the reach of any improper influences; in order that he

may approach the solemn responsibilities of the highest office in the gift
of a free people uncommitted to any other course than the strict line of
constitutional duty, and that the securities of this independence may be
rendered as strong as the nature of power and the weakness of its pos-
sessor will admit, I cannot too earnestly invite your attention to the pro-
priety of promoting such an amendment of the Constitution as will render him ineligible after one term of service.

Andrew Jackson (1830)
quoted in "American Enterprise Institute,"
Limiting Presidential and Congressional Terms (1979)

You do not have to be very smart to know that an office-holder who
is not eligible for reelection loses a lot of influence. So what have
you done? You have taken a man and put him in the hardest job in
the world, and sent him out to fight our battles in a life-and-death
struggle—and you have sent him out to fight with one hand tied behind his back, because everyone knows he cannot run for
reelection. . . .

If he is not a good President, and you do not want to keep him, you
do not have to reelect him. There is a way to get rid of him and it does
not require a constitutional amendment to do it.

President Harry S. Truman
testimony before the Senate Subcommittee on Constitutional Amendments
of the Committee on the Judicicary (1959)

Both at the beginning and the end of a congressional career the member
is unusually susceptible to interest group influence. To shrink the distance between these two points creates a bonanza for outside interests
organized to take advantage of it. Inexperience at legislative work for
members new to the job provides . . . a toe hold for interest groups who
can supply knowledge about issues and make up for the ignorance of
the newly arrived. The idea that advocates sometimes express that term
limits emancipate Congress from interest groups is dubious; indeed,
more likely exactly the opposite is the case.

Nelson W. Polsby, political scientist
"Term Limits," *The New Federalist Papers* (1997)

It's true, as the critics also say, that the term limit would deprive Congress of the service of legislators whom experience has made wise.
This would be a real cost. But it would be a cost worth paying to be
rid of the much larger number of time servers who have learned nothing from longevity in office except cynicism, complacency, and a
sense of diminished possibility. And it's not as if the job of being a
congressman is so difficult that it takes decades to master. It's easier
than being a first-rate school teacher, for example, and no harder than
such jobs as president, governor, or mayor—all of which are regularly

performed very well indeed by people who have had no on-the-job experience at all.

Hendrik Hertzberg, political writer
"Twelve Is Enough," *The New Republic* (1990)

Redistricting

Normally we think of democracy as voters choosing their representatives. Actually, the redistricting process is about representatives choosing their voters.

Nathaniel Persily, professor of law
quoted in *USA Today* (2002)

First they gerrymander us into one-party fiefs. Then they tell us they only care about the swing districts. Then they complain about voter apathy.

Gail Collins, columnist
"Other People's Elections," *New York Times* (2000)

Redistricting makes the inequities in campaign financing even worse. Most elections are so noncompetitive due to how the lines are drawn that big donors already know who's going to win. So they give to the likely winners to curry favor.

Douglas Amy
political scientist conference, Minneapolis, Minnesota (1997)

Gerrymandering invariably inflates the number of safe districts. Barring a successful primary challenge, the individual incumbent is virtually assured of continued reelection for as long as he or she cares to hold the seat. This has the effect of insulating the legislative body against the consequences of changing sentiments and circumstances, for gerrymandering has provided the individual legislator, the legislative leadership, and the legislature as a whole with rather strong guarantees of continued office and power. The political . . . composition of the legislature has been effectively frozen for a decade, and changes are possible only within a limited, narrow range. The representation system, because it has been made less politically sensitive and therefore less responsive, has thus been rendered less able to perform its most fundamental task—the translation of public sentiment into public policy as accurately as possible.

David Wells
Representation and Redistricting Issues (1982)

The real winners in the redistricting games are the incumbents. Nationwide in 2002 only eight incumbents were defeated in the general election. . . . the consequences of entrenched incumbency should concern us all. . . .

Primary elections in districts that are overwhelmingly Republican produce candidates that are generally to the right of the average Republican, while more liberal Democrats usually emerge from primaries in districts that are overwhelmingly Democratic. The political center—where most Americans are most comfortable—gets the least representation in Congress.

In short, the current system produces a House that is both more liberal and more conservative than the country at large. Members are less inclined to talk and cooperate, much less compromise. The legislative agenda is shaped more to energize the political base than to advance the common good.

> Earl Blumenauer, congressman (D-OR), and Jim Leach, congressman (R-IA)
> "Redistriciting: A Bipartisan Sport," *New York Times* (2003)

Nonvoting

They have such refined and delicate palates
That they can discover no one worthy of their ballots,
And then when someone terrible gets elected
They say, that's just what I expected.

> Ogden Nash

A statesman is an easy man,
He tells his lies by rote;
A journalist makes up his lies
And takes you by the throat;
So stay at home and drink your beer
And let the neighbors vote.

> William Butler Yeats
> *The Old Stone Cross* (1938)

I believe if you vote, you have no right to complain. People like to twist that around, I know. They say, well, if you don't vote you have no right to complain, but where's the logic in that? If you vote and you elect dishonest, incompetent people and they get into office and screw everything up, you are responsible for what they have done, you caused the problem, you voted them in, you have no right to complain. I, on the other hand, who did not vote, who, in fact, did not even leave the house on election day, am in no way responsible for what these people have done and have every reason to complain as loud as I want about the mess you created that I had nothing to do with.

> George Carlin, comedian
> quoted in Jack C. Doppelt and Ellen Shearer,
> *Nonvoters: America's No-Shows* (1990)

The American voter has been characterized as selfish, alienated, apathetic, irresponsible, and lazy in study after study of his voting participation behavior. . . . I contend the voter is getting a "bum rap." American voting participation among eligible voters, accurately defined as such, is high and Americans show themselves to be every bit as conscientious a voting population under their system as do the voters in other countries under their very different systems. Studies which indicate extraordinarily high degrees of nonvoting in America are really measuring other things. They reflect more accurately the statistical anomalies which emerge from diverse state registration methods and the unusual impact of the recent entrance of large numbers of historically low-voting young people into the "voting age population" than they do the apathy, alienation, or selfishness of the electorate of the United States.

Ronald C. Moe, political scientist
"The Empty Voting Booth: Fact or Fiction?" *Common Sense* (1979)

In the final analysis, electoral politics remains what it has always been—a game in which numbers determine results. And it is still played by the same basic rule: "people who don't vote don't count." Since it is disproportionately working-class citizens who "don't count," in this sense, their economic interests continue to remain outside the political agenda. They play no role in shaping the solutions, because they have become irrelevant to defining the problems. As a consequence, within a political context shaped by the twin economic and policy crises that began in the mid-1970s, working-class citizens can expect to bear a disproportionately greater share of the financial and social burdens involved in the "reindustrializing" and "rearming" of the capitalist state.

Paul Kleppner, political scientist
Who Voted? The Dynamics of Electoral Turnout, 1870–1980 (1982)

The Electoral College

The mode of appointment of the chief magistrate of the United States is almost the only part of the system, of any consequence, which has escaped without severe censure, or which has received the slightest mark of approbation from its opponents. The most plausible of these, who has appeared in print, has even deigned to admit that the election of the president is pretty well guarded. I venture somewhat further; and hesitate not to affirm, that if the manner of it be not perfect, it is at least excellent.

Alexander Hamilton
The Federalist, No. 68 (1787)

To lose their votes is the fate of all minorities, and it is their duty to submit; but this [the Electoral College] is not a case of votes lost, but of

votes taken away, added to those of the majority, and given to a person
to whom the minority is opposed.

Thomas Hart Benton, U.S. senator, Missouri (1824)
quoted in hearings before the Subcommittee on Constitutional Amendments,
of the Committee on the Judiciary, U.S. Senate (1961)

Most Americans, regardless of party, are agreed on the failings of the
electoral college. It is unfair, inaccurate, uncertain, and undemocratic.
Unfair, because the presidential candidate losing a state by even a close
margin forfeits all of that state's electoral votes. Inaccurate, because in
most elections the winner's electoral votes are inflated grotesquely out
of proportion to his popular vote. Uncertain, because Presidential electors are not legally bound to vote for the candidate who carries the
State. And undemocratic, because if no candidate wins a majority of the
electoral college the verdict is rendered in the House of Representatives,
where each State delegation, no matter how large, casts but a single vote
in choosing among the three top candidates.

James MacGregor Burns, political scientist
quoted in hearings before the Subcommittee on Constitutional Amendments,
of the Committee of the Judiciary, U.S. Senate (1961)

The electoral college method of electing a President of the United States
is archaic, undemocratic, complex, ambiguous, indirect, and dangerous.

American Bar Association
*Electing the President: A Report of the Commission
on Electoral College Reform* (1969)

In fact, presidential elections are already just about as democratic as
they can be. We already have one-man, one-vote—*but in the states.* Elections are as freely and democratically contested as elections can be—*but
in the states.* Victory always goes democratically to the winner of the raw
popular vote—*but in the states.* The label given to the proposed reform,
"direct popular election," is a misnomer; the elections have already become as directly popular as they can be—*but in the states.* Despite all
their democratic rhetoric, the reformers do not propose to make our
presidential elections more directly democratic, they only propose to
make them more directly *national,* by entirely removing the states from
the electoral process. Democracy is thus not the question regarding the
Electoral College, federalism is.

Martin Diamond, political scientist
The Electoral College and the American Idea of Democracy (1977)

Take away the electoral college and the importance of being black melts
away. Blacks, instead of being crucial to victory in major states, simply
become 10 percent of the electorate, with reduced impact.

Vernon Jordan, president, Urban League
quoted in Arthur Schlesinger Jr., "Not the People's Choice:
How to Democratize American Democracy," *The American Prospect* (2002)

Abolition of the electoral college would create the appearance of direct mass election and the reality of indirect elite manipulation. The proposal to replace the electoral college system with direct election is class legislation. It is fated to advantage elites, make voting choices for citizens more complex, threaten—indeed, more likely kill—our two-party system, force a proliferation of elections and candidates for the Presidency, and a similar proliferation of parties, many of which will be extreme or oriented to single causes.

The real questions posed by proposals for "electoral college reform" are not, therefore, about direct election of the President, which we already have, but about a mass society, without intermediaries like parties, which we do not want. The mediation of the major political parties presently structures choice through national conventions and competitive two-party elections. These would be replaced under so-called electoral college reform by crowds of candidates making their appeals to people solely through the media.

Aaron Wildavsky, political scientist
"The Plebiscitary Presidency: Direct Election as Class Legislation,"
Common Sense (1979)

I would not disguise, at the outset, my sense of the measure before the Senate today, proposing the abolition of the Electoral College, to state that in the guise of perfecting an alleged weakness in the Constitution, it in fact proposes the most radical transformation in our political system that has ever been considered—a transformation so radical and so ominous, in my view, as to require of this body the most solemn, prolonged, and prayerful consideration, and in particular a consideration that will reach back to our beginnings, to learn how we built and how it came about that we built better than we knew.

Daniel Patrick Moynihan, U.S. senator, New York
"The Electoral College and the Uniqueness of America,"
in Gary L. Gregg II, ed., *Securing Democracy:
Why We Need an Electoral College* (2001)

Perhaps the most fundamental bias of the Electoral College is this: It is not sufficient to win in a few big states by huge margins. Since almost all states give their votes on a winner-take-all basis, the system works in favor of candidates who win in a lot of places, even by modest margins, and against candidates whose support is deep but narrow. . . .

This bias cost Gore the presidency. Gore trailed in the aggregate popular vote from coast to coast until returns came in from California, where he pulled ahead only because he won that state by a 1.3 million vote margin. Gore lost the rest of America by nearly a million votes, winning only twenty of fifty states and about one-fifth of America's counties, so that one could fly from Washington DC to San Francisco without ever crossing a Gore state before reaching California.

James W. Ceaser and Andrew E. Busch
The Perfect Tie: The True Story of the 2000 Presidential Election (2001)

Ballot-Counting

Those who cast the votes decide nothing. Those who count the votes decide everything.

Joseph Stalin

Not everything that can be counted counts, and not everything that counts can be counted.

Albert Einstein

Direct Democracy (Initiative, Referendum, Recall)

For twenty years I preached to the students of Princeton that the Referendum and the Recall was bosh. I have since investigated and I want to apologize to those students. It is the safeguard of politics. It takes power from the boss and places it in the hands of the people.

Woodrow Wilson, political scientist (1911)
quoted in Thomas E. Cronin, *Direct Democracy:*
The Politics of Initiative, Referendum, and Recall (1989)

The value of the recall as an instrument of genuinely democratic government has not been sufficiently appreciated. . . . Above all else a democratic government must be kept closely in touch with public opinion. The recall makes it more possible . . . without any sacrifice of efficiency.

Herbert Croly (1914)
quoted in Thomas E. Cronin, *Direct Democracy:*
The Politics of Initiative, Referendum, and Recall (1989)

[The recall] tends to produce in every public official a nervous condition of irresolution as to whether he should do what he thinks he ought to do in the interest of the public, or should withhold from doing anything, or should do as little as possible, in order to avoid any discussion at all.

William H. Taft (1913), former president
quoted in Thomas E. Cronin, *Democracy:*
The Politics of Initiative, Referendum, and Recall (1989)

Our forefathers strongly believed in a fluid constitutional republic fed by the wishes of an informed citizenry dedicated to the furtherance of community action and well-being. Efforts to limit or abolish direct democracy should be opposed at every turn, and the free flow of ideas should be forever encouraged through these tools of direct democracy.

Douglas M. Guetzloe, president, Advantage Consultants
quoted in *Dangerous Democracy?*
The Battle over Ballot Initiatives in America (2001)

At the start of a new century—and millennium—a new form of government is spreading in the United States. It is alien to the spirit of the Constitution and its careful system of checks and balances.

Exploiting the public's disdain for politics and distrust of politicians, it is now the most uncontrolled and unexamined arena of power politics. It has given the United States something that seems unthinkable—not a government of laws but laws without government. The initiative process, an import now just over one hundred years old, threatens to challenge or even subvert the American system of government in the next few decades.

David S. Broder, newspaper columnist
Democracy Derailed: Initiative Campaigns and the Power of Money (2000)

By its very design, the [initiative] process ensures that concerns held by a minority—any minority—will be subjected to the will of the majority. It is not by accident that the founders of our nation considered and rejected this means of governance. Believing that government based solely on the unfiltered and unrefined views of the majority opens the door to tyranny, the founders based our republic upon the notion that lawmaking should be in the hands of those we elect.

Unlike the governing process debated and accepted by our founders, citizen lawmaking lacks the deliberation, refinement, and real citizen involvement that is essential for enlightened governance. . . . It is for these reasons, not the common misconception that moneyed special interests dominate the system, that we should reassess the initiative process.

Sue Tupper, vice president, APCO Worldwide
quoted in Larry J. Sabato et al., *Dangerous Democracy:*
The Battle over Ballot Initiatives in America (2001)

Political incivility feeds on itself. The attempt to recall California Gov. Gray Davis will encourage the idea that elections settle nothing—campaigning is permanent and ubiquitous.

George Will, newspaper columnist
"Careless People in Power," *Washington Post* (2003)

References

Best, Judith. 1971. *The Case against Direct Election of the President: A Defense of the Electoral College.* Ithaca, NY: Cornell University Press.

Brady, Henry E., Justin Buchler, Matt Jarvis, and John McNulty. 2002. *Counting All the Votes: The Performance of Voting Technology in the United States*. Berkeley: University of California Press.

Butterfield, Fox. 1997. "Many Black Men Barred from Voting, Study Shows." *New York Times*, (January 30): 148.

———. 2003. "Prison Rates among Blacks Reach a Peak Report Finds." *New York Times* (April 7): A11.

Caltech/MIT Voting Technology Project. 2001. *Voting: What Is, What Could Be*. Pasadena, CA, and Cambridge, MA: California Institute of Technology and Massachusetts Institute of Technology.

Ceaser, James W., and Andrew E. Busch. 2001. *The Perfect Tie: The True Story of the 2000 Presidential Election*. Lanham, MD: Rowman and Littlefield.

DiClerico, Robert E., and James W. Davis. 2000. *Choosing Our Choices: Debating the Presidential Nominating Process*. Lanham, MD: Rowman and Littlefield.

Dudley, Robert L., and Alan R. Gitelson. 2002. *American Elections: The Rules Matter*. New York: Longman.

Hyneman, Charles S., with the collaboration of Charles E. Gilbert. 1968. *Popular Government in America: Foundations and Principles*. New York: Atherton Press.

Keating, Dan. 2003. "New Voting Systems Assailed." *Washington Post* (March 28): A12 and A13.

Keyssar, Alexander. 2000. *The Right to Vote*. New York: Basic Books.

Maisel, L. Sandy. 2002. *Parties and Elections in America*, 3rd ed. Lanham, MD: Rowman and Littlefield.

McDonald, Michael P., and Samuel L. Popkin. 2001. "The Myth of the Vanishing Voter." *American Political Science Review* 95 (December): 963–971.

Nagourney, Adam. 2002. "Early Voting Puts Many Candidates in Early Overdrive." *New York Times* (October 14): A1.

Ornstein, Norman. 2001. "The Dangers of Voting Outside the Booth." *New York Times* (August 31): A25.

———. 2002a. "No Need to Repeal the Electoral College," in Bruce Stinebrickner, *Annual Editions: American Government 02/03*. Guilford, CT: McGraw-Hill/Dushkin.

———. 2002b. "No Need to Repeal the Electoral College." *State Legislatures* (February): 12–16.

Patterson, Thomas E. 2002. *The Vanishing Voter: Public Involvement in an Age of Uncertainty.* New York: Alfred A. Knopf.

Schwartz, John. "Computer Fraud Is Open to Easy Fraud, Experts Say." *New York Times,* July 24, 2003, A12.

Suro, Robert. 1998. "Felonies to Bar 1.4 Million Black Men from Voting, Study Finds." *Washington Post* (October 23): A12.

Teixeira, Guy. 1992. *The Disappearing American Voter.* Washington, DC: Brookings Institution.

Twohey, Megan. 2001. "Once a Felon, Never a Voter." *National Journal* (January 6): 46.

Washington Post. 2002. "Urging Voters to Stay Home." October 24, A35.

Wolfinger, Raymond E., and Steven J. Rosenstone. 1980. *Who Votes?* New Haven: Yale University Press.

6

Organizations, Associations, and Governmental Agencies

There follow some sixty-seven websites (and mailing addresses and phone numbers, where available) that are related to the voting process. They fall roughly into three general categories, one of which consists of those seeking to report, explain, and educate voters about the functioning of the electoral process, perhaps in one particular area, or in a broad range of areas. Websites in a second category provide information as well but for the purpose of trying to convince the viewer that a specific change or set of changes is necessary in the electoral process, be it in the area of term limits, campaign finance reform, voting systems, and so on. A third category includes those sites that have as their goal increasing the number of individuals participating in the political process, including elections. The emphasis here is on stimulating political participation per se, as opposed to directing it toward a particular political purpose.

Administration and Cost of Elections (ACE) Project
ACE Project Manager
United Nations
2 UN Plaza, Room DC2-1714
New York, NY 10017
http://www.aceproject.org/main/english/default.htm

ACE provides information on election administration. It is designed to be a research resource for policy makers, election professionals, political parties, academics and students, and many others worldwide.

Alliance for Better Campaigns
1990 M Street NW, Suite 200
Washington, DC 20036
(202) 659-1743
http://bettercampaigns.org/

The Alliance for Better Campaigns is a public interest group that seeks to improve elections by supporting campaigns in which the most information reaches the largest number of citizens. It advocates free broadcast airtime for candidates and other reforms to allow for an increased flow of information and communication, and to make it cheaper for candidates. The alliance aspires to open up the political process to more competition and to encourage voter participation.

Ballot Access News
P.O. Box 470296
San Francisco, CA 94147
(415) 922-9779
http://www.ballot-access.org/

A nonpartisan monthly newsletter reporting on legislative and legal developments about the access of candidates and parties to the ballot; includes essays and articles on ballot issues and links relevant to elections and voting systems.

Ballot Initiative Strategy Center (BISC)
1025 Connecticut Avenue NW, Suite 205
Washington, DC 20036
(202) 223-2373
http://www.ballot.org/

Founded to help defeat right-wing initiatives and to develop a proactive, national initiative strategy for progressives, BISC seeks to build a new funding, research, and training infrastructure to support progressive ballot measures.

Brennan Center for Justice
161 Avenue of the Americas, 12th Floor
New York, NY 10013
(212) 998-6730
http://www.brennancenter.org/

The Brennan Center for Justice promotes public education and legal action in the areas of democracy and poverty. Through the Center's "Voter Choice" and "Voting and Representation" projects, the site focuses on increasing choice at the ballot box and promoting policies that protect rights to equal electoral access and political participation.

California Clean Money Campaign
8800 Venice Boulevard, Suite 321
Los Angeles, CA 90034
(800) 566-3780
http://www.californiacleanmoney.org

Its purpose is to educate California voters on the problems of money in campaigns and to understand how it distorts public policy decisionmaking, undermines citizen motivation, deters potentially strong candidates from running, and compromises the entire democratic system. It also seeks to educate voters about Clean Money Reform through public financing of elections.

Campaign for Young Voters (CYV)
1301 K Street NW, Suite 450 West
Washington, DC 20005
(202) 728-0418
http://www.campaignyoungvoters.org/

The Campaign for Young Voters (CYV), formerly known as the Young Voter Initiative, assists candidates for public office in their efforts to reach out and engage younger voters. CYV publishes a "toolkit" and suggested campaign practices and materials to assist candidates at all levels in dealing with young adults about political participation and voting.

Center for Democracy and Citizenship
1301 K Street NW, Suite 450 West
Washington, DC 20005
(202) 728-0418
http://www.excelgov.org/displayMainSection2.asp?keyword=prcHomePage

The mission of the Center for Democracy and Citizenship is to identify and implement ways to improve the performance of America's representative democracy. The center is part of the nonprofit, nonpartisan Council for Excellence in Government, based in Washington, D.C. The center brings to the larger task of democratic and civic renewal a unique orientation and competence to deal directly with the men and women who run for and hold political office.

Center for Public Integrity
910 17th Street NW, Seventh Floor
Washington, DC 20006
(202) 466-1300
http://www.publicintegrity.org

This center's mission is to provide the American people with findings from its investigations and analyses of public service, government accountability, and ethics-related issues. Among the issues it tracks are the role of money in elections and voting procedures.

Center for Responsive Politics
1101 14th Street NW, Suite 1030
Washington, DC 20005-5635
(202) 857-0044
http://www.opensecrets.org/

The Center for Responsive Politics is a nonpartisan, nonprofit research group that tracks money in politics, as well as its effect on elections and public policy. The center conducts computer-based research on campaign finance issues for the news media, academics, activists, and the public at large. Its work is aimed at creating a more educated voter, an involved citizenry, and a more responsive government.

Center for Voting and Democracy (CVD)
6930 Carroll Avenue, Suite 610
Takoma Park, MD 20912
(301) 270-4616
http://www.fairvote.org/

The CVD is a nonprofit organization dedicated to fair elections where every vote counts and all voters are represented. It undertakes research, analysis, education, and advocacy to promote a more democratic voting system. Subjects currently under review include representation, instant runoff voting, redistricting, voting rights, and voter turnout.

Citizens for a Fair Vote Count
P.O. Box 11339
Cincinnati, OH 45211
(513) 481-1992
http://www.votefraud.org/

This is the nation's oldest organization seeking to restore fair and honest elections in the United States. To that end, it advocates a return to paper ballots, marked with an indelible marker and kept at all times in public view, and counted in public by all factions of neighborhood citizens.

Citizens for Term Limits
11300 N. Pennsylvania Avenue, #177
Oklahoma City, OK 73120
(775) 848-1193
http://www.termlimits.com/

The mission of Citizens for Term Limits is to mobilize American citizens to push for a constitutional amendment to limit the number of terms an individual may serve in each house of Congress and to push for enabling legislation for such an amendment by a two-thirds vote in each house, and then to campaign for its ratification by the states.

Clean Elections Institute, Inc.
2001 N. Third Street, Suite 210
Phoenix, AZ 85004-1439
(602) 840-6633
http://www.azclean.org/

The Clean Elections Institute encourages participation in the electoral process and seeks to build confidence in democratic institutions in Arizona. This is done by providing educational material on elections and monitoring political activities in Arizona.

Committee for the Study of the American Electorate (CSAE)
805 21st Street NW, Suite 401
Washington, DC 20052
(202) 994-6000
http://www.gspm.org/csae/

CSAE is a nonprofit, nonpartisan research institution that is focused on issues surrounding citizen engagement in politics.

CSAE has become the primary source of information and analysis on registration and voter participation, and a primary source on related issues including registration laws and their impact on participation, campaign advertising and finance, the impact of media on politics, and citizen education.

Common Cause Issue: Redistricting
1615 Guadalupe, #204
Austin, TX 78701
(512) 474-2374
http://www.ccsi.com/~comcause/position/pp_rr.html

Believing that redistricting should be as far removed from legislators as possible, Common Cause supports the establishment of an independent Redistricting Commission to draw congressional and state legislative districts. The website details the composition for such a committee and the criteria to be used in appointing it.

Community Networking and Political Participation
Kim Gregson
School of Library and Information Science
Indiana University
107 S. Indiana Avenue
Bloomington, IN 47405
(812) 855-4848
http://ezinfo.ucs.indiana.edu/~kgregson/teledemocracy.html

Here will be found print materials and a host of organizations created to foster expanded participation in the political process. A major theme of both the materials and the organization is that technology has now created the conditions for greater involvement.

Computer Professionals for Social Responsibility (CPSR)
P.O. Box 717
Palo Alto, CA 94302
(650) 322-3778
http://www.cpsr.org/

The CPSR is a national organization of computer professionals dedicated to raising awareness about the appropriate use of computer technology. The site features a fair number of analyses and reports relevant to computerized voting standards.

Congressional Research Service (CRS)
Penny Hill Press
6440 Wiscasset Road
Bethesda, MD 20816
(301) 229-8229
http://www.pennyhill.com/elections.html

Reports issued by the CRS provide a wealth of information on a range of topics, including campaign finance, reapportionment, citizen initiatives, political parties' delegate selection methods, election procedures and standards, voting technologies, and voter registration and turnout.

Democracy Network
http://www.dnet.org/

Democracy Network is a source for information on voting, elections, and issues. It encourages citizens to register to vote and to learn about democracy and elections. It is a project of the League of Women Voters Education Fund.

Democracy 21 Project
1825 I Street NW, Suite 400
Washington, DC 20006
(202) 429-2008
http://www.democracy21.org/

Democracy 21 is a nonprofit, nonpartisan organization dedicated to making democracy work for all Americans. It works toward eliminating the influence of big money in American politics and to ensure the integrity and fairness of government decisions and elections. It supports campaign finance reforms and other political reforms to accomplish these goals. Democracy 21 also pursues ways to use the Internet and other new media to strengthen democracy and involve citizens in government and politics.

Election Center
12543 Westella, Suite 100
Houston, TX 77077
(281) 293-0101
http://www.electioncenter.org/

The Election Center is a nonprofit organization dedicated to promoting, preserving, and improving democracy. Its members are government employees whose profession is to serve in voter registration and elections administrations.

Election.com
1001 Franklin Avenue, Suite 212
Garden City, NY 11530
(516) 248-4200
http://www.election.com

Election.com plans, designs, and manages traditional and Internet-based elections and surveys for private organizations and political jurisdictions around the world. The website contains information on voting technologies, voter registration, and absentee ballots.

Election Data Services
1401 K Street NW, Suite 500
Washington, DC 20005
(202) 789-2004
http://www.electiondataservices.com/home.htm

This is a consulting firm specializing in redistricting, election administration, and the analysis and presentation of census and political data. The website features a voting equipment study that enables local jurisdictions to assess their needs and analyze their requirements as they consider the acquisition of new voting equipment.

Electionline.org
1101 30th Street NW, Suite 210
Washington, DC 20007
(202) 338-9860
http://www.electionline.org/

This site is maintained by the Election Reform Information Project. It provides access to current news and analysis on U.S. elections and election reform, covering such issues as election administration procedures, electronic voting, and voter registration.

Election Reform Information Project
1101 30th Street NW, Suite 210
Washington, DC 20007
(202) 338-9860
http://www.electionline.org/index.jsp

The Election Reform Information Project provides the nation's only nonpartisan, nonadvocacy website providing up-to-the-minute news and analysis on election reform. The website is a forum for learning about, discussing, and analyzing election reform issues. The project also provides research on questions of interest to the election reform community and sponsors conferences where policymakers, journalists, and other interested parties can gather to share ideas, successes, and failures.

Elections Today
1101 15th Street NW, Third Floor
Washington, DC 20005
(202) 828-8507
http://www.ifes.org/research comm/publications.html

Elections Today is a newsletter published by the International Foundation for Election Systems. It provides access to new stories and articles about recent parliamentary and presidential elections.

Electionworld.org
http://www.electionworld.org/

This site provides information on the results of elections worldwide and offers a forum in which to discuss and to research those elections.

Electoral Reform Society
6 Chancel Street
London, SE1 OUU
United Kingdom
+44(0) 207-928-1622
www.electoral-reform.org.uk/

The mission of the Electoral Reform Society is to secure at all levels of representation an electoral system that will ensure all votes have equal value, give effective representation to all significant points of view within the electorate, allow electors to vote for their preferred candidates without fear of wasting their votes, and ensure the accountability of individual representatives to their electorates.

Electronic Voting
Rebecca Mercuri

P.O. Box 1166—Dept. EV
Philadelphia, PA 19105
http://www.notablesoftware.com/evote.html

Dr. Rebecca Mercuri's web page includes valuable resources (links, papers, statements, and articles) on voting technologies, e-voting in particular.

E-Voter Institute
http://www.e-voterinstitute.com/

The website of a trade association promoting online/digital services to government and political parties, it includes discussion about the use of the Internet in campaigning and voting.

Federal Election Commission (FEC)
999 E Street NW
Washington, DC 20463
(800) 424-9530
http://www.fec.gov/

The FEC was created to administer and enforce the Federal Election Campaign Act (FECA). Its duties are to disclose campaign finance information; to enforce the provisions of the law, such as limits and prohibitions on contributions; and to oversee the public funding of presidential elections. In addition to providing updates on contributions to federal candidates, it provides other useful information related to elections, including election results and information related to the functioning of the Electoral College. The website includes an informative Q&A section on the establishment of uniform voting system standards.

Federal Voting Assistance Program
Office of the Secretary of Defense
Washington Headquarters Services
1155 Defense Pentagon
Washington, DC 20301-1155
(800) 438-8683
http://www.fvap.gov/index.html

This website provides information to U.S. citizens covered by the Uniformed and Overseas Citizens Absentee Voting Act (UOCAVA).

Freedom's Answer
1233 20th Street NW, #203
Washington, DC 20036
(202) 785-5920
http://www.freedomsanswer.net

This is a nonprofit, nonpartisan movement started after September 11, 2001, to increase voter turnout by registering voters, taking pledges to vote, and providing voter information.

Freedom's Answer Youth Voter Corps
1010 Vermont Avenue NW, Suite 715
Washington, DC 20005
(202) 783-4751
http://www.freedomsanswer.net/yvc.home.shtml

Freedom's Answer Youth Voter Corps is a nonpartisan group of students who register new voters, including eighteen-year-old classmates; help increase voter turnout; and serve as poll workers to assist with the overflow of voters at the polls that their campaign will create. Every high school across the nation is invited to participate in Freedom's Answer and the Youth Voter Corps.

Global Initiative to Enfranchise People with Disabilities
1101 15th Street NW, Third Floor
Washington, DC 20005
(202) 828-8507
http://www. electionaccess.org

A project of the International Foundation for Election Systems (IFES), the initiative provides information gathered from countries around the world on voting for the disabled, including current laws and regulations; an IFES-proposed set of rights and standards; a list of countries with the best records; and a number of publications on the subject.

Government by the People
http://www.vote.org

This site promotes the use of technology in order for citizens to express themselves through voting and drafting of legislation. Its E-Government Project provides government with feedback on an ongoing basis.

Initiative and Referendum Institute
P.O. Box 6306
Leesburg, VA 20178
(703) 723-9621
http://www.iandrinstitute.org/http://www.ballotwatch.org/

The Initiative and Referendum Institute is a nonprofit, nonpartisan organization that provides information on the initiative and referendum process at the local, state, and national levels. Its mission is to research and develop clear analyses of the initiative process and its use, to inform and educate the public about the process and its effects, and to provide effective leadership in litigation—defending the initiative process and the right of citizens to reform their government.

Institute for Politics, Democracy, and the Internet (IPDI)
Graduate School of Political Management
George Washington University
805 21st Street NW, Suite 401
Washington, DC 20052
(800) 367-4776
http://www.ipdi.org/

IPDI's mission is to promote the development of U.S. online politics in a manner that upholds democratic values. Its goals are the establishment of a research base for the study of online politics, especially with respect to U.S. campaigns and elections; the design, testing, refinement, and promotion of appropriate standards of practice for the conduct of online campaigning; and the creation and public promotion of an online public space where good campaign practices and democratic values may thrive.

International Foundation for Election Systems (IFES)
1101 15th Street NW, Third Floor
Washington, DC 20005
(202) 828-8507
http://www.ifes.org

With a goal of encouraging national and international democracy, the IFES has been active in more than one hundred countries, providing technical assistance in all areas of election administration and management.

**International Institute for Democracy and
Electoral Assistance (IDEA)**
Stromsborg
S-103 34 Stockholm
Sweden
+468-698-3700
www.idea.int

IDEA is an intergovernmental organization that seeks to nurture and support sustainable democracy worldwide. Global in membership and independent of specific national interests, IDEA works with both new and long-established democracies, helping to develop the institutions and culture of democracy. It also provides a forum for dialogue between academics, policymakers, and democracy practitioners around the world, and helps countries build the capacity to develop and strengthen democratic institutions.

League of Women Voters
1730 M Street NW, Suite 1000
Washington, DC 20036-4508
(202) 429-1965
http://www.lwv.org/

The League of Women Voters seeks to encourage the informed and active participation of citizens in government, works to increase understanding of major public policy issues, and influences public policy through education and advocacy. The league provides voter information, information about civic participation, and information on current public policy issues such as election reform, campaign finance reform, and health care.

Lorrie Faith Cranor's Voting Web Page
http://lorrie.cranor.org/voting/

This site contains pointers to all the voting-related work and other relevant resources of Lorrie Faith Cranor, an associate research professor at the Carnegie Mellon School of Computer Science. Of special notice is the Electronic Voting Hotlist, which features a list of links to Internet sites with electronic-voting-related information.

National Association of Secretaries of State
Hall of States

444 N. Capitol Street NW, Suite 401
Washington, DC 20001
(202) 624-3525
http://www.nass.org/

This cite includes state election office contact information, state election laws and administration issues, and information about recent proposals adopted by the association, including programs to reengage young voters and increase voter registration election-day volunteering.

National Association of State Election Directors (NASED)
Council of State Governments
444 N. Capitol Street NW, Suite 401
Washington, DC 20001
(202) 624-5460
http://www.nased.org/

NASED's website includes a list of all voting systems that are NASED qualified. A directory of all state election officials and their URLs is also included.

National Commission on Federal Election Reform
Federal Election Reform Network
c/o The Century Foundation
41 E. 70th Street
New York, NY 10021
(212) 452-7750
http://www.reformelections.org

The National Commission on Federal Election Reform was orga-nized by the Miller Center of Public Affairs of the University of Virginia and the Century Foundation. Formed following the 2000 presidential election, it seeks to formulate concrete proposals for election reform that will help ensure a more effective and fair process in elections to come.

National Election Studies (NES)
Center for Political Studies
P.O. Box 1248
Ann Arbor, MI 48106-1248
(734) 764-5494
http://www.umich.ed/~nes/

The NES strives to produce high-quality data on voting, public opinion, and political participation. These data are used to serve the research needs of social scientists, teachers, students, policy-makers, and journalists concerned with the theoretical and empirical foundations of mass politics in a democratic society.

National Initiative for Democracy
http://www.vote.org

This is a national organization seeking to bring about the adoption of a constitutional amendment establishing a national initiative process.

National Voting Rights Institute (NVRI)
27 School Street, Suite 500
Boston, MA 02108
(617) 624-3900
http://www.nvri.org/

The NVRI is a prominent legal center in the campaign finance reform field. Through litigation and public education, the institute aims to redefine the issue of private money in public elections as the nation's newest voting rights barrier, and to vindicate the constitutional right of all citizens, regardless of their economic status, to participate in the electoral process on an equal and meaningful basis.

New Democracy's List of Election Reforms
http://www.mich.com/~donald/reassign.html

This site calls for and discusses proposals to reform the single-member district and plurality methods of election.

Office of Election Administration
999 E Street NW
Washington, DC 20463
(800) 424-9530
http://www.fec.gov/pages/OEArole.htm

A division of the Federal Election Commission, this office provides information and advice to state and local officials on such matters as election case law, computerizing election management, ballot access procedures, contested elections and recounts, and recent innovations in the administration of elections.

President Elect
http://www.presidentelect.org/

President Elect serves as the unofficial homepage for the Electoral College. It provides information on the election of U.S. presidents and facts about the Electoral College.

Project Vote Smart
One Common Ground
Philipsburg, MT 59858
(406) 859-8683
http://www.vote-smart.org/

Administrators of Project Vote Smart provide carefully researched data on elected officials at the national and state levels—their voting records, campaign finances, issue positions, position statements, and backgrounds. Included on the website is information on registration procedures in individual states.

Proportional Representation Library
Douglas J. Amy
Department of Political Science
Mount Holyoke College
Skinner Hall, Room 110
South Hadley, MA 01075
(413) 538-2667
http://www.mtholyoke.edu/acad/polit/damy/prlib.htm

This is a good source of information on proportional representation elections, including beginning readings, in-depth articles by scholars and activists, an extensive bibliography, and a guide to related websites.

Rock the Vote
http://action.rockthe
vote,org/action/index.asp?step=2&item=10044

Designed to motivate young people, this website includes voter registration information, surveys, and a facility to e-mail Congress.

Secure Electronic Registration and Voting Experiment (SERVE)
Office of the Secretary of Defense
Washington Headquarters Services

1155 Defense Pentagon
Washington, DC 20301-1155
(800) 438-8683
http://www.fvap.gov/index.html

This website is an Internet Voting System for the 2004 elections and is the latest in a series of technology initiatives undertaken by the Federal Voting Assistance Program as part of its mission to improve access to the polls for uniformed and overseas citizens.

Social Science Information Gateway (SOSIG)
Institute for Learning and Research Technology
University of Bristol
8-10 Berkeley Square
Bristol BS8 1HH
United Kingdom
http://www.sosig.ac.uk/roads/subject-listing/
worldcat/eleccampaigns.html

SOSIG's website contains a host of material related to the conduct of elections, including books, papers, reports, and journal articles, as well as links to other relevant organizations within the United States and around the world.

Strategic Taskforce to Organize and Mobilize People (STOMP)
320 First Street SE
Washington, DC 20003
(202) 479-7000
http://stomp4victory.org/

STOMP is a Republican organization made up of volunteers whose main purpose is to mobilize voters. It encourages people to register and vote Republican and provides information about candidates.

Term Limits Home Page
10 G Street NE, Suite 410
Washington, DC 20002
(800) 733-6440
http://www.termlimits.org/

This website seeks to rally Americans to the cause of limiting the terms of service of elected officials at the national, state, and local levels. To this end, the site provides information and articles on term limits, as well as on relevant organizations for those who want to become involved.

Vanishing Voter Project
Joan Shorenstein Center on the Press, Politics, and Public Policy
John F. Kennedy School of Government
79 JFK Street, Second Floor Taubman
Cambridge, MA 02138
(617) 495-8269
http://www.vanishingvoter.org/

The Vanishing Voter Project seeks to reinvigorate the presidential campaign through research-based proposals designed to improve its structure. The project has the goal of broadening and deepening citizens' involvement in the presidential selection process.

Votehere.net
http://www.votehere.net/

The website of this vendor of electronic voting systems contains technical information on computerized voting.

Voting Task and Voting Systems
http://accurate democracy.com/voting_systems.htm

This site explains improvements for democracy of any size, from schoolroom to nationwide, and at all steps in the process from nominating candidates to allocating funds.

Your Vote Counts
http://www.yourvotecounts.org/flashsite.html

Your Vote Counts is an organization that focuses on encouraging people to vote. Its website, which is provided as a public service by the Ad Council and the Federal Voting Assistance Program, provides links to voter information on such subjects as candidates, issues, and voter registration.

Your Vote Matters
http://www.yourvotematters.com/

Your Vote Matters is an organization created to encourage and facilitate the active participation of young Americans in the political process. Its goal is to translate the inner workings of the government into a format that makes it easy to understand what the government is doing and how it affects young people.

Youth Vote Coalition
1010 Vermont Avenue NW, Suite 715
Washington, DC 20005
(202) 783-4751
http://www.youthvote.org/

Youth Vote Coalition is a nonprofit coalition that seeks to increase the political involvement of 18–30-year-olds. The coalition is made up of over ninety diverse organizations.

7

Print and Nonprint Resources

This chapter begins with an annotated list of books, monographs, and reports related to the subject of voting. The first section contains entries focusing primarily on the initial quest for the *right* to vote, including the people and organizations playing a prominent role, and the variety of forces that both impeded and facilitated the movement toward universal suffrage. Also included here are entries related to the expansion of that right beyond the general election to include nominations and decisions on initiatives and referenda, and recalls.

The second section identifies a number of sources that bear more directly on the *value* of the franchise, recognizing, of course, that some of these may, for purposes of providing historical context, open with discussions that address some aspect of the right to vote as well. Within this second section are a number of subsections, each of which deals with a subject matter relevant to the value of the vote: the configuration of the ballot and voting systems; the current functioning of the presidential nominating process; the procedures for redistricting and reapportionment, and their consequences; participation in, and the policies decided by, initiatives and referenda; the level of participation in elections; the role of money in elections; and the Electoral College.

The third and final section lists a number of video and audio cassettes currently available that address one or more subjects related to the right to vote and/or the value of the vote. These subjects include why we should vote, voter apathy, the implications of new voting technology, controversy over the Florida vote in the 2000 presidential election, the Electoral College, term limits, the role of money, and the consequences of elections.

Print Resources

The Right to Vote

Howard Ball, Dale Krane, and Thomas P. Lauth. *Compromised Compliance: Implementation of the 1965 Voting Rights Act.* Westport, CT: Greenwood Press, 1982.

This book focuses on the Section 5 enforcement provision of the 1965 Voting Rights Act. It addresses the roles of the Justice Department, political leaders at all levels of government, civil rights groups, federal judges, county and city officials, and voter groups in rectifying violations of the Voting Rights Act. As the authors reveal, the record has been far from perfect, due in part to the nature of the act itself and partly also to the actors charged with enforcing it.

Constance Buel Burnett. *Five for Freedom.* New York: Greenwood Press, 1968.

Here are chronicled the lives of five women of preeminent importance in rousing the nation to recognize the injustice being done to women by denying them the right to vote. It was Quaker preacher Lucretia Mott who inspired Elizabeth Cady Stanton to take up the cause, only to be followed by Lucy Stone and Susan B. Anthony. On their heels came Carrie Chapman Catt, who would transform a disjointed movement into an effective, functioning organization.

Jane Jerome Cambi. *Women against Women: American Anti-Suffragism, 1880–1920.* Brooklyn: Carlson Publishing, 1994.

Suffragettes, as this book vividly demonstrates, had to confront not only skeptical males but a group of vehemently opposed women. Included in this examination is the philosophy of these antisuffrage women, the strategies and tactics they employed to defeat the right to vote, and the role of one of its most prominent, if less dogmatic, members, Ida Tarbell.

Marchette Gaylord Chute, ed. *The First Liberty: A History of the Right to Vote in America, 1619–1850.* New York: Dutton, 1969.

Traces the right to vote over some two and a half centuries, commencing with the forces that precipitated the creation of the first elected assembly in 1619 and ending shortly after the Dorr rebellion—the last significant effort to prevent white males from voting.

Nancy F. Cott, ed. *History of Women in the United States, Vol. 19: Women Suffrage.* Munich: K. G. Saur, 1994.

Part of a twenty-volume series on the history of women in the U.S., this particular volume contains a collection of thirty essays, nearly all of which are devoted to state-specific examinations of the women's suffrage movement.

William J. Crotty. *Political Reform and the American Experiment.* New York: Thomas Y. Crowell, 1977.

Although addressing a number of subjects related to the electoral process, it contains a good opening chapter on the expansion of the suffrage from colonial times to the mid-twentieth century.

Wendell W. Cultice. *Youth's Battle for the Ballot: A History of Voting Age in America.* Westport, CT: Greenwood Press, 1992.

Tracing advocacy for the youth vote all the way back to ancient Greece, the author shows that throughout history there have been calls to enfranchise the young, and he notes the practice of conferring the military franchise on youth in Athens and in Rome, as well as in Europe during the Middle Ages, and in the colonies of the New World. The focus then turns to efforts by the states and federal government to lower the voting age, public and political opinion on this issue, the role of the three branches in advancing and/or retarding the movement, and how youth groups organized to bring pressure to bear on the political system.

Chandler Davidson and Bernard Grofman, eds. *Quiet Revolution in the South: The Impact of the Voting Rights Act, 1965–1990.* Princeton, NJ: Princeton University Press, 1994.

These essays examine the impact of the Voting Rights Act on each of eight southern states, focusing first on brief histories of voting in the state, then litigation arising out of the Voting Rights Act, the impact of at-large election systems on minority representation, how the act impacted on the election of minority candidates at the local level, and the success of minority candidates in white-dominated districts.

James W. Davis. *Presidential Primaries: Road to the White House.* New York: Thomas Y. Crowell, 1967.

In this classic work on presidential primaries, the author considers the forces that gave rise to the presidential primary, how our method of nomination differs from other Western democracies, types of primaries used in states, primary financing, how different types of candidates fare in primaries, and the overall impact of primaries on who is likely to win. The underlying theme of the book is that the primaries, in conjunction with a national party convention, constitute a superior method for nominating candidates than the party convention by itself. The former, Davis argues, requires candidates to demonstrate both their vote-getting ability and their skill at negotiating in the "smoke-filled room" with party leaders, while the latter tests only their negotiating skills.

Kenneth L. Eshleman. *Where Should Students Vote? The Courts, the States, and Local Officials.* Lanham, MD: University Press of America, 1989.

It is contended here that the issue of whether students should vote where they matriculate or where they live raises thorny constitutional, administrative, and political questions for courts, legislatures, and local officials. Also included are data on the actual and potential impact of student voting in college communities.

John Hope Franklin. *From Slavery to Freedom,* 3rd ed. New York: Alfred A. Knopf, 1967.

This definitive work deals comprehensively with the black condition from the time of slavery through 1966. Included in this examination is an excellent analysis of the right to vote granted blacks following the Civil War, how it was frustrated by southern states over a period of many years, and how it was won back in the 1960s.

Marvin E. Gettleman. *The Dorr Rebellion: A Study in American Radicalism, 1833–1849.* New York: Random House, 1973.

Described here are the movement and ultimate rebellion led by Thomas Wilson Dorr of Rhode Island as he fought to wrest from conservatives the right to vote, and more, for the white male population of his state. This rebellion, which was ultimately suppressed, represented the last major attempt in the states to prevent white males from voting.

William Gillette. *The Right to Vote: The Politics and Passage of the Fifteenth Amendment.* Baltimore: Johns Hopkins University Press, 1965.

A brief account of the background, passage, and ratification of the Fifteenth Amendment, focusing on the campaign for ratification in the South, border states, Midwest, New England, and West.

Sara Hunter Graham. *Woman Suffrage and the New Democracy.* New Haven, CT: Yale University Press, 1996.

Arguing that the National American Woman Suffrage Association was one of the most effective single issue groups in U.S. history, the author examines this association as a "pressure group," employing the conceptual framework of the pressure group literature. The first portion of the book (1890–1915) examines the formation of the organization; the second focuses on the strategies and tactics it employed as a pressure group and details how these strategies and tactics affected the internal workings of the organization itself.

Bernard Grofman and Chandler Davidson, eds. *Controversies in Minority Voting: The Voting Rights Act in Perspective.* Washington, DC: Brookings Institution, 1992.

Scholars and practitioners explore a number of controversies surrounding the historic 1965 Voting Rights Act, including how both the Justice Department and the courts have interpreted the act, whether amendments to it (1970, 1975, 1982) by Congress have kept faith with its original intent, and the degree to which the act has actually fueled racial and ethnic animosities.

Miriam Gurko. *The Ladies of Seneca Falls: The Birth of the Women's Rights Movement.* New York: Macmillan, 1974.

This book examines the roles and impact of such giants in the women's suffrage movement as Susan B. Anthony and Elizabeth Cady Stanton, and also the importance of such less-attended-to figures as Mary Wollstonecraft, the Grimke sisters, and Margaret Fuller.

Charles V. Hamilton. *The Bench and the Ballot: Southern Federal Judges and Black Voters.* New York: Oxford University Press, 1973.

Focusing on the critical eight-year period between the Civil Rights Act of 1957 and Voting Rights Act of 1965, Hamilton examines some fifteen cases brought before the federal courts in the South, doing so in the context of the particular judicial styles and temperaments of the presiding judges.

Patricia Greenwood Harrison. *Connecting Links: The British and American Woman Suffrage Movements, 1900–1914.* Westport, CT: Greenwood Press, 2000.

To a far greater extent than previously realized, there was considerable cross-pollination going on between the British and American suffrage movements, including visits, speaking tours, and organizational participation, as well as the sharing of strategies and tactics. This said, the author also maintains that after 1906 the influence flowed much more heavily from England to the United States than vice versa.

David Michael Hudson. *Along Racial Lines: Consequences of the 1965 Voting Rights Act.* New York: Peter Lang, 1998.

Provides a concise and useful examination of the Voting Rights Act of 1965 and subsequent amendments to it, including the debate over them, and how they were reshaped by the federal courts. Particularly useful are the case studies of how these laws impacted three minority groups: blacks (Dallas, Texas), Hispanics (Dade County, Florida), and American Indians (Navajo Reservation, Arizona).

Harold Hyman and Stuart Bruchey. *Women Vote in the West: The Women Suffrage Movement, 1869–1896.* New York: Garland, 1986.

While Congress was debating the merits of testing out women's suffrage in the territories, the territorial legislatures of Dakota, Wyoming, Utah, New Mexico, and Colorado considered whether to grant women the right to vote, with only Wyoming and Utah deciding to do so. This book examines these efforts in the states of Wyoming, Utah, Colorado, and Idaho.

Julia E. Johnsen, ed. *Lowering the Voting Age.* New York: H. G. Wilson, 1944.

A wonderfully organized book beginning with a series of essays offering a general discussion of extending the franchise, followed by a second set of essays that argues for lowering the voting age, and then a final set of essays coming out against it. At the end of the book is an excellent, detailed fourteen-page outline summarizing all the points pro and con.

V. O. Key Jr. *Southern Politics in State and Nation.* New York: Alfred A. Knopf, 1950.

Although this groundbreaking work deals comprehensively with the politics in each of ten southern states, eight chapters are devoted to black voting and the methods used to prevent it, including detailed analyses of the literacy test, poll tax, and white primary.

Alexander Keyssar. *The Right to Vote: The Contested History of Democracy in the United States.* New York: Basic Books, 2000.

In this magisterial work, Keyssar examines exhaustively the expansion of the right to vote from the time of the American Revolution up to the present, focusing on the struggles of various groups (women, African Americans, Native Americans, immigrants) to win the vote, as well as on how changing social and economic forces at times frustrated or facilitated the movement toward universal suffrage.

Charles Sumner Lobingier. *The People's Law, Or Popular Participation in Law-Making.* New York: Macmillan Press, 1909.

An exhaustive examination of direct legislation (initiative and referendum) beginning first with its use in Europe, after which the author turns his attention to the United States, noting that direct legislation was, in fact, employed in colonial America and in the revolutionary period, well before its first formal adoption in South Dakota in 1897. A significant section of the book examines its adoption and use in the southern and western states.

Susan E. Marshall. *Splintered Sisterhood: Gender and Class in the Campaign against Woman Suffrage.* Madison: University of Wisconsin Press, 1997.

It is argued here that the antisuffrage movement among women, which equaled in intensity the sentiment for it, was energized by wealthy, educated women who exercised considerable political influence through their husbands and their membership on social service committees. Extending the vote to women of the lower class would, these antisuffragettes believed, further increase the "ignorant vote" and ultimately lead to the removal of these well-placed women from positions of influence.

Donald R. Matthews and James W. Prothro. *Negroes and the New Southern Politics.* New York: Harcourt, Brace, and World, 1966.

Relying on what was arguably the largest collection of data ever compiled up to that time on black political behavior in the South, this study attempted to determine the extent to which blacks were participating in a broad range of political activities, including voting; why some were more involved than others; and the consequences of this involvement for southern politics and race relations.

Dudley O. McGovney. *The American Suffrage Medley: The Need for a National Uniform Suffrage.* Chicago: University of Chicago Press, 1949.

The author discusses the philosophical underpinnings that informed the Founding Fathers' views on voting, and their views on citizen participation in the election of representatives, senators, and president. He then discusses the "medley" of restrictions placed on voting by the states at the midpoint of the twentieth century, noting weaknesses in the Fourteenth, Fifteenth, and Twentieth Amendments that made them possible. He concludes that a further amendment is necessary to require a national uniform standard of voting in the United States.

National American Woman Suffrage Association. *Victory: How Women Won It, 1840–1940.* New York: H. W. Wilson, 1940.

A collection of eleven essays that sequentially deal with the initial agitation by women for the vote, their first victory in Wyoming, the campaign state by state, cracks in the opposition, and the campaign to persuade Congress. Despite the title of the book, scarcely any attention is given to events beyond 1920.

Ellis P. Oberholtzer. *The Referendum in America.* Freeport, NY: Books for Libraries Press, 1893.

A discussion of the referendum in Switzerland, where it originated, is followed by an examination of its incorporation into some state constitutions, which required the use of the referendum on such issues as the location of state capitals, a state's territorial area and jurisdiction, city charters, and certain tax issues. The concluding chapter assesses how the courts have handled questions arising from the use of referenda.

Frederic D. Ogden. *The Poll Tax in the South.* Tuscaloosa: University of Alabama Press, 1958.

An in-depth examination of the poll tax in the eleven states of the former Confederacy, focusing upon its origins, form, how it was collected, its relationship to political corruption, impacts on registration, and the efforts to repeal it. Although concluding that the poll tax was not responsible for preventing as many people from voting as has been claimed, Ogden nevertheless acknowledges that it is wholly incompatible with a democratic process.

Byron Shaffer. *Quiet Revolution: The Struggle for the Democratic Party and the Shaping of Post-Reform Politics.* New York: Russell Sage Foundation, 1983.

Shaffer details the campaign, precipitated by the battle for the Democratic Party presidential nomination in 1968, by reformist elements within the party to bring about sweeping changes in how delegates to its national convention are selected—changes that would ultimately revolutionize the presidential nominating process in both parties by expanding the role of the rank and file while reducing that of the party elites.

Elizabeth Cady Stanton, Susan B. Anthony, and Matilda Joslyn Gage, eds. *History of Woman Suffrage.* 6 vols. New York: Fowler and Wells, 1881.

An extraordinary chronicle of the women's suffrage movement from 1848 to 1920. Early volumes contain reminiscences by and about prominent members of the movement as well as activities in various states. Later volumes focus primarily on progress state by state, national conventions, and even the women's rights movement in Europe.

Donald S. Strong. *Negroes, Ballots, and Judges.* Tuscaloosa: University of Alabama Press, 1968.

The focus here is on how the 1957 and 1960 Civil Rights Acts impacted three states (Alabama, Mississippi, and Louisiana) most resistant to the full incorporation of blacks into American society. The author details efforts by their state legislatures and judges to render both acts ineffective.

Abigail Thernstrom. *Whose Votes Count? Affirmative Action and Minority Voting Rights.* Cambridge, MA: Harvard University Press, 1987.

A history of the 1965 Voting Rights Act and how it has been amended by judicial interpretation, administrative action, and Congress. These subjects are examined in the context of the book's underlying theme—how to discern electoral inequality and the circumstances that justify federal intervention in state and local elections. In the course of this discussion, it becomes clear that the author does not in every instance accept the received wisdom on what constitutes electoral inequality.

U.S. Commission on Civil Rights. *Report of the United States Commission on Civil Rights 1959.* Washington, DC: U.S. Government Printing Office, 1959.

Although this report addresses the condition of blacks in the areas of education and housing, Part Two is devoted to the issue of voting and provides an excellent summary of voting in the South from 1865 on, statistical analyses of black voting over this period, and practices still in use by states to impede black voting. It concludes with a set of recommendations mandating the U.S. Census to compile registration and voting statistics, requiring states to maintain public voting records, and calling for the establishment of more effective procedures to allow the Civil Rights Commission to pursue infringements upon the right to vote.

Alan Ware. *The American Direct Primary.* New York: Cambridge University Press, 2002.

An excellent treatment on the origins and spread of the direct primary in the United States. In the course of this examination Ware rejects the conventional wisdom that reformers advocated the direct primary to weaken what were seen as corrupt political parties. He argues instead that the impetus for the use of the direct primary came from within the parties themselves.

Marjorie Spruill Wheeler. *New Women of the New South: The Leaders of the Women's Suffrage Movement in the Southern States.* New York: Oxford University Press, 1993.

In the region of the country where the fight for woman's suffrage had the toughest road to hoe, this author describes the robust women's suffrage movement that developed in the 1890s, fueled primarily by the argument being made by suffragettes that granting women the vote would act as a counterweight to black voting strength.

Chilton Williamson. *American Suffrage from Property to Democracy.* Princeton, NJ: Princeton University Press, 1960.

A classic on the evolution of the suffrage from 1760 to the eve of the Civil War. Williamson traces the struggle in the several states between advocates of the property qualification for voting and those in favor of manhood suffrage, noting that even when the property qualification was in effect, male suffrage was more widespread than some scholars have claimed.

The Value of the Vote
Ballots and Voting Systems

Spencer D. Albright. *The American Ballot.* Washington, DC: American Council on Public Affairs, 1942.

An examination, in both primary and general elections, of the ballot forms in use during the first part of the twentieth century, as well as the extent to which states were moving toward the adoption of voting machines, and with what results.

Douglas J. Amy. *Real Choices and New Voices: The Case for Proportional Representational Elections in the United States.* New York: Columbia University Press, 1993.

According to Amy, our current single-member district plurality elections are outmoded, unfair, and undemocratic, fostering low turnout elections, undifferentiated candidates, two-party monopoly, wasted votes, issueless campaigns, underrepresentation of women, lack of minority representation, and gerrymandering—all of which would be ended under a system of proportional representation.

————. *Behind the Ballot Box: A Citizen's Guide to Voting Systems.* Westport, CT: Praeger Publishers, 2000.

A concise analysis of various voting systems (plurality, majority, proportional, semiproportional) along with a suggested set of criteria for evaluating voting systems and how well each voting system meets each criterion.

Henry M. Bain and Donald Hecock. *Ballot Position and Voter's Choice.* Detroit: Wayne State University Press, 1937.

These authors demonstrate through empirical analysis that candidates enjoy a significant advantage over their opponents as a result of where their names are placed on a paper ballot or voting machine.

Henry E. Brady, Justin Buchler, Matt Jarvis, and John McNulty. *Counting All the Votes: The Performance of Voting Technology in the United States.* Berkeley: University of California Press, 2002.

An empirical analysis (based upon data from 2,219 counties in the 2000 election) that seeks to determine those voting systems that do the best job of registering and tabulating votes by minimizing the percentage of ballots recording no vote for president, due to either undervotes or overvotes. Five different voting systems are compared—direct record electronic, lever machines, optical scan, paper ballot, and punchcard. Punchcards are found to perform the worst, while optical scans and direct record electronic perform best.

David Butler, Howard R. Penniman, and Austin Ranney, eds. *Democracy at the Polls: A Comparative Study of Competitive National Elections.* Washington, DC: American Enterprise Institute, 1981.

Examines elections in twenty-eight Western democracies, including the United States, focusing on how votes are translated into seats in the legislature, how political parties are organized, candidate selection, financing of elections, the role of media and polls, turnout, and the impact of elections on public policy.

Caltech/MIT Voting Technology Project 2001. *Voting: What Is, What Could Be.* Pasadena, CA, and Cambridge, MA: California Institute of Technology and Massachusetts Institute of Technology, 2001.

An excellent examination of current voting systems along several dimensions—cost, equipment, registration, absentee and early voting, polling places, and ballot security. In the concluding section is proposed a Modular Voting Architecture designed to overcome the limitations of current voting equipment.

The Democracy Online Project. *Voting in the Information Age: The Debate over Technology.* Washington, DC: Graduate School of Political Management, George Washington University, 2001.

An excellent discussion of whether to establish national voting standards and the benefits and drawbacks of employing technologies such as ATM machines and the Internet as methods of voting.

Robert L. Dudley and Alan Gitelson. *American Elections: The Rules Matter.* New York: Longman, 2002.

A concise overview of the electoral process, including the expansion of the franchise, apportionment and districting, gaining access to the ballot, types of ballots and ballot counting procedures, and a concluding section on the Electoral College—how it operates, who benefits, and proposals for change.

L. E. Fredman. *The Australian Ballot: The Story of an American Reform.* East Lansing: Michigan State University Press, 1968.

Following a discussion of the British and Australian experience with the secret ballot, the author considers how the movement toward this profound reform developed in the United States, the reasons it was adopted, the individuals and groups promoting it, and its dissemination throughout the states.

Lani Guinier. *The Tyranny of the Majority: Fundamental Fairness in Representative Democracy.* New York: Free Press, 1995.

Taking turns, redesigning electoral districts on the basis of interests, and cumulative voting are explored as ways out of the quagmire in which minorities repeatedly find themselves, namely, having their interests routinely ignored by electoral majorities.

Steven Hill. *Fixing Elections: The Failure of America's Winner Take All Politics.* New York: Routledge, 2002.

Hill argues that the geography-based winner-take-all system of electing presidents and legislatures is at the root of many pathologies in the American political system, including low turnout, expensive and negative campaigns, the absence of proper minority and majority representation, gridlock in Congress, regional balkanization, and the differences existing between the inhabitants of our cities and middle America.

Arend Lijphart and Bernard Grofman, eds. *Choosing an Electoral System: Issues and Alternatives.* New York: Praeger, 1984.

In this collection of essays by leading scholars from six countries, the battle over the desirability of plurality rule versus proportional representation is joined with some arguing that the former insures, among other things, a stronger government, while others maintain that the latter guarantees a fairer representation of interests in the legislature. Still others suggest that by way of impact there may be fewer differences between the two systems than might appear.

Samuel Merrill III. *Making Multicandidate Elections More Democratic.* Princeton, NJ: Princeton University Press, 1988.

In order to avoid the possibility in multicandidate races whereby the candidate most acceptable to the majority of voters actually loses, the author proposes the adoption of "approval voting," allowing voters to vote for as many candidates as they wish, but casting only one ballot per candidate.

Dick Morris. *VOTE.com.* Los Angeles, CA: Renaissance Books, 1999.

Political consultant and onetime pollster for Bill Clinton, Dick Morris argues that growing access to the Internet will usher in an era of direct democracy, enabling voters to regularly transmit their sentiments to elected officials, bring an end to the influence of special interest groups, and remove the importance of money in campaigns, as the Internet replaces paid political TV advertising.

The National Commission on Federal Election Reform. *To Assure Pride and Confidence in the Electoral Process.* Charlottesville, VA: Miller Center of Public Affairs, 2001.

Formed in reaction to disputes arising over the balloting in Florida during the 2000 presidential election, the commission made a series of recommendations for improving the voting process. Included were the maintenance of accurate voting lists, the use of reliable voting equipment, procedures for handling close elections in a fair manner, ensuring that eligible voters can participate effectively through "provisional voting," and the establishment of a limited federal oversight role to ensure the achievement of these goals.

Douglas W. Rae. *The Political Consequences of Electoral Laws.* New Haven, CT: Yale University Press, 1971.

A sophisticated empirical analysis of several democracies to see how electoral laws governing the translation of votes into seats in the legislative chambers affect the degree of two-party competition.

Andrew Reynolds, John Carey, and Ben Reilly. *International IDEA Handbook of Electoral System Design.* Stockholm: International IDEA, 2002.

Provided herein is a useful and accessible overview of both the design and administration of election systems in more than two hundred states and territories around the world.

Robert Richie and Steven Hill, eds. *Whose Vote Counts?* Boston, MA: Beacon Press, 2001.

A brief but excellent collection of essays on proportional representation—its benefits, potential limitations, and where and how it ought to be tried in the American political system.

Wilma Rule and Joseph Zimmerman, eds. *United States Electoral Systems: Their Impact on Women and Minorities.* New York: Praeger, 1992.

The articles in this volume examine how the election of both women and minorities to public office at all levels is affected by various voting systems, including cumulative voting, multi- and single-member districts, reapportionment, and judicial election systems.

Steven E. Schier. *You Call This an Election? America's Peculiar Democracy.* Washington, DC: Georgetown University Press, 2003.

Schier argues that a properly functioning electoral system should promote political, governmental, and regime stability; accountability of elected officials; higher voter turnout; and careful consideration of public policy. As the title of the book suggests, he finds the American electoral process wanting in all of these areas. The way out of our problems lies in strengthening our political parties, broadening voter registration, giving parties free TV time, adopting one-punch partisan ballots, doing away with initiatives that clutter up the ballot, and greater party efforts to get out the vote.

Sue Thomas and Clyde Wilcox, eds. *Women and Effective Elective Office.* New York: Oxford University Press, 1998.

The authors consider the success women have had in winning election to the statehouses and national legislature of this country, what sort of an impact they have had in these positions, and what advantages and disadvantages they face as they seek to do so. The book concludes with an assessment of future goals, challenges, and hopes.

Dennis F. Thompson. *Just Elections: Creating a Fair Electoral Process in the United States.* Chicago: University of Chicago Press, 2002.

Whether our elections may be considered just, Thompson argues, is a function of the extent to which they incorporate three fundamental democratic principles—equal respect, free choice, and popular sovereignty. These principles, as he shows, although enjoying broad support in the abstract, generate considerable disagreement in their application to the electoral process.

Ted Wachtel. *The Electronic Congress: A Blueprint for Participatory Democracy.* Pipersville, PA: Piper's Press, 1992.

In view of the public cynicism about government, fueled by a Congress awash in money and under the control of special interests, Wachtel proposes an electronic Congress. By this he means instituting a system of national referenda—some binding, others advisory—allowing citizens to vote by telephone on specific resolutions adopted by Congress.

Nominating Process

Andrew E. Busch. *Outsiders and Openness in the Presidential Nominating Process.* Pittsburgh: University of Pittsburgh Press, 1997.

Starting with the late nineteenth century, the author examines how the presidential nominating process has evolved over time and how these changes have affected the receptiveness of the process to political outsiders. Particular attention is given to the revolutionary changes in the process following the Democratic National Convention of 1968.

James W. Ceaser. *Reforming the Reforms: A Critical Analysis of the Presidential Selection Process.* Cambridge, MA: Ballinger Publishing, 1982.

Although the author devotes some attention to assessing the impact of campaign finance reforms on presidential selection, his primary focus is the post-1968 reforms of the presidential nominating process. Believing that the process of nomination should foster legitimacy, attract and nominate qualified candidates, and contribute to the governing process, he finds the reformed process wanting on all three criteria. He concludes by pointing to further possibilities for changing the process, including, on the one hand, even more direct democracy, and, on the other, restoring greater influence to the party elites.

James W. Davis. *U.S. Presidential Primaries and the Caucus-Convention System.* Westport, CT: Greenwood Press, 1997.

A sourcebook on the two principal methods (caucus-convention, primary) by which delegates to our national party conventions are selected. Included are discussions of the nomination reforms post-1968, demographic data on delegates, campaign strategies, financing nominations, polls, debates, and primary turnout. Also considered are possible alternatives to the current primary system, including regional primaries and a single national primary.

Robert E. DiClerico and James W. Davis. *Choosing Our Choices: Debating the Presidential Nominating Process.* Lanham, MD: Rowman and Littlefield, 2000.

Following an opening chapter on how the presidential nominating process has evolved from 1800 to the present, Davis argues that the current president-by-primary process has left us with a nomination system decidedly less desirable than the party-dominated system of old. DiClerico, in contrast, disputes the validity of several indictments made against the current president-by-primary system and argues as well that it has several strengths not found in the old (i.e., pre-1972) nominating system.

John Haskell. *Fundamentally Flawed: Understanding and Reforming Presidential Primaries.* Lanham, MD: Rowman and Littlefield, 1996.

Drawing on social choice theory, Haskell concludes that our president-by-primary process violates democratic principles of fairness and fosters a campaign environment that scarcely contributes to a careful weighing of candidates and issues. He also provides a useful analysis of alternatives to the current primary arrangements, including approval voting, which would allow voters to rank their candidate preferences, thereby eliminating what he regards as the greatest weakness of the current primary system—distortion of voter preferences.

James I. Lengle. *Representation and Presidential Primaries: The Democratic Party in the Post-Reform Era.* Westport, CT: Greenwood Press, 1981.

The major argument here is that the voters who come out to vote in presidential primaries are, as a group, unrepresentative of the rank and file in their party on factors such as ideology, issue concerns, and candidate preferences—a fact that could have both short- and long-term harmful consequences for the parties.

Nelson W. Polsby. *Consequences of Party Reform.* New York: Oxford University Press, 1983.

The reforms of the presidential nominating process undertaken by the Democratic Party following its tumultuous national convention in 1968 were designed to expand participation in the process. It is argued here, however, that the reforms have made the process less responsive to majorities, more hospitable to special interest influence, and contributed little to the process of governing.

Howard Reiter. *Selecting the President: The Nominating Process in Transition.* Philadelphia: University of Pennsylvania Press, 1985.

Rejecting the conventional wisdom that the post-1968 reforms of the presidential nominating process themselves altered it in a profound way, Reiter insists that the forces behind change actually began back in the early 1950s and made possible the reforms that would come later in the early 1970s.

Hugh Winebrenner. *The Iowa Precinct Caucuses: The Making of a Media Event.* Ames: Iowa State University Press, 1987.

Here is explained how the Iowa caucus emerged from obscurity and became a major media event on the road to the presidency. The author concludes with an assessment of whether this new-found attention has been good for the caucus itself and for the presidential nominating process as a whole.

Redistricting, Reapportionment

Michel L. Balinsky and H. Peyton Young. *Fair Representation: Meeting the Ideal of One Man, One Vote.* Washington, DC: Brookings Institution, 2001.

Anticipating the reapportionment slated to occur on the basis of the 2000 census, these authors formulated a theory of fair representation employing principles for converting state populations into congressional seats. Their analysis concludes that the current apportionment formula favors smaller over larger states and fails to live up to the "one-man, one-vote" principle.

Chandler Davidson, ed. *Minority Vote Dilution.* Washington, DC: Howard University Press, 1984.

A collection of twelve essays devoted primarily to attempts by some jurisdictions to dilute the black vote through gerrymandering, reapportionment, and at-large elections, and how the voting rights acts were used to remedy these problems. Also included is an essay on the desirability, though unlikelihood, of moving to a system of proportional representation.

Robert D. Dixon Jr. *Democratic Representation: Reapportionment in Law and Politics.* New York: Oxford University Press, 1968.

An exhaustive examination of the reapportionment issue in the aftermath of *Baker v. Carr.* The book is organized around nine major themes: the central place of population in any formula for representation; the weighting of votes equally does not by itself guarantee equal representation; the other components of representation are appropriate for judicial review; preservation of county lines can minimize gerrymandering; reapportioners must establish a mathematical boundary within which reapportionment compromises need to be reached; reapportionment should be left to the state legislatures and the courts; courts should not shy away from ruling on reapportionment issues merely because their decisions have political implications; courts should also relax normal rules on standing and intervenor policies in order to maximize the introduction of relevant data and issues; and finally, except in the South, there is little relationship between malapportionment and bad public policy.

Elmer C. Griffith. *The Rise and Development of the Gerrymander.* Chicago: Scott Foresman, 1907.

Contrary to the accepted wisdom that the gerrymander originated in 1812 in the state of Massachusetts, Griffith shows that it actually dates back to over one hundred years prior (1705) in connection with the creation of assembly districts in Pennsylvania. There followed gerrymanders in several other states prior to the high-profile one in Massachusetts. He continues his analysis up through 1840, by which time gerrymandering had become a generally accepted practice.

Bernard Grofman, Lisa Handley, and Richard Niemi. *Minority Representation and the Quest for Voting Equality.* New York: Cambridge University Press, 1992.

Three major areas of concern command the attention of these authors: laying out the voting rights case law and the confusion that attends its explication in the district and circuit courts, the issues that face the courts as they confront the questions of alleged vote dilution in single-member districts, and the implications that voting rights case law has for the issue of representation in the future.

Andrew Hacker. *Congressional Districting: The Issue of Equal Representation.* Washington, DC: Brookings Institution, 1963.

This brief examination of congressional districting places the issue in historical and constitutional context and considers actions by the states and courts as they apply to Congress, the reasons for malapportionment, and its consequences.

Howard D. Hamilton, ed. *Legislative Apportionment: Key to Power.* New York: Harper and Row, 1964.

A brief and highly accessible treatment of malapportionment— its origins, the battle in the court to correct it, with particular attention given to *Baker v. Carr,* and proposed correctives for the problem.

Leroy Hardy, Alan Heslop, and Stuart Anderson, eds. *Reapportionment Politics: The History of Redistricting in the 50 States.* Beverly Hills, CA: Sage Publications, 1980.

This compendium of essays examines the history of redistricting in each of the fifty states, noting how the uniqueness of each state has also carried over to how it has approached redistricting. Except for the chapter on Massachusetts, which addresses congressional districting only, all focus on redrawing lines in state legislative districts.

Nancy Maveety. *Representation Rights and the Burger Years.* Ann Arbor: University of Michigan Press, 1991.

Arguing that although the Burger Supreme Court's decisions on representation have been overshadowed by both its predecessor (the Warren Court) and successor (the Rehnquist Court), Maveety insists that the Burger Court's "group-balancing" approach to issues of representation in fact brought an expanded role for the Court, and the incorporation of the concept of "aggregate political rights" into constitutional law.

Anthony Peacock, ed. *Affirmative Action and Representation: Shaw v. Reno and the Future of Voting Rights.* Durham, NC: Carolina Academic Press, 1997.

Taking the view that the Supreme Court's *Shaw v. Reno* decision was a bellwether in equal protection litigation, these twelve essays—written by both proponents and opponents of affirmative action—examine the implications of the *Shaw* decision, possible alternative models of representation given the Court's sensitivity to race-conscious districting, and the appropriateness of applying the Voting Rights Act to the election of judges—a matter not reached in the *Shaw* decision.

Richard K. Scher, Jon L. Mills, and John J. Hotaling. *Voting Rights and Democracy: The Law and Politics of Districting.* Chicago: Nelson-Hall, 1997.

An amendment to the Voting Rights Act of 1982, while not widely appreciated at the time, was destined to create a "second revolution in civil rights" arising from its impact on how the re-districting/reapportionment cycle of 1991–1992 played out in reconfiguring state legislatures, the U.S. House of Representatives, and local legislative bodies. This book explains how the 1991–1992 cycle worked, why it happened the way it did, and how it ought to work in future rounds.

The Initiative, Referendum, and Recall

John A. Allswang. *The Initiative and Referendum in California, 1898–1998.* Palo Alto, CA: Stanford University Press, 2000.

Tracing the use of direct legislation over a one-hundred-year period in one of the nation's most influential states, Allswang shows how the politics of initiatives and referenda today are not markedly different from the past with respect to campaign strategies, interest group participation, big money, paid signature gatherers, professional campaign managers, participation by citizens and business groups, and attempts to reform the process.

Shawn Bowler, Todd Donovan, and Caroline J. Tolbert, eds. *Citizens as Legislators: Direct Democracy in the United States.* Columbus: Ohio State University Press, 1998.

The twelve essays in this book address the modern initiative campaign industry, whether it fulfills the original goals behind the initiative, how effectively voters cope with the array of decisions they confront on the ballot, and why certain policy outcomes are different in those states with direct legislation.

David S. Broder. *Democracy Derailed: Initiative Campaigns and the Power of Money.* New York: Harcourt, 2000.

The dean of American political journalists argues that while the initiative process was intended to provide voters with a more direct means of influence over the policy-making process, it has in fact become the plaything of moneyed interests, often from out of state, who manipulate public opinion to suit their own agendas.

Thomas E. Cronin. *Direct Democracy: The Politics of Initiative, Referendum, and Recall.* Cambridge, MA: Harvard University Press, 1989.

Although acknowledging that direct democracy mechanisms have worked better than some might have imagined, Cronin sees room for considerable improvement. Drawing upon Gallup surveys and interviews with 200 political activists and elected officials in ten states, he examines how informed voters are about the petitions they sign and the ballots they cast, whether majority rule infringes on minority rights, the influence of those campaigning for and against ballot measures, and the desirability of expanding these direct democracy mechanisms to the national level.

Richard J. Ellis. *Democratic Delusions: The Initiative Process in America.* Lawrence: University Press of Kansas, 2002.

The author readily acknowledges that ordinary citizens, fueled by the passion of a burning issue, may brave the elements and citizen rebuffs in order to secure the necessary signatures to get an initiative placed on the ballot. But much more common in his view is the practice of for-profit companies securing signatures on petitions—sometimes peddling several petitions at once—for special interests and the well-heeled. He also notes that initiatives, which take political judgments out of the hands of the legislature, are instead shaped by the least democratic branch (courts), for they are called upon to rule on how attorney generals label or define a proposed initiative and then rule again on legal challenges, if they get passed.

Elisabeth R. Gerber. *The Populist Paradox: Interest Group Influence and the Promise of Direct Legislation.* Princeton, NJ: Princeton University Press, 1999.

Based upon an examination of 168 direct legislation campaigns in eight states, Gerber concludes that, contrary to the conventional wisdom, initiatives and referenda backed by wealthy interests are not all that successful in gaining adoption, while those sponsored by citizen groups are.

David B. Magleby. *Direct Legislation: Voting on Ballot Propositions in the United States.* Baltimore: Johns Hopkins University Press, 1984.

Relying upon survey and aggregate data from four states (Massachusetts, California, Florida, and Washington) as well as national surveys, this study examines who participates in initiatives and referenda, and why, how they learn about the propositions under consideration, and how well they comprehend them. Also considered in this study are the mechanics of the direct legislation process and state variations, the success rate of such legislation, and, very importantly, who benefits from the process.

Matthew Mendelsohn and Andrew Parkin, eds. *Referendum Democracy: Citizens, Elites and Deliberation in Referendum Campaigns.* New York: Palgrave, 2001.

Eleven essays examine the growing use of referenda in democracies; their impact on political parties, legislative bodies, and minorities; and how referenda affect deliberation and decision-making by voters.

Larry J. Sabato, Howard Ernst, and Bruce A. Larson, eds. *Dangerous Democracy? The Battle over Ballot Initiatives in America.* Lanham, MD: Rowman and Littlefield, 2001.

Scholars who have written about initiatives, journalists who have covered initiative campaigns, and consultants who have worked on them all weigh in on the state of the initiative process as it has grown in popularity over the past twenty years. In the concluding chapter, the editors outline a series of proposals for improving the process, including financial disclosure, voter guides, subsidies for public dialogue, and ballot changes.

M. Dane Waters. *The Battle over Citizen Lawmaking: A Collection of Essays.* Durham, NC: Carolina Academic Press, 2001.

With one notable exception, the essays in this volume, while noting room for improvement in the initiative process, are generally supportive of direct democracy and critical of attempts to neutralize the process—attempts coming from the very groups whom the Progressives sought to check with the initiative.

Laura R. Woliver. *From Outrage to Action: The Politics of Grass-roots Dissent.* Urbana: University of Illinois Press, 1993.

This book contains four case studies of how grassroots organizations attempted to challenge decisions and actions of the criminal justice system in the cities of Milwaukee and Madison, Wisconsin. One of these studies focuses on the successful mobilization of citizens to recall a local judge in Madison who made a number of sexist comments in the course of a sentencing procedure.

Joseph F. Zimmerman. *The Recall: Tribunal of the People.* Westport, CT: Praeger, 1997.

An examination of the recall of state and local officers over the course of U.S. history, after which the author provides a balanced assessment of the strengths and weaknesses of the recall process. In the final chapter he offers a "model for voter sovereignty" in which he sets forth how a recall process ought to work.

Term Limitations

American Enterprise Institute. *Limiting Presidential and Congressional Terms.* Washington, DC: American Enterprise Institute, 1979.

This monograph considers how proposals to limit presidents to a single six-year term and members of Congress to twelve years of consecutive service would impact on various groups both inside and outside government.

Gerald Benjamin and Michael J. Malbin, eds. *Limiting Legislative Terms.* Washington, DC: Congressional Quarterly Press, 1992.

This collection of twelve essays addresses the Founding Fathers' thinking on term limits, the campaign for term limits waged in Washington and at the grass roots, and the effects of term limits on political officials in states where they have already been instituted, as well as their effects on legislative bodies and government.

John M. Carey. *Term Limits and Legislative Representation.* New York: Cambridge University Press, 1996.

To a debate that has been heavily speculative, this author attempts to bring some hard evidence on the impact of term limits, comparing the legislative branch in Costa Rica, where term limits are constitutionally mandated, to the U.S. Congress, where they are not. He concludes that the imposition of term limits does not necessarily eliminate political careerism or personal electioneering among legislators. What it does do, however, is reduce the level of party cohesion within the legislature.

James K. Coyne and John H. Fund. *Cleaning House: America's Campaign for Term Limits.* Washington, DC: Regnery Gateway, 1992.

Fed up with congressional careerists more interested in pork barreling than the public interest, the author chronicles the pathologies associated with a House full of professional politicians. He sets forth a point-by-point refutation of arguments made against term limits and insists that they are constitutional and in keeping with American tradition.

Foundation for the Study of Presidential and Congressional Terms. *Presidential and Congressional Term Limitation: The Issue That Stays Alive.* Washington, DC: Foundation for the Study of Presidential and Congressional Terms, 1980.

In this monograph, the nation's oldest organization pushing for term limits provides a concise summary of the arguments made for and against limiting the president to a single six-year term and members of Congress to no more than twelve years of consecutive service.

Victor Kamber. *Giving up on Democracy: Why Term Limits Are Bad for America.* Washington, DC: Regnery Publishing, 1995.

Rejecting the concept of the "citizen legislator," the author examines the campaign for term limits in Oklahoma, California, and Washington state; the motives behind those pushing for this change; why these actions are ill-conceived; and the decision of the Supreme Court to strike down term limits at the federal level.

George Will. *Restoration: Congress, Term Limits, and the Recovery of Democracy.* New York: Free Press, 1992.

Political commentator George Will argues that members of Congress focus primarily on protecting their incumbency by being overly responsive to public whims, while at the same time ignoring the public interest. Term limits, he believes, would restore the appropriate constitutional distance between representative and constituent, intended by the Founding Fathers, allowing members of Congress to behave as statesmen rather than as politicians.

Voting Participation

Jack C. Doppelt and Ellen Shearer. *Non Voters: America's No-Shows.* Thousand Oaks, CA: Sage Publications, 1999.

In the 1996 presidential election, one hundred million voting-age Americans declined to vote, making it the first time since 1924 that more Americans stayed away from the polls than voted. The authors of this study traveled to fifteen states and conducted in-depth interviews with thirty of these nonvoters. A good portion of the book allows these nonvoters to speak in their own words. Based upon these interviews, the authors develop a typology of nonvoters: "doers," "unpluggeds," "irritables," "don't knows," and "alienateds."

Arthur T. Hadley. *The Empty Voting Booth.* Englewood Cliffs, NJ: Prentice-Hall, 1978.

Based upon polling a random sample of 2002 eligible voters, Hadley divides nonvoters into six categories (Positive Apathetics, Bypassed, Politically Impotent, Physically Disenfranchised, Naysayers, and Crosspressured), arguing that the nonvoters he uncovered in many ways do not fit the conventional stereotype of those who fail to vote.

Ron Hirschbein. *Voting Rites: The Devolution of American Politics.* New York: Praeger, 1999.

Hirschbein attributes the fall in voting turnout not only to the decline in its instrumental value (i.e., that it has little impact) but, much more important, to the decline in its expressive value. In short, it no longer provides the ritualistic gratification and entertainment that voters sought and used to find in the act of voting.

Paul Keppner. *Who Voted? The Dynamics of Electoral Turnout, 1870–1980.* New York: Praeger, 1982.

The goal of this sophisticated book is to identify the social and political/structural predictors of turnout during a period of over one hundred years. Examining the votes for president and Congress, Keppner discerns four distinct eras in the non-South where the level of turnout resembled neither what came before nor after, and four largely different turnout eras in the South as well.

William C. Mitchell. *Why Vote?* Chicago: Markham, 1971.

Responding to the 1970 U.S. Supreme Court decision declaring that eighteen-year-olds could vote in national elections, the author attempts to show that young people have very real political stakes in elections, and that it makes a difference which party and candidate are elected. He also identifies conditions under which the casting of a vote could be critical to the outcome, and suggests ways voters should go about evaluating their political choices in an election.

Thomas E. Patterson. *The Vanishing Voter: Public Involvement in an Age of Uncertainty.* New York: Alfred A. Knopf, 2002.

Despite the fact that education levels have risen and legal barriers to voting have been eliminated, voting turnout continues to decline. Patterson concludes, based upon some 80,000 interviews conducted during the 2000 presidential election, that the explanation for declining turnout lies with the nature of our partisan politics, media coverage, candidate strategy, and electoral reforms. As a solution to these problems, the author outlines a "model campaign," which is designed to foster political involvement.

Frances Fox Piven and Richard A. Cloward. *Why Americans Still Don't Vote: And Why Politicians Want It That Way.* Boston: Beacon Press, 2000.

Unpersuaded by the arguments that social and psychological factors explain the decline in turnout, the authors instead argue that procedural requirements for voting instituted at the turn of the century, *and* party response to them, are the major sources of the problem. Themselves active participants in efforts to reduce voting barriers, the authors detail the campaign to ease voter registration requirements via adoption of the National Voter Registration Act, and they assess its impact to date.

Richard G. Smolka. *Election Day Registration: The Minnesota and Wisconsin Experience in 1976.* Washington, DC: American Enterprise Institute, 1977.

Although determining that election-day registration increased turnout a couple of points and did not advantage one party over the other, this author concludes that the costs were high—long lines, confusion at polling places, and considerable potential for corruption.

Harold W. Stanley. *Voter Mobilization and the Politics of Race: The South and Universal Suffrage, 1952–1984.* New York: Praeger, 1987.

Conventional wisdom had it that the increases in voter turnout in the South since the 1950s were mostly a black phenomenon resulting primarily from the elimination of the poll tax, and that the elevated turnout among whites was fueled by a racist backlash, along with the arrival of whites from the North. This study finds little support for these claims. The effect of racial backlash, according to the author, had a minor impact on the increase in white turnout, with factors such as increased political competition, changing attitudes toward the parties and candidates, easing of registration requirements, increasing levels of education, and greater use of media all having a much greater impact on white turnout. These factors were instrumental in raising the level of black turnout as well.

Ruy A. Teixeira. *Why Americans Don't Vote: Turnout Decline in the United States, 1960–1984.* New York: Greenwood Press, 1987.

One of the most thoughtful scholars on political participation finds that today's nonvoters are not to be found primarily at the bottom of the social structure but rather are present in all demographic and partisan groupings. His statistical analyses suggest that the primary causes of declining turnout are decreased political efficacy, decline in campaign involvement, and decline in party identification. He is not optimistic about reversing the decline.

————. *The Disappearing American Voter.* Washington, DC: Brookings Institution, 1992.

Who is voting? Who is not? and Does it really matter? are the fundamental questions that drive this examination of turnout. Teixeira also considers various proposals for making voting easier, as well as their likely impact. The final chapter is reserved for the most challenging problem, namely, how to motivate Americans to vote.

Ben Wattenberg. *Where Have All the Voters Gone?* Cambridge, MA: Harvard University Press, 2002.

Arguing that even the most efficient of registration systems would have little impact on voting participation, Wattenberg insists that we must look elsewhere for declining turnout. The culprits, he suggests, are the complexity of our elections and the steady decline of the party system. His proposals for increasing turnout include changing the date of our presidential elections, switching to proportional representation, and possibly compulsory voting.

Raymond E. Wolfinger and Steven J. Rosenstone. *Who Votes?* New Haven, CT: Yale University Press, 1980.

Drawing upon surveys of 88,000 people conducted by the Bureau of the Census in 1972 and 1974, these authors conclude that level of education is far and away the most important factor in determining who votes, followed by age. Although these findings suggest that some groups are underrepresented in the electorate while others are overrepresented, this fact is of relatively minor significance because the political preferences of voters differ little from nonvoters.

Financing Campaigns

Bruce Ackerman and Ian Ayres. *Voting with Dollars: A New Paradigm for Campaign Finance.* New Haven, CT: Yale University Press, 2002.

Highly skeptical of efforts to curb the influence of money by contribution and spending limits, the current public financing option, and disclosure requirements, the authors instead propose two novel approaches to the problem. One is a Patriot credit card funded by Congress in the amount of $50 to be contributed by the voter to the candidate of one's choice. The other, a *secret* donation booth, would allow unlimited contributions to be made to candidates, but without their knowledge of who the contributors were.

David W. Adamany and George E. Agree. *Political Money.* Baltimore: Johns Hopkins University Press, 1975.

A useful general treatment of the role of money in campaigns, including the distinctiveness of money as a political resource, the costs of campaigning, the limitations of the campaign finance reforms passed in the early 1970s, and how other countries (Germany, Finland, Sweden, Norway) have attempted to address the problem. The authors come down on the side of public financing—although continuing to allow limited private contributions as well—and in the final chapter consider in great detail options for the raising and distributing of public funds.

Clifford W. Brown Jr., Lynda W. Powell, and Clyde Wilcox. *Serious Money: Fundraising and Contributing in Presidential Nomination Campaigns.* New York: Cambridge University Press, 1995.

Drawing their data from the 1988 and 1992 nomination campaigns, these authors consider direct mail solicitation and personal solicitation networks as approaches to raising money, along with how the resources of a candidate determine which approach will be used. Also considered are the motives—purposive, solidarity, and material—behind those who contribute, and finally, the relationship between the method of raising money and the motives of the contributors.

Dan Clawson, Alan Neustadtl, and Mark Walker. *Dollars and Votes: How Business Campaign Contributions Subvert Democracy.* Philadelphia: Temple University Press, 1998.

Although a number of books address the question of how campaign contributions lead to access and influence over policy, this study is particularly noteworthy for its extensive interviews with members of the corporate world and the remarkable candor with which they discuss the motives that lay behind corporate giving. The authors conclude that the only way out of the morass of money and influence is through a system of full public financing of elections, a proposal that, they note, is gaining greater support.

Anthony Corrado. *Paying for Presidents: Public Financing in Presidential Elections.* New York: Twentieth Century Fund Press, 1993.

Public financing of presidential elections, the most innovative aspect of campaign finance reform, has been defended by some as an equalizer in presidential election campaigns and condemned by others as a failure, a regulatory nightmare that is easily circumvented by various kinds of backdoor spending and contributions. The author of this report, both a scholar and veteran of three presidential campaigns, attempts to take the measure of both the criticisms and defenses of public financing. He concludes that it is well worth preserving, but urges reform of the tax check-off, the matching funds formula, and soft money contributions.

Elizabeth Drew. *Politics and Money: The New Road to Corruption.* New York: Macmillan, 1983.

A brief but compelling account of the role of money in our politics—the extent to which raising it is a constant preoccupation of members of Congress, how the givers navigate around campaign finance regulations, and the costs to citizens in the form of laws passed and appointments made that operate to the advantage of special interests.

Daniel N. Friedenberg. *Sold to the Highest Bidder: The Presidency from Dwight D. Eisenhower to George W. Bush.* New York: Prometheus Books, 2002.

In this examination of the administrations of ten presidents, the author argues that the government's policy decisions are driven by the need to reward the wealthy few—the result of an electoral process corrupted by the influence of those very interests through their financial backing of candidates and their control of the means of communication. Abolishing the Electoral College, term limits, reforming presidential primaries, and changing representation in the U.S. Senate are considered in the final chapter as ways of improving the electoral process.

Thomas Gais. *Improper Influence: Campaign Finance Law, Political Interest Groups, and the Problem of Equality.* Ann Arbor: University of Michigan Press, 1998.

This study makes the rather unorthodox argument that campaign finance laws currently on the books serve to prevent many groups of citizens from forming PACs to advance their views and interests, but do not similarly disadvantage business groups. The result is a campaign finance system skewed in favor of economic interests. The solution to this imbalance, Gais writes, is to completely deregulate campaign financing.

Charles Lewis and the Center for Public Integrity. *The Buying of the President.* New York: Avon Books, 1996.

This book lays out through numbers, revelations, and analyses the extent to which candidates (Dole, Clinton, Alexander, Graham, Wilson, Buchanan, Lugar, Spectre, and Keyes) have been beholden to special interests for bankrolling their campaigns, and how much the special interests are beholden to the candidates as well.

Michael J. Malbin and Thomas L Gais. *The Day after Reform: Sobering Campaign Finance Lessons from the American States.* New York: Rockefeller Institute Press, 1998.

With more than half the states having revamped their campaign finance laws, the authors have undertaken an extensive study to determine how successful they have been after candidates, parties, and individuals have had an opportunity to adapt to them. Based upon a fifty-state survey and extensive interviews with political officials, the authors call for campaign finance reformers to be more realistic about what is achievable, and to be more attentive to how proposed reforms are likely to be used by those they are designed to regulate. These concerns guide their concluding chapter, in which they lay out a series of suggestions for further changes in the regulation of money in campaigns.

Frederick G. Slabach. *The Constitution and Campaign Finance Reform: An Anthology.* Durham, NC: Carolina Academic Press, 1998.

A collection of essays written over a twenty-year period, mostly by legal scholars, addressing the question of whether money constitutes speech and thus is not susceptible to regulation, or, alternatively, whether the government has a legitimate and compelling interest in regulating the flow of money into election campaigns.

Bradley A. Smith. *Unfree Speech: The Folly of Campaign Finance Reform.* Princeton, NJ: Princeton University Press, 2001.

Smith is wholly opposed to any limits on the raising and spending of money in election campaigns not only because he judges them to be violations of free speech but also because they protect incumbents, burden grassroots political activity with excessive regulations, and drain campaign dialogue of its vitality. He further makes the unconventional point that money does not corrupt. On the contrary, more money in the political process would, in his view, enhance equality in the political process, not reduce it.

Frank J. Sorauf. *Inside Campaign Finance: Myths and Realities.* New Haven, CT: Yale University Press, 1992.

An excellent overview of the history of campaign finance regulations and problems with laws currently on the books. The book also develops several interesting points that do not fit squarely with the conventional wisdom. These include the contentions that money may not be quite as decisive in determining election outcomes nor PACs as influential in the policy process as many believe, and the assertion that incumbent officeholders are becoming increasingly dominant in their relationship with contributors. Sorauf also examines potential options for further reform, and why public opinion, parties, and officeholders may make further significant change difficult.

The Electoral College, the 2000 Election

David W. Abbott and James P. Levine. *Wrong Winner: The Coming Debacle in the Electoral College.* New York: Praeger, 1991.

In a book that proved to be prescient, the authors argue that the Electoral College is a time bomb waiting to go off, as they detail the number of elections in which the Electoral College very nearly gave us a president with a minority of the popular vote. After enumerating its biases and distortions of election results, the authors consider various alternatives, finding all wanting except for direct popular election.

Judith Best. *The Case against Direct Election of the President: A Defense of the Electoral College.* Ithaca, NY: Cornell University Press, 1971.

A staunch defender of the Electoral College, Best refutes the alleged drawbacks leveled against it (contingency election, inequalities in voting power, faithless elector, minority president) while also arguing that the widely popular direct-election alternative would create more problems than it solves. The Electoral College, she insists, is a most appropriate method of election in a federal system and has the very real advantage, unlike direct election, of assuring electoral certainty.

James W. Ceaser and Andrew E. Busch. *The Perfect Tie: The True Story of the 2000 Presidential Election.* Lanham, MD: Rowman and Littlefield, 2001.

Here is offered a comprehensive look at the 2000 election, beginning with the invisible primary followed by the nomination and general election campaigns, and the post-election campaigns of each candidate as he sought to emerge victorious from the Florida stalemate. The book concludes with a thoughtful discussion of reform proposals related to vote casting and counting, the Electoral College, reporting of election results, campaign finance, and the major party nominating process.

Alan M. Dershowitz. *Supreme Injustice: How the High Court Hijacked Election 2000.* New York: Oxford University Press, 2001.

This impassioned critique of the Supreme Court's rulings on the 2000 election not only finds fault with the reasoning of the majority but argues that their rationale actually contradicts positions taken by some of the justices in previous cases, thereby inviting the inference that the decision was motivated by political considerations.

Martin Diamond. *The Electoral College and the American Idea of Democracy.* Washington, DC: American Enterprise Institute, 1977.

In this monograph, one of the Electoral College's leading defenders provides a point-by-point refutation of the American Bar Association's characterization of the Electoral College as "archaic, undemocratic, complex, ambiguous, and dangerous." Such conclusions, he suggests, arise from a too simplistic view of what *democracy* means.

Gary L. Gregg III. *Securing Democracy: Why We Have an Electoral College.* Wilmington, DE: ISI Books, 2001.

A collection of essays by a distinguished group of scholars, including the late Daniel Patrick Moynihan. The essays place the Electoral College in the context of the Founding Fathers' thinking about democracy, assess how the institution performed in the crisis elections of the past three centuries, and argue that the Electoral College has contributed greatly to the stability of the two-party system and succeeded admirably in marginalizing demagogues.

Also considered is how changing the election process might in turn change—and not necessarily for the better—the kinds of candidates who would emerge victorious.

Lawrence D. Longley and Neal R. Peirce. *The Electoral College Primer.* New Haven, CT: Yale University Press, 1996.

An excellent and superbly organized examination of why the Electoral College was created, how it functions today, and, in the authors' view, its many drawbacks.

Richard Posner. *Breaking the Deadlock: The 2000 Election, the Constitution, and the Courts.* Princeton, NJ: Princeton University Press, 2001.

This leading scholar and federal appeals court judge, although critical of some of the Supreme Court's reasoning in *Bush v. Gore*, nevertheless concludes that the Court's decision to step in and settle the dispute was the prudent course of action.

Jack N. Rakove, ed. *The Unfinished Election of 2000.* New York: Basic Books, 2001.

An excellent collection of essays that variously address the 2000 presidential election in the context of our electoral history; the political forces that produced such a close election; the role of the Supreme Court in settling the outcome, and the potential consequences of that decision for lower courts; and the weaknesses of the Electoral College.

Larry J. Sabato, ed. *Overtime: The Election 2000 Thriller.* New York: Longman, 2002.

Essays written by academics, journalists, and members of the Bush and Gore campaign staffs address the primaries, conventions, the general election, the problems associated with counting the Florida ballots, and the post-election political and legal strategies pursued by the Bush and Gore campaigns.

Paul Schumaker and Burdett A. Loomis, eds. *Choosing a President: The Electoral College and Beyond.* New York: Chatham House, 2002.

Thirty-seven experts on American politics have contributed to this volume their views on the Electoral College and the numerous proposals to alter or abolish it. Their considered judgment is that while the college is not without its faults, it is preferable to the risks we would run—some knowable, some not—were we to turn to any of the alternatives proposed, including direct election.

Cass R. Sunstein and Richard A. Epstein. *The Vote: Bush, Gore, and the Supreme Court.* Chicago: University of Chicago Press, 2001.

Written by leading legal scholars, the eleven essays in this volume both challenge and defend the reasoning set forth by the Supreme Court in its landmark ruling in *Bush v. Gore.*

Twentieth Century Fund. *Winner Take All: Report of the Twentieth Century Fund Task Force on Reform of the Presidential Election Process.* New York: Holmes and Meier, 1978.

Believing the Electoral College to be fatally flawed but recognizing as well that direct election could produce a number of undesirable consequences, including endless recounts and a proliferation of minor parties, the task force proposes a "national bonus plan" that would award an additional two electoral votes to each state, all of which would be given to the presidential candidate receiving the most popular votes nationwide.

Nonprint Resources

The Best Campaign Money Can Buy
Date: 1992
Media: VHS
Length: 60 minutes
Cost: $19.98
Source: Public Broadcasting Service, (415) 543-1200

This *Frontline* documentary shows the overriding importance of money in the 1992 presidential election, revealing the time and resources that candidates devote to raising money and their interactions with fat-cat contributors.

Computer Votefraud and the 1996 Elections
Date: 1996
Media: Audiocassette
Length: 45 minutes
Source: Cincinnatus

Pointing to the voter fraud alleged to have occurred in a number of elections, this film concludes that the culprits are computerized voting and exit polls. The solution? Return to the paper ballot.

Congressional Elections
Date: 1983
Media: VHS
Length: 28 minutes
Source: WETA, Washington, DC, and the American Political Science Association

Discusses the role of political parties, the increased importance of financing, voting turnout, and the consequences of elections.

Cyber Politics
Date: 1996
Media: VHS
Length: 30 minutes
Source: PCTV, Inc.

Examines how political parties, lobbyists, candidates, campaign managers, and political activists are using computer technology to affect the outcome of elections and how the media uses computer technology to report on elections.

The Decline of Politics: The Superficial Democracy
Date: 1995
Media: VHS
Length: 29 minutes
Cost: $89.95
Source: Films for the Humanities and Sciences, (800) 257-5126

Discussion of the ramifications of an American political arena that favors the superficial exchange of slogans, personal attacks, and orchestrated appearances over the serious discussion of issues, problems, and ideas.

The Decline of Politics: Voter Apathy
Date: 1992
Media: VHS
Length: 30 minutes
Source: Golden Dome Productions

This program examines the lack of participation in the political process by Americans. It considers some of the factors contributing to voter apathy and offers insights into political reform.

Democracy in a Different Voice
Date: 1995
Media: VHS
Length: 54 minutes
Cost: $95.00
Source: Insight Media, (800) 897-0089

Outlining the views expressed in her 1995 book (*The Tyranny of the Majority*), Lani Guinier maintains that winner-take-all elections can have the effect of leaving minorities as permanent losers in the electoral process. She suggests a number of ways to remedy this problem.

Electing the President
Date: 1996
Media: VHS
Length: 5 hours
Source: University of California at Davis, Washington Center

This series of programs explores a host of issues involved in how we elect our president. The issues are not linked to any one particular election or candidate, but rather apply to the election process itself.

Electing the President: Six Steps to the Summit
Date: 1995
Media: VHS
Length: 45 minutes
Cost: $87.72
Source: Insight Media, (800) 897-0089

This film examines the impact of the crucially important early primaries and caucuses on the national conventions and campaigns, as well as how the political parties and Electoral College fit into the presidential selection process.

Election 2000: The Florida Squeeze
Date: 2001
Media: VHS

Length: 30 minutes
Cost: $89.95
Source: Films for the Humanities and Sciences, (800) 257-5126

The sensational 2000 presidential election that made "butterfly ballot" and "chad" household words caused an uproar over the malfunctioning mechanics and the validity of America's electoral process. What is being done to see that major voting irregularities cease to occur again? David Gergen, adviser to four former presidents; David Leahy, supervisor of elections for Miami-Dade County; and Mark Seibel, managing editor of the *Miami Herald,* suggest ways to reform America's voting system.

Election Day
Date: 1996
Media: VHS
Length: 25 minutes
Cost: $29.95
Source: Schlessinger Video Productions,
http://www.amazon.com

From campaigning and debates to rallies and voting, this program explains the activities that precede Election Day. Different levels of public office elections are reviewed along with the constitutional amendments that gave the right to vote to all groups. Children also explore the history of voting and examine the attributes of a good leader by watching as a group of middle school students elect their class president.

The Election Process in America
Date: 2002
Media: VHS
Length: 50 minutes
Cost: $19.95
Source: Full Circle Entertainment, Inc., http://www.amazon.com

Explains the Electoral College and how government officials are elected.

Elizabeth Cady Stanton and Susan B. Anthony
Date: 1988
Media: VHS
Length: 24 minutes

Cost: $89.95
Source: Films for the Humanities and Sciences, (800) 257-5126

This film provides a brief overview of the formation of the National Woman Suffrage Association, focusing on the roles of Susan B. Anthony, Elizabeth Cady Stanton, and Lucretia Mott—the three women who were arguably the most influential figures in the women's rights movement.

Hail to the Chief: Electing the President
Date: 1993
Media: VHS
Length: 14 minutes
Source: Lucerne Media

Explains how the Electoral College works and why this method was formulated. Also covers changes in elections due to more voters, political parties, and TV.

Listening to America: Getting Out the Vote
Date: 1992
Media: VHS
Length: 55 minutes
Source: Public Affairs Television

Bill Moyers interviews Kathleen Hall Jamieson, Fr. Andrew Greely, and Michael Frante concerning voting among minorities, youth, and the general apathy of voters.

The National Commission on Federal Election Reform Report
Date: 2001
Media: VHS
Length: 30 minutes
Source: University Relations, Television News Office, University of Virginia
http://www.researchchannel.org/program/displayevent.asp?riel=763

Dr. Zelikow, executive director of the National Commission on Federal Election Reform, discusses election administration and summarizes the recommendations given in the commission's report. These include statewide voter registration systems, an election holiday, voting rights restored for convicts who have served their terms, simplifying absentee voting, a 2 percent maximum for overvotes and undervotes per precinct, and federal voting system standards. States would need to meet certain goals to receive federal funds but could determine how to meet their goals; specific voting methods were not mandated.

The Price of Politics: Electing our Leaders
Date: 1997
Media: VHS
Length: 60 minutes
Cost: $89.95
Source: Public Broadcasting Service, (415) 543-1200

This program centers on such topics as the influence of special interest monies, America's party system, adherence to campaign platforms, reform initiatives such as term limits, and the media's role in shaping the current system.

So You Want to Buy a President?
Date: 1996
Media: Videocassette
Length: 60 minutes
Source: Public Broadcasting Service, (415) 543-1200

Big contributors to presidential election campaigns are not giving simply to express their support for a candidate but rather because they expect to be provided with access to the councils of power, should their candidate win.

A Third Choice
Date: 1996
Media: VHS
Length: 60 minutes
Cost: $129.95
Source: Public Broadcasting Service, (415) 543-1200

How third-party and independent presidential candidates have affected electoral politics is the major focus of this film documentary.

View Smart to Vote Smart
Date: 2000
Media: VHS
Length: 60 minutes
Cost: Free

Source: The Family and Community Critical Viewing Project, (202) 775-3680

Designed to educate current and future voters on the role of television during elections.

Visions of America
Date: 1994
Media: Videocassette
Length: 60 minutes
Source: Hoover Institution of War, Revolution, and Peace

Panel discussion of the merits of term limits, their effect on states that have enacted term limits, and their legality and potential effect upon the U.S. Congress if imposed.

Vote Fraud in the '96 GOP Primaries
Date: 1996
Media: Audiocassette
Length: 30 minutes
Source: Cincinnatus

In this interview, James Condit Jr., director of Citizens for a Fair Vote, details several instances of what he regards as vote fraud in Republican Party presidential primaries in 1996.

Voter Participation and New Information Technologies
Date: 1994
Media: VHS
Length: 84 minutes
Source: CSPAN and the Benton Foundation

This program explains how the new information technology (national information infrastructure and the information superhighway) will help voter participation.

Voting: A Right and a Responsibility
Date: 2003
Media: DVR-R
Length: 40 minutes
Cost: $94.95
Source: Films for the Humanities and Sciences, (800) 257-5126

This film is a wide-ranging examination of the electoral process, including a history of voting, with particular attention to the struggle of women and African Americans in gaining the franchise. It gives examples of close elections and guidance on how to register to vote, absentee voting, and the use of voting machines. Primary as well as general elections are considered, as well as national, state, and local elections, along with referendums.

Why Bother Voting?
Date: 1992
Media: VHS
Length: 57 minutes
Source: Public Broadcasting Service, (415) 543-1200

Encourages young people to vote, speaking to them in their own language and showing them how their voice can make a difference. Employs humor, celebrity cameos, graphics, and music to explain the mechanics of voting and the importance of the decision-making process.

Why Vote? A Right and a Responsibility
Date: 1996
Media: VHS
Length: 38 minutes
Cost: $69.95
Source: Cambridge Educational, (800) 468-4227

Answers many questions young people or first-time voters have about voting and their role in the political process. Begins with a short history of voting and a discussion of why it is important to vote. Shows how the right to vote has been fought for throughout history, and why the struggle for universal suffrage has been so long and hard. Examples of close elections illustrate how history would have been changed if these elections had different results. Includes registering to vote, precincts, absentee voting, voting machines, write-in votes, and an overview of the various kinds of elections (local, state, and national; primary and general; referendums; bond issues; constitutional amendments). Shows how to take a thorough and critical look at candidates and their positions, their experience, their campaign platforms, and other factors.

Why Vote? Questions on Democratic Participation and Political Reform: A Town Hall Meeting
Date: 1995
Media: VHS

Length: 70 minutes
Cost: $7.54
Source: LegiSchool Project, (916) 327-2155

A roundtable discussion in which California high school students and legislators discuss the political process itself, the factors that discourage people from participating in it, voter registration, term limits, and campaign financing. The forum took place at the California state capitol in September 1995.

Your Vote Counts
Date: 1992
Media: VHS
Length: 30 minutes
Source: Cablevision of Connecticut

A look at why candidates choose to run and why Americans choose not to vote.

Glossary

absentee voting   A practice dating back to the Civil War when Union soldiers in the field were allowed to vote by absentee, whereby individuals who will be away from their place of residence on election day are allowed to mail in their ballot. Over the years, the states varied considerably in the procedures they instituted for absentee voting, but the 1970 Voting Rights Act required all states to adopt uniform rules for absentee registration and voting in presidential elections.

approval voting   A voting system in which voters may select as many candidates as they wish in a multicandidate election, but only one vote per candidate. The candidate receiving the most votes wins.

at-large election   An electoral system in which one or more candidates for a representative body are selected by all the voters in a given jurisdiction instead of by some smaller unit within it. Thus, voters are represented by several individuals as opposed to one.

Australian ballot   A ballot of uniform shape and size, printed by the state, and cast in secret.

automatic plan   Calls for retaining the system of electoral votes used to elect a president but eliminating the presidential electors who cast those votes. Thus, the electoral votes of a state would be awarded automatically to the candidate who received the most popular votes in that state. This reform is seen as a corrective for the problem of the "faithless elector." (*See* faithless elector.)

***Baker v. Carr*, 369 U.S. 186 (1962)**   Reversing a decision it had made twenty-six years earlier that apportionment of legislative districts was a "political question" not appropriate for adjudication by the Court, the Supreme Court now ruled that redistricting was appropriate for review under some circumstances. This ruling opened the door to a host of Supreme Court decisions on redistricting.

Bipartisan Campaign Reform Act (2002) Also known as McCain-Feingold, it prohibits national parties from accepting any soft money contributions while allowing state and local parties to accept up to $10,000 per year per individual for party-building activities. The individual contribution limit was raised from $1,000 to $2,000 and indexed to the rate of inflation. Also, unions, corporations, and nonprofit groups are prohibited from paying for broadcast advertisements with soft money if they refer to a specific candidate and appear within thirty days of a primary and sixty days of a general election.

blanket primary A primary election open to all voters, who may vote for a candidate of any party for each office.

bloc voting A pattern of voting in which members of one group (e.g., racial or ethnic) vote for a candidate of their group while members of another group vote against that candidate.

Buckley v. Valeo, **424 U.S. 1 (1976)** Asked to rule on the constitutionality of the 1974 amendments to the Federal Election Campaign Act, the Supreme Court upheld the disclosure requirements and contribution limits but found unconstitutional the limits on campaign expenditures, limits on how much individuals and groups could spend on behalf of candidates, and limits on how much of their own money candidates could spend on their campaigns. The Court also found the composition of the Federal Election Commission to be in violation of the separation-of-powers principle.

Bush v. Gore, **531 U.S. 98 (2000)** In this recent decision, the U.S. Supreme Court overturned the Florida State Supreme Court's order for a recount of the 2000 presidential vote in Florida. It found that issuing such an order without also specifying standards for what constitutes a valid vote was to deny Florida voters the equal protection of the laws guaranteed under the Fourteenth Amendment.

canvassing board A state or local government board charged with the responsibility of securing the vote counts from election precincts, tabulating the votes, and certifying the winners.

caucus convention A method for choosing delegates to the national party presidential nominating conventions. Party members convene at the precinct level and select individuals to a county-level caucus, who in turn select individuals to a district-level caucus, who choose individuals to the party's state convention, which then selects delegates to the party's national convention. This method of selection is used in Iowa, the most famous of all the caucuses because it traditionally leads off the presidential nominating process.

challenge primary The candidate nominated by the state party convention is the official party nominee unless challenged in a primary following the convention. Those who lose at the party convention but receive a certain percentage of the vote are accorded an automatic right to challenge.

Citizenship Act (1924) Specifies that any American Indian born in the United States is a U.S. citizen.

Civil Rights Act (1957) This act made intimidation in connection with the right to vote a federal crime. Also, the U.S. attorney general was authorized to take action against interferences with the right to vote, and a Civil Rights Commission was created to investigate voting irregularities based upon race.

closed primary A primary election open only to those registered in the party holding the primary.

Congressional Apportionment Act (1842) Required states to use single-member districts for the election of members to the U.S. House of Representatives.

congressional caucus Also derisively referred to as "King Caucus," this was the procedure used for nominating presidential candidates from 1796 through 1820. The members of each party in Congress caucused and chose a nominee from their respective parties.

contingency presidential election If no presidential candidate wins a majority (270 or more) of the electoral votes, the election is then forced into the House of Representatives, where each state has only one vote to cast for any one of the top three finishers in the Electoral College vote. This is viewed by many as highly undemocratic since the voting power of Delaware, for example, becomes equal to the voting power of California.

cross-filing In some states, candidates are allowed to seek the nomination of more than one political party, provided the state party committee of the second party accepts the candidate.

cumulative voting Used in some localities in the United States, under this semiproportional voting system voters have as many votes as there are seats in their constituency and can allocate those votes as they choose, including casting more than one vote for a particular candidate.

direct primary Unique to the United States, it is a voting method that allows rank-and-file party members to vote for their party's nominees, rather than leaving the determination to be made by the party organization itself.

district plan A proposal to reform the Electoral College that calls for awarding electoral votes by congressional district rather than statewide. Advocates of this change argued that it would prevent a president from being elected with a minority of the popular vote. Subsequent scholarly analysis, however, has shown this not to be the case.

Electoral College The 538 presidential electors apportioned among the states according to their congressional representation (plus three for the District of Columbia) whose votes officially elect the president and vice president.

Electoral Count Act (1887) Specified procedures to be followed for raising and resolving challenges to presidential ballots. This law was passed in response to the controversy over votes cast in the election of 1876.

electoral system A procedure for converting popular votes into control of public offices.

electoral votes Allocated to each state for purposes of electing the president and vice-president, and based upon the number of representatives a state has in Congress (i.e., the number of representatives in the U.S. House, plus its two U.S. senators).

Enforcement Act (1870) Made it a federal crime to interfere with the right to vote.

faithless elector A presidential elector who declines to vote in the Electoral College for the presidential candidate receiving the most popular votes in the elector's state. Critics of the Electoral College see this as yet another one of its flaws.

Federal Election Campaign Act (1971) This act limited media expenditures and how much of their own money candidates could use in running for office, and it imposed stricter requirements on disclosure of contributions and expenditures. Some of these regulations would later be overturned in *Buckley v. Valeo.*

Federal Election Campaign Act (1974) The most sweeping campaign finance reform legislation in U.S. history, it imposed contribution and spending limits on candidates, individuals, and groups; created a system of partial public financing of presidential nomination campaigns and full funding of presidential general election campaigns; set down further disclosure requirements; and created a Federal Election Commission to supervise and enforce these rules.

Federal Election Commission (FEC) Created by the 1974 amendments to the Federal Election Campaign Act (1971), the FEC is charged with enforcing federal election laws and disbursing public presidential campaign funds.

filing deadline The last day a candidate for office can file official papers and pay the required fee to appropriate state election officials in order to secure a place on the ballot.

Fifteenth Amendment Prohibits the federal and state governments from denying or abridging the right to vote on the basis of race, color, or previous condition of servitude.

franchise The right to vote.

frontloading Because the early contests in the nominating process have come to be seen as so decisive in determining the fate of presidential candidates, more and more states have moved their primaries and caucuses to the *front* end of the process in order to have an impact before the race is decided.

fusion parties Minor parties that, in an effort to increase their influence, endorse candidates in another party. Twenty states prohibit such parties.

general election An election to choose among the candidates nominated by the two major parties, and any independent and third-party candidates who meet the requirements necessary to gain access to the ballot.

gerrymandering The drawing of district boundary lines for partisan advantage.

grandfather clause Instituted after Reconstruction as one of several ways southern states sought to prevent blacks from voting, it limited the franchise to anyone whose grandfather had been eligible to vote.

Gray v. Sanders, 372 U.S. 368 (1963) This Supreme Court case determined that in primary elections for U.S. senators and state executive officers, the weight of each person's vote must be equal.

Guinn v. U.S., 238 U.S. 347 (1915) Supreme Court case in which "grandfather laws" were ruled a violation of the Fifteenth Amendment.

Harper et al. v. Virginia State Board of Elections, 383 U.S. 663 (1966) The Supreme Court found that the poll tax creates an invidious distinction on the basis of wealth and is thus in violation of the Equal Protection Clause of the Fourteenth Amendment.

Help America Vote Act (2002) Provides money to states in meeting new national standards with respect to voting. To qualify, states must take steps to provide voters an opportunity to check their ballots, provide one voting machine per precinct for the disabled, define what constitutes a legal ballot for each type of voting machine used, create a centralized and computerized voter registration database, and allow provisional voting to those whose eligibility is in question, pending a final determination.

incumbent gerrymandering The drawing of district boundary lines to favor legislators in office.

indirect initiative Allows statutes to be proposed by petitions containing a required number of valid citizen signatures, and then presented to the legislature for action. If the legislature fails to act or unacceptably alters the original proposal, then supporters may gather additional signatures and present the proposal to voters for acceptance or rejection.

initiative Used in twenty-five states, it allows voters to propose a legislative measure by filing a petition with a required number of valid citizen signatures.

initiative industrial complex Refers to the vast group of consultants who have sprouted up to manage the initiative process. They are involved in drafting the initiatives, circulating the signature petitions, conducting polls and focus groups, and running the ad campaigns.

instant registration Four states (Maine, Minnesota, Oregon, and Wisconsin) allow their residents to register right up to and including election day.

instant runoff voting Each voter has only one vote but can rank candidates in order of preference (e.g., 1-Bush, 2-Nader, 3-Kerry). The ballot count acts as a series of runoff elections, with the candidate receiving the fewest first-place votes being eliminated and his/her ballots transferred to second choices as reflected on voters' ballots. The process of transferring votes is repeated until one candidate emerges with a majority.

Jim Crow laws A series of laws adopted by southern states in the aftermath of Reconstruction to discriminate against blacks, including literacy tests, tests on interpreting the U.S. Constitution, "white primaries," poll taxes, and residency requirements.

Lane v. Wilson, **524 U.S. 908 (1939)** The Supreme Court ruled unconstitutional efforts by states to punish individuals for not voting.

limited voting Used in some voting systems with multimember districts (e.g., Boston, New York, and Philadelphia); voters are allowed at least one vote shy of the number of individuals to be elected. Advocates of this system of election maintain that it gives minorities a greater chance to win representation.

literacy test   A test administered to determine an individual's ability to read and write as a condition for voting registration. One of several devices used by southern states to prevent blacks from voting, it was suspended by the Voting Rights Acts of 1965 and 1970 and ruled unconstitutional by the Supreme Court in *Oregon v. Mitchell* (1970).

Ludlow Amendment   An unsuccessful attempt to place in the Constitution an amendment requiring that war be declared only if a majority of Americans so approved in a nationwide referendum.

majority rule   The election of individuals by more than 50 percent of the votes cast.

McCain-Feingold   *See* Bipartisan Campaign Reform Act.

***McConnell v. Federal Election Commission,* 124 S.Ct. 619 (2003)**   The Supreme Court upheld the major provisions of the Bipartisan Campaign Reform Act (McCain-Feingold), including raising the individual contribution limit from $1,000 to $2,000; banning national political parties from accepting "soft money" contributions; and prohibiting labor unions and corporations from using money in their general treasuries for ad campaigns.

McGovern-Fraser Commission   Created following the tumultuous 1968 Democratic Convention to investigate delegate selection procedures. It proposed a series of sweeping reforms designed to expand rank-and-file participation in the delegate selection process. These changes, which were ultimately adopted by the Democratic Party, significantly reduced the role of its party elites in the presidential nominating process.

malapportionment   Legislative districts with unequal numbers of individuals, and therefore in violation of the one-person, one-vote doctrine.

Motor Voter Act   *See* National Voter Registration Act (1993)

multimember district   An electoral district represented by more than one individual, thus providing those living in the district with the opportunity to vote for more than a single individual.

***Myers v. Anderson,* 238 U.S. 368 (1915)**   Supreme Court case that ruled unconstitutional tax and property qualifications for voting.

national bonus plan   A reform that calls for retaining the Electoral College system, but with a new provision that would award the winner of the national popular vote an additional block of 102 electoral votes, thereby assuring that the electoral vote winner would also be the popular vote winner.

national party convention A national meeting of delegates chosen by primary, caucus-convention, or appointment, convening for the purpose of nominating the presidential and vice-presidential candidates, and adopting a party platform.

national presidential primary Each party would hold its own national presidential primary on the same day, thereby providing voters in each party with the same set of choices for president, unlike the current primary process where candidates are eliminated as the process runs its course.

National Voter Registration Act (1993) Requires that citizens be allowed to register while licensing their car, at welfare offices, or by mail, and prohibits purging of voter rolls except for change of residency.

Nineteenth Amendment (1920) Granted women the right to vote.

Nixon v. Herndon, **273 U.S. 536 (1927)** Ruled unconstitutional the exclusion of blacks from voting in primary elections.

nonbinding primary A primary that allows voters to register their preferences though the results are not binding. In a few states the Republican and Democratic parties hold nonbinding presidential primaries, even while choosing their delegates separately through the caucus-convention method. The delegates chosen are free to take into account the primary results but are not bound by them.

nonpartisan elections Often used in city, county, school board, and judicial elections, these elections do not require that candidates officially indicate their party affiliation.

nonpartisan primary This peculiar form of election is unique to Louisiana. All candidates for office in *both* parties are listed on one ballot, and voters are allowed to cast a single vote for the candidate for each office. If any candidate receives a majority of the vote, then he/she is elected to that office. If no candidate receives a majority, a general election is held between the two highest vote-getters, regardless of their party affiliation.

office block ballot A ballot that lists all candidates under the office for which they are running, thereby making split-ticket voting easier.

one person, one vote As articulated in *Reynolds v. Sims,* the Supreme Court declared that when undertaking reapportionment, a good-faith effort must be made to create legislative districts as nearly equal in population as possible. Failure to do so constitutes a violation of the Equal Protection Clause of the Fourteenth Amendment.

open primaries Primary elections open to members in either party and to independents.

overvotes Ballots disqualified because they show more than one vote cast for candidates running for a given office, or because the voter voted for one candidate and then went on to write in the name of that very same candidate.

party column ballot A ballot listing all of a party's candidates for all offices in a single column, thereby facilitating straight-ticket voting.

plurality rule Election of an individual receiving one more vote than any of his/her opponents, but with less than 51 percent of the vote.

political efficacy Individuals' sense that they have the ability to influence their political environment. Some have argued that individuals with a low sense of efficacy are less likely to participate in the political process.

poll taxes Payment required as a condition of voting. Declared impermissible in federal elections by the Twenty-fourth Amendment and ruled unconstitutional by the Supreme Court in *Harper v. Virginia Board of Education* (1966).

***Pope v. Williams*, 193 U.S. 621 (1904)** Upheld the constitutionality of residency laws for voting.

precinct The smallest political subdivision used for the purpose of both organizing the vote in elections and organizing political parties.

pre-primary convention Used by parties in some states (e.g., Colorado), a state party convention is held before the primary to endorse the nomination of some of the several candidates who will be running in the party's primary.

presidential ticket Listing of the presidential and vice-presidential candidates on the same ballot, as required by the Twelfth Amendment.

Progressive Era Refers to a reform movement that flowered around the turn of the twentieth century. So-called Progressives sought to reduce government corruption and expand political participation, and to this end championed such reforms as direct primaries; the initiative, referendum, and recall; nonpartisan local elections; and civil service reform.

property qualification for voting Beginning in colonial America and disappearing roughly around the mid-1800s, individuals in most states were required to prove ownership of some property (defined, depending upon the state, as land, ownership of certain possessions, and/or financial worth) in order to be eligible to vote.

proportional plan Another proposal to reform the Electoral College, calling for awarding the electoral votes of a state on a proportional rather than a winner-take-all basis. Such a change, it has been argued, would increase turnout, provide third parties with greater leverage in the political process, and prevent a president from being elected with a minority of the popular vote. Although the first two effects seem likely to occur under such a plan, scholarly analysis has demonstrated that the third would not be assured.

proportional representation An election system in which the proportion of seats allocated to a party in the legislative body is in proportion to the number of votes it receives.

provisional voting Allowing an individual whose eligibility to vote cannot be definitively determined at the time of an election to cast a provisional vote, to be counted once eligibility is proven.

racial gerrymandering The practice of drawing district boundaries in such a way as to ensure that members of a certain race constitute a minority. Declared unconstitutional in *Gomillion v. Lightfoot* (1960).

reapportionment The reallocation of congressional seats to the states by Congress following the U.S. Census constitutionally required every ten years. This procedure is also followed by state legislatures.

recall A procedure used in eighteen states whereby the removal of a public official, before completion of his or her term, is submitted to a popular vote.

redistricting The redrawing of congressional and other legislative district lines after each ten-year census in order to achieve districts that are as equal in population as possible.

referendum Employed in twenty-four states, it is a procedure allowing measures passed by the legislature, or proposed amendments to the state constitution, to be submitted to the voters for their approval.

regional primary A contiguous group of states holding its primaries on the same day. It has the advantages of reducing wear and tear on candidates as well as travel expenses—advantages lost when candidates are forced to prepare for primaries scattered around the country and held on the same day.

residency A qualification for voting based upon domicile. The amount of time one must reside in a location to establish residency has in the past varied by level of jurisdiction, with one year typically required at the state level, ninety days at the county, and thirty at the local level. In 1972, however, the Supreme Court (in

Dunn v. Blumstein) ruled that a one-year residency requirement was excessive, suggesting instead that thirty days would be more appropriate. The 1970 Civil Rights Act also mandated a residency requirement of no greater than thirty days to be eligible to vote in a federal election.

Revenue Act (1971) Created a tax check-off system on the federal income tax form allowing voters to designate $1 of their federal income taxes to be put into a Presidential Campaign Fund for the purpose of funding presidential campaigns beginning in 1976.

Reynolds v. Sims, **377 U.S. 533 (1964)** This Supreme Court case ruled that both houses of a bicameral state legislature must be apportioned on the basis of population.

runoff primary If no candidate receives a majority of the vote in the initial primary, a runoff primary is held among the top two finishers. Runoff primaries have been most common in southern states, with some black leaders charging that it is a device used by whites to prevent blacks from gaining nomination to public office.

semiclosed primary A primary that is closed to members from the other party but open to those registered as Independents.

Seneca Falls Convention (1848) A historic gathering of women who in a Declaration of Sentiments asserted their equality with men and set forth a series of demands, including the right to vote.

Seventeenth Amendment (1913) Requires that U.S. senators be directly elected by the people.

Shaw v. Reno, **509 U.S. 630 (1993)** According to the decision of this Supreme Court case, whites have cause to claim gerrymandering against them if district lines are drawn in such a bizarre fashion as to be explainable only as an effort to insure the election of a minority group.

short counting A dishonest practice whereby voting results are purposely misreported in order to advantage a particular candidate. The intended presence of poll watchers is to prevent the occurrence of such actions.

single-member district An electoral district represented by only one individual chosen by the voters.

Smith v. Allwright, **321 U.S. 649 (1944)** The Supreme Court ruled that barring blacks from voting in primaries is a violation of the Fifteenth Amendment.

soft money Money raised by the political parties in unlimited amounts for party-building purposes. Prohibited to the national political parties by the Bipartisan Campaign Reform Act (2002), known as McCain-Feingold, but state and local political parties are allowed to accept a limited amount of soft money each year for party-building purposes.

Soldier Voting Act (1942) Granted military personnel the right to vote absentee in federal elections and exempted them from the poll tax.

sore loser law On the books in nine states, it prohibits candidates who run and lose in a state's primary from then running as a third-party or independent candidate in the general election.

suffragists Those individuals, mostly but not entirely women, who led the fight for over seven decades to secure women the right to vote.

Thornburgh v. Gingles, **478 U.S. 30 (1986)** The Supreme Court set down criteria for determining when at-large or multimember districting plans unfairly dilute the votes of African Americans.

three-fifths compromise For purposes of establishing representation in the U.S. House of Representatives, the Constitution required that slaves be counted as three-fifths of a person. Rendered null and void by the Fourteenth Amendment.

turnout The number of individuals who come out to vote, whether determined on the basis of the voting-age population, the number eligible to vote, or the number of registered voters. The U.S. Census employs the first standard, a number of scholarly studies rely on the second, and European countries generally use the third.

Twelfth Amendment Changed the Constitution to require presidential electors to vote separately for president and vice president, and in the event that an election is forced into the House of Representatives, members of that body are required to choose among the three candidates with the highest number of electoral votes.

Twenty-second Amendment (1951) No individual may be elected to more than two terms as president. In addition, if an individual has served more than half of an unexpired term, then he/she may be elected to only one additional term.

Twenty-third Amendment (1961) Assigned to the District of Columbia electoral votes to be cast for president that could not exceed in number those of the least populous state (Alaska, with three electoral votes).

Twenty-fourth Amendment (1964) Prohibits the use of a poll tax in any federal election, primary or general.

Twenty-sixth Amendment (1971) Lowered the legal voting age to eighteen in all elections.

undervotes   Ballots that show no vote for a given office.

Uniformed and Overseas Citizens Absentee Voting Act (1986)   Requires that states and territories permit U.S. citizens and military personnel living overseas to register and vote by absentee.

U.S. Term Limits v. Thornton, **514 U.S. 779 (1995)**   The Supreme Court ruled that states lack the authority under the Constitution to impose term limits on representatives elected to Congress.

Voter Accessibility for the Elderly and Handicapped Act (1984)   Requires that polling places be accessible to the handicapped in federal elections and that they provide the handicapped with registration and voting aids.

voter registration   In order to become eligible to vote, individuals are required in all but one state (North Dakota) to establish their identity and place of residence by completing a registration form. First instituted by the state of Massachusetts in 1801; most states adopted the practice in the 1870s as a protection against corruption of the voting process.

voter roll-off   When voters mark their ballots for candidates seeking the more important offices appearing at the top of the ticket but fail to vote for candidates seeking relatively less important offices listed further down the ticket. The longer the ballot, the more likely roll-off is to occur.

Voting Rights Act (1965)   Suspended literacy tests for five years, dispatched federal examiners to southern states to register blacks and observe registration practices, and prohibited southern states (i.e., those with a history of discrimination against blacks) from altering election procedures unless cleared by the Justice Department. The Justice Department was also instructed to test the constitutionality of the poll tax.

Voting Rights Act (1970)   Extended the Voting Rights Act for five years, lowered the minimum voting age to eighteen, prohibited a residency requirement greater than thirty days in federal elections, and required uniform national rules for absentee registration and voting in federal elections.

Voting Rights Act (1975)   Extended the Voting Rights Act for an additional seven years, expanded its provisions to include "language minorities," and required that ballots and voter registration materials be bilingual.

Voting Rights Act (1982)   Extended the Voting Rights Act for an additional twenty-five years and stipulated that voting procedures might be in violation of the law if their effect served to discriminate, even though there was no intent to do so.

Wesberry v. Sanders, **376 U.S. 1 (1964)** Supreme Court ruled that congressional districts must be substantially equal in population.

white primary One of many practices intended to prevent blacks from voting, instituted by the Democratic Party in southern states after Reconstruction. It excluded them from voting in primary elections and was ultimately declared unconstitutional in *Smith v. Allwright* (1944).

winner-take-all voting A voting procedure whereby the side winning the largest number of votes receives all of whatever is at stake, be it delegate votes, legislative seats, or a state's electoral votes.

Index

About the Author

Robert E. DiClerico is an Eberly Distinguished Professor of Political Science at West Virginia University, where he specializes in the American presidency and political parties and elections. Professor DiClerico received his undergraduate degree from Hamilton College and doctorate from Indiana University (Bloomington). He coauthored *Choosing Our Choices: Debating the Presidential Nominating Process* (2000) and *Few Are Chosen: Problems in Presidential Selection* (1984) and is the single author of *The American President* (2000), now in its fifth edition. In addition, he edited *Political Parties, Campaigns, and Elections* (2000), *Analyzing the Presidency* (1990), and coedited *Points of View: Readings in American Government* (2003), now in its ninth edition.

Professor DiClerico was selected as the state of West Virginia Professor of the Year by the Faculty Merit Foundation (1995), and the Council for the Advancement and Support of Education (1990) and was the first-year recipient of the West Virginia Foundation Award for Outstanding Teaching (1986).

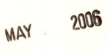